GLOBALIZATION AND ECONOMIC DEVELOPMENT

Experience of Developing Countries

GLOBALIZATION AND ECONOMIC DEVELOPMENT

Experience of Developing Countries

DR. MANJIT SINGH
M.Sc.(Hons.), Ph.D.
Lecturer of Economics
Guru Nanak Dev University
Amritsar (Punjab)

Foreword by

PROFESSOR P.S. RAIKHY
Former Professor and Head
Former Dean, Faculty of Economics and Business
Punjab School of Economics
Guru Nanak Dev University
Amritsar (Punjab)

DEEP & DEEP PUBLICATIONS PVT. LTD.
F-159, Rajouri Garden, New Delhi - 110 027

GLOBALIZATION AND ECONOMIC DEVELOPMENT
Experience of Developing Countries

ISBN 978-81-8450-270-1

Printed in India at MAYUR ENTERPRISES
WZ Plot No. 3, Gujjar Market, Tihar Village, New Delhi - 110 018

Published by DEEP & DEEP PUBLICATIONS PVT. LTD.,
F-159, Rajouri Garden, New Delhi - 110 027 • Phone : 25435369, 25440916
E-mail : ddpubs@gmail.com • ddpbooks@yahoo.co.in
Showroom :
2/13, Ansari Road, Daryaganj, New Delhi - 110 002 • Telefax : 23245122

Dedicated

To

My Grandfather

(Sant Dall Singh Ji)

Contents

Foreword xi

Preface xv

1. INTRODUCTION **1**

2. GLOBALIZATION AND ECONOMIC DEVELOPMENT : SOME ISSUES **12**

History of Globalization 16

Positive Impact of Globalization 17

Dangers/Pitfalls of Globalization 26

Conclusion 32

3. REVIEW OF LITERATURE **36**

4. DATA BASE AND METHODOLOGY **62**

Methodology 64

Tabular Analysis 64

Chi-Square Test 64

Correlation Analysis 65

Rank Correlation Analysis 66

Factor Analysis 66

Composite Index 69

Bridging of Gap 69
Regression Analysis 69
PQLI 70
Coefficient of Variation 72
Chow Test 73

5. ECONOMIC GROWTH AND STRUCTURAL CHANGES 75

Level of Growth and Share of Agriculture in GDP 76
Level of Growth and Average Annual Growth Rate of Agriculture 78
Level of Growth and Share of Industry in GDP 79
Level of Growth and Average Annual Growth Rate of Industry 81
Level of Growth and Share of Services in GDP 82
Level of Growth and Average Annual Growth Rate of Services 83
Level of Growth and Average Annual Growth Rate of GDP 85
Level of Growth and GNI Per Capita (PPP) 86
Level of Growth and Private Consumption Expenditure (% of GDP) 87
Level of Growth and Gross Domestic Savings (% of GDP) 89
Level of Growth and Gross Capital Formation (% of GDP) 90
Level of Growth and Energy Use Per Capita 92
Level of Growth and Share of Fuel, Ores and Metal Exports in Merchandise Exports 93
Level of Growth and Share of Food and Agricultural Raw Material Exports in Merchandise Exports 94
Level of Growth and Share of Manufacture Exports in Merchandise Exports 96
Level of Growth and Exports-GDP Ratio 97
Level of Growth and Imports-GDP Ratio 99

Level of Growth and Degree of Openness (Trade-GDP Ratio) 100
Level of Growth and Average Annual Growth Rate of Export Volume 101
Level of Growth and Average Annual Growth Rate of Import Volume 102
Level of Growth and Merchandise Trade-GDP Ratio 104
Level of Growth and Trade in Services-GDP Ratio 105
Level of Growth and Gross Private Capital Flows-GDP Ratio 107
Level of Growth and FDI Net Inflows-GDP Ratio 107
Level of Growth and FDI Net Outflows-GDP Ratio 109
Level of Growth and Total Debt Services-GNI Ratio 110
Level of Growth and Daily Calorie Supply Per Capita 112
Level of Growth and Employment in Agriculture (% of Total Employment) 113
Level of Growth and Employment in Industry (% of Total Employment) 114
Level of Growth and Employment in Services (% of Total Employment) 116

6. ECONOMIC GROWTH AND DEMOGRAPHIC CHANGES 123
Level of Growth and Birth Rate (Per 1000 People) 124
Level of Growth and Death Rate (Per 1000 People) 125
Level of Growth and Infant Mortality Rate 127
Level of Growth and Life Expectancy at Birth 128
Level of Growth and Number of Physicians (Per 1000 People) 129
Level of Growth and Adult Literacy Rate 131
Level of Growth and Primary School Enrolment 132
Level of Growth and Secondary School Enrolment 134
Level of Growth and Percentage of Population of Working Age (15-64 Yrs.) 135
Level of Growth and Urban Population (% of Total) 137

Level of Growth and International Migration Stock (% of Population) 138

7. FACTORS IN ECONOMIC DEVELOPMENT : AN EMPIRICAL INVESTIGATION 143

Correlation Matrices 144

Factor Analysis 154

Measuring Economic Development : Composite Index, GNI Per Capita, PPP and PQLI 166

Rank Correlation Analysis 201

Correlation Analysis of the Selected Variables with Composite Index of Economic Development 203

Conclusion 205

8. GLOBALIZATION AND ECONOMIC DEVELOPMENT : CONVERGENCE AND STABILITY 208

GNI Per Capita of Different Groups of Countries 209

GNI Per Capita of Developing Countries 210

Hogendorn's Concept of Bridging the Development Gap 215

Coefficients of Variation of Development Indicators 217

Step-wise (Step-up) Regression Analysis 221

Correlation Analysis 228

Rank Correlation Analysis 228

Fastest and Slowest Growing Countries 231

Stability of Regression Parameters (Chow Test) 235

9. SUMMARY AND CONCLUSIONS 238

Appendices 259

Bibliography 295

Index 306

Foreword

Globalization is a multifaceted and multidisciplinary topic in its broadest reaches. KOF Index of Globalization (prepared by Swiss Economic Institute) has tried to measure its economic, social and political dimensions. The recent wave of globalization has generated an intense debate among economists, attracting both strong supporters and opponents. Some countries and categories of people have benefited from this, but some countries have been left out. Amongst the latter are many Least Developed Countries (LDCs) and the poor and unemployed people. Many LDCs have been marginalized in the world economy during the globalization period. The main message that comes across is that globalization and liberalization have increased heterogeneity across countries, sectors, and types of firms. Some have been able to take advantage of new opportunities, while others have only encountered more obstacles.

Many studies have been undertaken to study and measure globalization and its impact. The classics on the subject include the works of Joseph Stiglitz, James Petras & Henry Veltmeyer, Jagdish Bhagwati, Deepak Nayyar, Peter Isard and Soumyen Sikdar, who have highlighted the impacts and discontents of globalization.

Globalization has brought about revolutionary changes worldwide. The most significant changes brought about by the process of globalization are the increasing interdependence and integration at a worldwide scale. Its impact has touched upon political, cultural, economic and ideological aspects of society.

In economic globalization, the impact relates to production, consumption, commercial exchange and distribution aspects. Globalization may affect employment levels, living standards, consumer's product choice, exchange opportunities and national income levels. Thus, globalization definitely has profound impact on the subject of Economics as a whole and on the field of Development Economics, in particular in view of its significant implications for economic development.

The present book by Dr. Manjit Singh is an endeavour in this direction and it deals with the contemporary issues of globalization which is attracting attention all over the world. The main objective of the book is to examine the impact of globalization on economic development of developing countries. The work has been structured into nine chapters, including a brief review of literature. It is based on secondary data and covers the period of 1980 to 2004 at four points of time and the number of countries varies between 66 to 113. In all, 42 variables were considered. Many simple and advanced statistical techniques, including Factor Analysis, Composite Index of Economic Development and Chow Test, etc. have been employed to meet the objectives.

The study showed that structural and demographic changes have taken place along with economic development in developing countries. The results of Factor Analysis bring out multi-dimensional nature of economic development. The increase in 'variations' explained by the variables related to globalization showed the increased role of globalization in the economic development of developing countries. The author has also developed a Composite Index of Economic Development as a measure of economic development, using different economic, structural and demographic indicators.

The most fascinating part of the book is the study of issues of convergence and stability in growth rates of developing countries. Using different measures of convergence/divergence, the author reported that the developing economies are not converging, the gap between the developed and developing countries is in fact increasing rather than decreasing and the developing countries have not been able to 'catch-up' the developed countries. However, the findings show that there is relative stability in the growth rate of developing countries, which could be attributed to globalization.

The author rightly points out that 'globalization is not a zero-sum game so that some countries benefit at the cost of others'; in fact, all countries could gain from it. He cautions that 'globalization itself is neither good nor bad. It is like a two-edged sword, which can cut for you and also which can cut you, if not properly managed'. He observes that 'governance is critical in the process of economic development. With due attention to their problems, developing countries should manage the process of globalization so as to drive maximum benefits while minimizing the risks.'

I congratulate Dr. Manjit Singh for bringing out such an excellent, up-to-date and immensely useful book for the students, teachers, researchers, policy-makers and those interested in the field of Development Economics in general and Globalization, in particular.

DR. P.S. RAIKHY
Professor
Former Professor and Head
Former Dean
Faculty of Economics and Business
Punjab School of Economics
Guru Nanak Dev University
Amritsar (Punjab)

Preface

Since early nineties, most of the developing countries have followed policies of liberalization, privatization and globalization. Over the past several decades, the economies of the world have become increasingly linked through expanded international trade in services as well as primary and manufactured goods. These linkages have had a marked effect on the developing world. Though globalization has been taking place in the world economic system since the second half of 19th century but the recent wave of 1990s has been very fast and involves different dimensions like globalization of financial markets, internationalization of corporate strategies, diffusion of technology, transformation of consumption pattern, growing global politico-economic system and diminished role of national governments in designing rules for global governance. Under globalization, the changes in one country have effects on others immediately which may affect the pattern and pace of structural and demographic changes and thereby the rate of growth in other countries.

The objective of this book is to examine the impact of Globalization on the Economic Development of the developing countries. It also covers theoretical issues relating to globalization and its impact. Chi-Square Analysis was used to establish the relationship between level of development and structural and demographic indicators of developing countries. The study showed that as globalization progressed, the structural and demographic changes took place at a relatively faster pace, which in general, raised the pace of economic development in the developing countries. Factor analysis was used to empirically study the factors in economic development. The results of Factor Analysis showed that globalization has positive impact on economic development of developing countries. Also, economic development of developing countries was measured using different measures. Composite Index of economic development was developed using structural, demographic and social indicators.

Further, the book analyzes the issues of convergence and stability. Step-wise regression analysis, coefficient of variation, simple and multiple regression analysis, etc. were used for examining convergence. The results showed no clear-cut indication of convergence between developed and developing countries and also within developing countries. Also, the income gap is not bridging. Correlation analysis, rank correlation analysis and Chow Test were used to examine the stability in growth rates. The study showed that there is relative stability in growth rates of developing countries. On the whole, the developing countries have not been able to gain much in the process of globalization. This may be partly due to their chosen policies and partly due to factors outside their control.

This book would not have been possible without the guidance, support and help of many personalities. First of all, I wish to express my deep sense of gratitude and indebtedness to my esteemed teacher Dr. P.S. Raikhy, Professor, Punjab School of Economics, Guru Nanak Dev University, Amritsar, for his encouraging and enthusiastic guidance and helpful criticism during the course of this study. I am grateful to him for introducing me to the World of Research. Prof. Raikhy has been the driving force behind this work. During the work, many times when I did not know which path to take, he was there to guide me and show me the way. He has freely given me his precious time and I have always felt that my work has been his first priority. The success of this research work is solely due to his generosity, ideas and amazing intellect.

I have been supported by a number of people within Punjab School of Economics, Guru Nanak Dev University, Amritsar. I am thankful to Prof. A.S. Sethi who helped me in solving conceptual doubts in the quantitative analysis at various stages of study. Thanks are due to Prof. Sharanjit Singh Dhillon who has been extremely interested in this work. It has been a great pleasure to have discussions with both of them.

I am also thankful to all the library staff of Punjab School of Economics, Guru Nanak Dev University, Amritsar, Indian Institute of Economic Growth, New Delhi, RIS (Indian Habitat Centre, New Delhi), IIFT, New Delhi, World Bank Library, New Delhi, Indian Council of World Affairs, New Delhi and Rattan Tata Library of New Delhi for help in making best use of the libraries.

I will be failing in my duty, if I do not thank various economists from whose work I benefitted a lot during this work.

Words are not sufficient to express the feelings in my heart for my family and friends who encouraged and supported me during this research work. Their love, continuous encouragement, prayers, words of praise as well as suggestions often boosted my courage and determination to complete this research work. A few lines are too short to make a complete account of my sense of deep appreciation for their contribution.

I am grateful to my parents for their unconditional support and encouragement to pursue my interests. My father S. Gurbachan Singh has been a moving spirit behind all my achievements. He has been reminding me that my research should always be useful and serve good purposes for all humankind, researchers and policy-makers. My dear mother Smt. Balwinder Kaur has been a constant source of encouragement for me. I feel that without the encouragement and moral support of my parents, I could never have been what I am today.

However, the one person who made it possible for me to pursue this dream is my brother S. Jaswant Singh who has made my life wonderful in all respects. He helped me in every possible manner to complete this research work. I must also thank my lovely nephew Gurbir Singh for always reminding me how lucky I am.

I am thankful to my uncles S. Raghbir Singh, Secretary, SGPC, S. Harbhajan Singh and other family members, S. Harjinder Singh and S. Mandeep Singh for their inspiration and moral support.

Last, but not the least, I warmly appreciate S. Sarbjit Singh, S. Sukhdev Singh and all my friends for their invaluable cooperation, inspiration and ever-present support. I sincerely thank them all.

DR. MANJIT SINGH
Lecturer of Economics
Guru Nanak Dev University
Amritsar (Punjab)

Introduction

Economic development has been a major challenge for the society, at least since early twentieth century, even when its meaning has been changing. According to Meier and Baldwin (1957), "Economic development is a process whereby an economy's real national income increases over a long period of time." However, if the rate of population growth is higher than that of the rise in national income, per capita income may be falling instead of rising. Meier (1970), therefore, redefined economic development as "the process whereby the real per capita income of a country increases over a long period of time." Again, it was realized that with increase in per capita income, it is not necessary that standard of living of the general masses will improve. Per capita income indicates the wealth in the hands of people but it does not indicate that they all have the same amount. It is the average of the rich and poor. Thus, per capita figure also may not indicate the amount of well-being within a country or even within a state or region. It was, therefore, considered essential to redefine economic development in terms of economic welfare.

Seers (1969) posed the basic question about the meaning of development in terms of level of poverty, unemployment and inequality in the economy. Seers opined that, "if all three of these have declined from high levels, then beyond doubt this has been a period of development for the country concerned. If one or two of these central problems have been becoming worse, especially if all three have, it would be strange to call the result 'development' even if per capita income doubled." Thus, it is necessary that with increase in per capita income, economic welfare should also increase.

'Growth trickles down and spreads' was the wide-spread belief amongst many developing countries when they treaded on the path of development. As a consequence of this belief, initially no need was felt for improving people's quality of life, reducing income inequalities and protecting the quality of regional and global environmental commons. But the hope of solving these problems with growth got belied with the failure of 'trickle down' hypothesis. According to the World Bank Report (1992), "Development is about improving the well-being of people. Raising living standards and improving education, health and equality of opportunity are all essential components of economic development." Economic development has also been redefined as an attack on the chief evils of the world today; malnutrition, diseases, illiteracy, slums, unemployment and inequality (Streeten, as quoted in Todaro and Smith, 2003). Thus, 'Economic Development' is a multi-dimensional process involving major changes in the social structures, popular attitudes, and national institutions as well as the acceleration of economic growth, the reduction of inequality and the eradication of absolute poverty (Todaro and Smith, 2003).

For a long time, the terms economic development and economic growth have been used as synonymous. But Schumpeter (1934) made the distinction when he defined development as a discontinuous and spontaneous change in the stationary state which forever alters and displaces the equilibrium state previously existing; while growth as a gradual and steady change in the long-run which comes about by a gradual increase in the rate of savings and population. Kindleberger (1965) also made the distinction stating that "Economic growth means more output, while economic development implies both more output and changes in the technical and institutional arrangement by which it is produced and distributed." Friedman as quoted in Hansen (1972) defined growth as an expansion of the system in one or more dimensions without a change in its structure, and development as an innovative process leading to the structural transformation of social system.

Thus economic growth is a quantitative and sustained increase in the country's per capita income accompanied by expansion in its labour force, consumption, capital and volume of trade. On the other hand, economic development is a wider concept than economic growth. It is taken to mean growth plus change. It is related to qualitative changes in economic wants, goods, incentives, institutions, productivity and knowledge or the "upward movement of the entire social system" (Myrdal, 1957). It describes the underlying determinants of growth such as technological and structural changes.

Economic development is the primary objective of the majority of the world's nations. This truth is accepted almost without controversy. Economic development is necessary for underdeveloped countries because it helps them in solving the problems of general poverty, unemployment, backwardness and low standard of living. On the other hand, economic growth is equally significant to developed countries as it helps them to maintain their existing growth rate. On the whole, development in all societies is needed for the fulfilment of the following objectives:

(i) To increase the availability and widen the distribution of basic life-sustaining goods such as food, shelter, health and protection.
(ii) To raise levels of living, including higher incomes, the provision of more jobs, better education and greater attention to cultural and humanistic values.
(iii) To expand the range of economic and social choices available to individuals and nations by freeing them from servitude and dependence. (Todaro and Smith, 2003)

Development strategy may vary from one country to another, depending upon the nature, structure and degree of interdependence among its primary, secondary and tertiary sectors. During the last four decades of developmental efforts, the most important achievement of some of the countries, has not been just development, but an understanding of what we really mean when we speak of development. Another thing that the people living in developing countries have come to know is that the path of development is strewn with vicious circles, which require quick and drastic measures to break. Experience has also proved that there are no short-cuts to development and that at macro economic level, the process of development becomes time-consuming and difficult. It is essential to identify the political, social and institutional framework that imparts the necessary impetus to the overall development in general and different sectors like agriculture, industry, trade, transport, etc., in particular.

Fisher (1935) and Clark (1940) undertook a systematic study of economic structure and their changes leading to emergence of Fisher-Clark hypothesis on structural change. Economic structures, divided into three broad sectoral economic activities, i.e. the primary, the secondary and the tertiary, differ significantly from each other in use of natural resources, in the scale of operation of the productive units common to each in production process, in final output and trends in their shares in total output and resources used. According to this hypothesis, economic growth leads to rise in the share of income and employment in the secondary and the tertiary sectors while that of the primary sector would decline. Evidence of long-term trends in the developed countries confirmed this hypothesis.

Economic development involves structural changes in composition of output, employment, consumption, trade and other related aspects. This internal process of structural changes is necessary for generating and sustaining the process of rapid economic growth (Todaro and Smith, 2003). The character of a developing economy changes due to these structural changes. Structural changes may take place at the level of activities, thereby changing the structure of sub-sectors and sectors of an economy. These structural changes may go a long way in shaping the future growth rate and pattern, and thereby the quality of life of the people. Structural change is a complex, intertwined phenomenon, not only because economic growth brings about complementary changes in various aspects of the economy, such as the sector compositions of output and employment, organization of industry, etc., but also because these changes in turn affect the growth process.

The structural changes can be expedited through policy actions. Such policy actions are vital, because of the 'widening gap' between developed and developing countries and the developing countries may have to 'run fast to stand still'. The concept of structure itself implies a set of interrelated elements, where a change in one element leads to change in others. The structure of an economy changes due to changing tastes and demand which get reflected in the changing income elasticity of demand. On the supply side, these changes may be effected through technological changes. On the whole, government policies—industrial, commercial, investment, labour, regional, locational, monetary and fiscal, etc.—may act as catalysts for structural changes in the economy. (Bawa and Raikhy, 1993)

The structural changes are the important ingredients of economic development and the concept can also be defined as planned alteration of the structure of production and employment. There may be a significant change in the scale or average size of productive units (away from small family and personal enterprises to the impersonal organization of huge national and multi-national corporations); and finally, a corresponding shift in the spatial location and occupational status of the labour force away from rural, agricultural and related non-agricultural activities toward urban-oriented manufacturing and service pursuits (Todaro and Smith, 2003). At sub-sectoral level there is shift in manufacturing from less to more durable goods, and to a limited extent from consumer to producer goods, increase in share of some service groups (personal, professional and governmental) and decline in share of others (domestic services). It is the effect of combination of these shifts in industrial origin of aggregate output along with the trends in efficiency within the various sectors that produced marked shifts in the sectoral allocation of labour force. These shifts are important, for they mean changes in conditions of life and work of the population, affecting the use of income and other links in the mechanism of economic growth.

Models of development and transformation of dual economy explain at theoretical level the transfer of agricultural surpluses and migration of workforce as two most important and integrated ingredients initiating development process in the advanced sector in the initial phases and for its subsequent sustained growth. In fact, the growth and modernization of agriculture enables out-migration and modern manufacturing in the economy. (Ranis and Fei, 1961)

A high rate of growth in per capita product implies a rapid shift in the structure of final demand—whether due to persistent income elasticities or due to technological changes. Also, the factors that induce a high rate of growth of per capita product usually make for a greater rate of expansion of foreign trade and of changes in international division of labour. According to Bagchi (1987), "Sustained economic development in a particular region leads to changes in economic structure. The basic elements of economic structure are taken to be goods and services of different kinds, and the employment provided by the production of such goods and services."

There is a close and two-way relationship between trade and structural changes. Structural changes brought by the process of industrialization significantly influence the export potential as well as import demand of the industrializing country. The correction of structural disequilibria is a common ingredient of trade policies, particularly those of third world countries, However, correct direction of structural changes also depends significantly on trade policies. (Neena and Raikhy, 1993)

An obvious reason for studying structural change is that it is at the center of modern economic growth. It is, therefore, an essential ingredient for describing the process and the construction of any comprehensive theory of development (Syrquin, 1988). An important aspect of measuring the structural changes is to examine the sources of economic growth, which may change in importance due to changes in policy emphasis and, in turn, have significant implications for future rate and pattern of economic growth. (Sethi and Raikhy, 2001)

Population has also become one of the major issues in economic development. There is a complex relationship between population growth and economic development. Both are interrelated and interdependent. Basic issue is to know how population growth affects and is in turn affected by general level of economic development. The conventional argument is that population growth is an essential ingredient to stimulate economic development. Larger population provides the needed consumer demand to generate favourable economies of scale in production, to lower production costs, and to provide a sufficient and low-cost labour supply to achieve higher output levels. Population "revisionist" economists of the neo-classical counter-revolution school argue, for example, that free markets will always adjust to any scarcities created by population pressures. Such scarcities will drive up prices and signal the need for new cost-saving production technologies. In the end, free markets and human ingenuity will solve any and all problems arising from population growth. (Simon, 1981)

But, on the other hand, population growth adversely affects the economic development in many ways. First, faster population growth makes the choice more scarce between higher consumption now and the investment available to bring higher consumption in the future. In developing countries, the resources available for investment are limited. Therefore, population growth retards investment needed for higher future consumption. Second, rapid population growth tends to over-use the country's natural resources. This is particularly the case where the majority of people are dependent on agriculture for their livelihood. With rapidly rising population, agricultural holdings become smaller and unremunerative to cultivate. There is no possibility of increasing farm production through the use of new land. Consequently, many households continue to live in poverty. Lastly, with rapidly growing population, it becomes difficult to manage the adjustments that accompany economic and social change. Urbanization in developing countries creates such problems as housing, power, water, transport, etc.

The term population explosion has been coined to describe the fundamental imbalance between resources and the population of the developing countries. It is apprehended that unless accepted means are found for checking population growth, the desired targets of economic development will remain unfulfilled (McNamara, 1984). The problem of population growth is not simply a problem of numbers. It is a problem of human welfare and of development. (Todaro and Smith, 2003)

Economic development is a relative term and its precise measurement is a difficult proposition. Earlier attempts of measuring development have focused on a single aspect of development, i.e. growth of real PCI/GNP per capita. However, disenchantment with GNP measures and failure of this measure to reflect fully the other aspects of development and welfare of the masses, led to some refinements/modifications in the GNP measures. This too could not fully reflect the multifaceted aspects of development and welfare of the people at large. Therefore, attempts were made to develop alternative measures of development based on a variety of indicators relating to economic, social and demographic aspects. These indicators have been weighted in a variety of ways to construct composite indices of development. Some economists are not contented with this approach of composite indices of development; as to them the focus of this approach is on structural changes rather than on the end results of development, i.e. the welfare of the masses. They have developed an alternate approach called Physical Quality of Life Indices (Morris, 1979).

The purpose of development is to offer people more options. One of the options is access to income not as an end itself but as means to acquiring human well-beings. There are other options including longevity of life, knowledge, community participation and guaranteed human rights (UNDP, 1990). It is now believed that improvement in the quality of people as productive agents must be central objective of development policies. It is also important to note that demographic variables have an important bearing on the level of living and standards. PQLI (Physical Quality of Life Index) measures the economic development by considering 3 indicators—infant mortality, life expectancy at age one and literacy. PQLI is a measure that can help policy makers to determine the extent to which their policies actually benefit their societies (Morris, 1979). Also, in this context, the Human Development Index (HDI), a composite index prepared by United Nations Development Programme, measured by 3-key components—longevity, knowledge and income, is an important measure of level of living and development. Each component is measured by several parameters. Thus, PQLI and HDI measure economic development by considering only three indicators. But economic development is a multidimensional process and cannot be measured on the basis of three indicators. Thus, there is a need of composite index which is based on several indicators of economic development and effort has been made to develop a composite index of development.

Most of the developing countries have followed policies of liberalization at least since early nineties. Over the past several decades, the economies of the world have become increasingly linked through expanded international trade in services as well as primary and manufactured goods, through portfolio investments such as international loans and purchases of stock, and through direct foreign investment, especially on the part of large multinational corporations. These linkages have had a marked effect on the developing world. Developing countries are exporting and importing more from one another as well as from the developed countries. The countries have also opened up more and world is heading towards a single entity 'global village' where the changes in one country have effects on others immediately.

The term 'globalization' broadly signifies the process of increased trade, flow of capital and human resources and transfer of technology between nations. Global integration, which started after the Second World War, accelerated over the last two decades. Rapid technical change has facilitated the process of globalization by creating a conducive atmosphere.

The strong performance of the global economy and of developing countries in particular, in the recent years, has raised the issue of its sustainability in the long period. Next wave of globalization will involve deeper integration with the world economy through trade, flow of information technology, finance and migration and will offer renewed and enhanced opportunities to raise productivity and income. (World Bank, 2007)

NEED AND OBJECTIVES OF THE STUDY

Globalization—the integration of the world economy—has been a widely debated theme in the past two decades or so. The growth of cross-border economic activity has changed the structure of economies and the political and social organization of countries. Not all effects of globalization can be measured directly. But the scope and pace of change can be monitored along four important channels: trade in goods and services, financial flows, the movement of people, and the diffusion of technology and knowledge.

Many factors have accelerated the pace of globalization. Barriers to international trade and investment are coming down. Technological progress has dramatically cut transportation and communication costs, enabling production processes and distribution networks to move from local to global. Some previously non-tradable services can now be traded easily around the world. Efficiency gains due to resource allocation at global scale have made globalization an increasingly powerful source of growth. Thus trade, financial flows, domestic policies, financial policy, investment policies, migration of persons and technical diffusion, etc. have tremendous effect on the process of economic development. The structure of economies is changing fast. Under globalization, the changes in one country have effects on others immediately. Globalization has important bearing on growth, structural and demographic changes and the effect is expected to have strengthened since early nineties.

In the above-mentioned context, the present study aims to examine the relationship of Globalization and Economic Development and their correlates at four points of time, i.e. in early eighties, early nineties, early 2K and in the recent past and also to construct alternative measures of economic development in this context.

OBJECTIVES OF THE STUDY

The present study has following specific objectives:

1. To examine the relationship of structural and demographic variables with level of per capita income, particularly since early nineties.
2. To construct and compare alternative measures of economic development on the basis of economic, structural and demographic variables.

3. To examine whether development levels are converging, especially since early nineties.
4. To establish relationship between rate of growth and level of growth and examine stability of rate of growth, especially since early nineties.

HYPOTHESES OF THE STUDY

In the light of the above mentioned objectives, the study attempts to test the following hypotheses:

1. Structural and demographic changes have taken place with economic growth in the developing countries.
2. Different measures of economic development are consistent with each other.
3. There is a positive impact of globalization on the economic development of developing countries.
4. Globalization has led to convergence between the developing and developed countries, and also within the developing countries.
5. Globalization has led to stability in growth rate of the developing countries.

To meet the objectives, the study has been organized in nine chapters, including the present one. The second chapter deals with the issues of globalization and economic development. The third chapter reviews the empirical studies pertaining to various aspects and dimensions of globalization and economic development. Data base and methodology used in the study have been described in the fourth chapter. The relationship between economic growth and structural changes has been established in fifth chapter, while that of economic growth and demographic changes has been taken up in the sixth chapter. The seventh chapter deals with the empirical investigation of the factors in economic development and presents a comparative study of different measures of economic development. The eighth chapter examines the issues of convergence and stability of rate of growth. The last chapter presents the summary and brings out implications of the study.

Globalization and Economic Development : Some Issues

The term 'globalization' has become a buzzword. Everyday impassioned authors and activists, whether anti- or pro-globalization, put their oars into these agitated waters. Magazines and newspapers also write incessantly on the issue, and polls are taken and discussed on 'global rage'. There are evidently many who think that globalization may be economically benign, increasing economic prosperity in the conventional economic sense of enlarging the cake, but it has negative dimensions also as it diminishes, not enhances, the war on poverty, the assault on gender discrimination, the protection of culture both indigenous and mainstream, and indeed many such aspects (Bhagwati, 2004). For many advocates of the globalization thesis, the scope and depth of the flows have created a New World Order, with its own institutions and configurations of power that have replaced the previous structures associated with the nation-state (Petras and Veltmeyer, 2001).

Globalization is a process by which the economies of the world increasingly get integrated, leading to a global economy and global economic policymaking. Globalization also refers to increased openness of economies to international trade, financial flows and direct foreign investment (Todaro and Smith, 2003), and involves integration of national economies through international market for products and factors, resulting in enhanced cross-border flows of goods, capital and labour; and flows of information, technology and management know-how (Thorbecke and Nissanke, 2006).

Globalization is not limited to economic globalization. Economic globalization and information technologies affect global culture. The free flow of goods, establishment of manufacturing facilities, spread of the restaurants, internet, satellite and cable TV are sweeping away cultural boundaries. Thus, globalization has many aspects such as economic, political, social, cultural, etc., but this study focuses mainly on economic globalization and the term 'globalization' in the study means economic globalization. Economic globalization constitutes integration of national economies into the international economy through trade, direct foreign investment (by corporations and multi-nationals), short-term capital flows, international flows of workers and humanity in general, and flows of technology (Bhagwati, 2004). Economic globalization refers to the intensification and stretching of economic interrelations across the globe. Gigantic flows of capital and technology have stimulated trade in goods and services. Markets have extended their reach around the world, in the process creating new linkages among national economies. Huge transnational corporations, powerful international economic institutions, and large regional trading systems have emerged as the major building blocs of the 21st century's global economic order (Steger, 2006). Economic openness is not simply confined to trade flows, investment flows, and financial flows. It also extends to flows of services, technology, information and ideas across national boundaries. However, the cross border movement of people is closely regulated and highly restricted. Economic integration straddles national boundaries as liberalization has diluted the significance of borders in economic transactions. It is, in part, an integration of markets (for goods, services, technology, financial assets, and even money) on the demand side, and in part, an integration of production (horizontal and vertical) on the supply side. (Nayyar, 2006)

Globalization is both a description and a prescription, and as such it serves as both an explanation and description. As an explanation, though a poor one, it is an ideology that currently dominates thinking, policy-making and political practice. As a description, "globalization" refers to the widening and deepening of the international flows of trade, capital, technology and information within a single integrated global market. With terms such as "the global village", it identifies a complex of changes produced by the dynamics of capitalist development as well as the diffusion of values and cultural practices associated with this development (UNRISD, 1995). In this context, reference is generally made to changes in the capitalist organization of production and society, extensions of a process of capital accumulation hitherto played out largely at the national level and restricted to the confines (and regulatory powers) of the state. As a prescription, "globalization" involves the liberalization of national and global markets with the belief that free flows of trade, capital and information will produce the best outcome for growth and human welfare (UNDP, 1992).

The process of globalization accelerated during the last quarter of twentieth century. There are three main manifestations of this phenomenon—international trade, international investment, and international finance—which also constitute its cutting edge. But there is much more to globalization. It refers to the expansion of economic transactions and the organization of economic activities across the political boundaries of nation states. More precisely, it can be defined as a process associated with increasing economic openness, growing economic interdependence, and deepening economic integration between countries in the world economy (Nayyar, 2006).

The concept of globalization—the 'integration of the economies of the world' in the context of 'global neighbourhood' or 'global village'—involves three major components. One, it emphasizes market mechanism and reduction in the role of the state. In this context, it involves growing internationalization of production, increasing knowledge-intensity of production, increasing trade flows of goods and services, growing integration of capital markets, shifts in industrial organization and resulting structural changes in production and trade. Second, it involves information technology and resulting comprehensive and fast flow of information around the world. This has led to shrinking of the geographical distances. Third component is technological revolution involving bio-technology, micro-electronics, new materials and goods, etc. It may have implications for technological capabilities and distribution of benefits (Panchmukhi, 1998).

According to Sikdar (2002) there are four principal factors that set the spiral of globalization moving and keep it moving, these are:

(i) Increasing pace of technological innovation that has dramatically shortened the economic life cycle of processes and products. Rapid obsolescence implies that the investments in research and expensive machinery have to be recovered in shorter and shorter period. This necessitates continuous discovery of sale outlets.

(ii) The IT revolution that has swept through the world in the last decade has radically transformed production processes and made the management of production facilities scattered over several countries much easier.

(iii) Advancing production technology and easier communications have enabled multinational corporations to fine-tune the value chain. Parts and components are routinely sourced from different countries and intra-firm trade among affiliates and subsidiaries of the multinationals account for a substantial potion of global trade.

(iv) It is also believed that IT revolution has led to the collapse of socialism. The collapse gave a blow to the Soviet model of planned economic development and left the field uncontested for capitalism. This forced countries from the developing world to move out of planning and regulation and build market friendly, outward-oriented economic structures.

HISTORY OF GLOBALIZATION

Globalization, however, is not new. There was a similar phase of globalization which began a century earlier, i.e. 1870, and gathered momentum until 1914 when it came to an end. In many ways, the world economy in the late twentieth century closely resembled the world economy in the late nineteenth century.

Though globalization has been taking place in the world economic system since the second half of 19th century but the recent wave of 80s and 90s has been very fast and involves different dimensions like globalization of financial markets, internationalization of corporate strategies, diffusion of technology, transformation of consumption pattern, growing global politico-economic system and diminished role of national governments in designing rules for global governance.

The intervening period since the World War II and the Great Depression of thirties to the seventies was the period of increased government intervention, controls, regulations, tariffs and import substitution.

The parallels between the two periods are striking. The integration of the world economy through international trade, reflected in the share of world exports in world GDP, was about the same. The story was similar for international investment, as the stock of direct foreign investment at constant prices or as a proportion of world output was about the same. The integration of markets for international finance was also comparable, in so far as cross-national ownership of securities, international bank lending and net international capital flows, in relative terms, were about the same. In the late nineteenth century, the missing dimension was international transactions in foreign exchange, which are massive now, given the past regime of fixed exchange rates under the gold standard. In the late twentieth century, the missing dimension was the almost unrestricted movement of people across national boundaries, which was massive then, given the present regime of restrictive immigration laws and consular practices. In terms of governance, however, there is a fundamental difference between these two phases of globalization. The late nineteenth century was the age of empire. The rules of the game were set by the military strength of a few imperial powers. The risks associated with trade, investment and finance across national boundaries were, in effect, underwritten by the imperial nation states. The early twenty-first century is a different world. The earlier forms of governance are neither feasible nor desirable, in part because the nation state does not have the same strength and in part because the contemporary world would prefer to set the rules of the game to manage the risks associated with globalization (Nayyar, 2006).

POSITIVE IMPACT OF GLOBALIZATION

Globalization has different implications at micro and macro levels. At micro-level there is more pressure on business enterprises to continuously innovate and improve quality of products. The link between producers and consumers is quickly established through electronic media, Internet and E-commerce. At macro level, more and more countries have followed policies of liberalization, privatization, deregulation of markets, removing structural distortions and liberalizing FDI, etc. Thus rapid shift towards market-oriented policies has taken place, where profit motive and price mechanism determine the allocation of resources (Bawa, 2002).

Globalization has far-reaching economic, social, political, cultural, environmental and technological consequences. Now-a-days global forces play important role in the determination of cropping pattern, investment level and pattern, price structure, quality of production, occupational structure and direction of economic activities. Globalization may raise employment level, improve living standards, increase consumer's product choice, expand exchange opportunities and raise national income levels. Thus globalization has significant implications for economic development.

In view of far-reaching effects of globalization, not surprisingly, therefore, the term "globalization" has acquired many emotive connotations and become a hotly contested issue in current political discourse. At one extreme, globalization is seen as irresistible and benign force for delivering economic prosperity to people throughout the world; at the other, it is blamed as a source of all contemporary ills.

Globalization has opened the door to many benefits. It has promoted open societies and open economies and encouraged a freer exchange of goods, ideas and knowledge. In many parts of the world, innovation, creativity and entrepreneurship have flourished. Globalization has set in motion a process of far-reaching change that is affecting everyone. New technology, supported by more open policies, has created a world more integrated than ever before. This spans not only growing interdependence in economic relations—trade, investment, finance and the organization of production globally—but also social and political interaction among organizations and individuals across the world.

Globalization has created opportunities for developing countries. The experiences of China, India, Indonesia, Thailand, and some other countries have demonstrated that integration into the global economy is necessary for long-term growth and poverty reduction (World Bank, 2006).

Essentially, there are four channels of globalization process through which there is interaction with the development process—trade in goods and services, movement of persons, financial flows and technological diffusion. The expected benefits of these four channels need to be discussed in detail.

Trade dimension of globalization is the most prominent. In the past two decades or so growth in trade has outpaced the growth in production by at least a factor of two and this phenomenon is likely to sustain in the next two decades. Over the last forty years, a six-fold rise in world gross national product (GNP) has been accompanied by a twelve-fold increase in world trade (Sikdar, 2002). Income growth, changing comparative advantage and push towards greater openness will continue expanding trade. Import tariffs have dropped dramatically on account of multilateral trade agreements except in case of agriculture and this has also led to rapid expansion in trade. (Pietro and Sawhney, 2002)

The foreign trade plays considerable role in economic development and has great importance for developing countries. It provides the urge to develop, the knowledge and experience that make development possible, and the means to accomplish it (Cairncross, 1962). Also, in this regard, Haberler (1959) opined that "My overall conclusion is that international trade has made a tremendous contribution to the development of less developed countries in the 19th and 20th centuries and can be expected to make an equally big contribution in the future, and that substantial free trade with marginal, insubstantial corrections and deviations, is the best policy from the point of view of economic development."

Opening up to the international trade has helped many countries grow far more quickly than they would otherwise have done. International trade helps economic development when a country's exports drive its economic growth. Export-led growth was the centerpiece of the industrial policy that enriched much of Asia and left million of people there far better-off (Stiglitz, 2002).

Supporters of free trade claim that it increases economic prosperity as well as opportunity, especially among developing nations, enhances civil liberties and leads to a more efficient allocation of resources. Economic theories of comparative advantage suggest that free trade leads to a more efficient allocation of resources, with all countries benefiting which are involved in the trade. In general, it leads to lower prices, more employment, higher output and a higher standard of living for those in developing countries. (Sachs, 2005)

Standard trade theory focussed on comparative advantage in trade expansion but new trade theory places more emphasis on role of specialization. Consumers' love for variety has also provided producers the opportunity to export. The production networks have allowed breaking up of the production process across multiple firms and countries. Technological advances in telecommunications and transport and new management processes have led to rise in export-GDP ratio from 12 percent in 1985 to 25 percent in 2005 and is likely to jump to 34 percent by 2030 (World Bank, 2007), even if there is no change in trade policies. Further reduction in tariffs will push the ratio further. Now fresh-cut flowers, perishable broccoli and strawberries, live lobsters and even ice-cream are sent between countries (Frankel, 2000).

Globalization promotes markets which in turn become efficient through competition, the division of labour and specialization. This allows people and economies to focus on what they can do best. Global markets offer greater opportunity for people to participate more and more in the larger markets around the world. It means that they can have access to more capital flows, modern technology, cheaper imports, and larger export markets.

Participation in the global production networks established by MNCs provided developing countries with the means to enhance their economic performance by accessing global know-how and integrating their markets with world markets. Such a production now accounts for one-fifth of world production, two-third of trade and is integrating developing countries further into world markets.

Under WTO policy regime, dismantling of quota system, converting it into tariffs, tariff binding and reduction, market access, etc. has further led to expansion of trade. GATS has also played some role in expansion of trade in services especially relating to finance, telecommunications and transport, etc., which are major inputs in production of goods in agricultural and manufacturing sectors. Experience regarding trade-related policies indicates that:

(i) Possibility of achieving export competitiveness is more in domestic resource industries, alongwith locally available inputs and skills.
(ii) Industrialization in developing countries draws impetus from international production networks.
(iii) Domestic and foreign investment in services exposes local suppliers to competition, leading to rise in productivity and exports.
(iv) Building export capability is an important component of policy before negotiating reduction in trade barriers (Yusuf, 2001).

Migration is another channel of globalization which is of widespread concern for countries of in-migration and out-migration alike. International migration of persons has increased rapidly in the past 20 years or so. Immigration to United States consisted largely of Latin Americans and Caribbeans, and Asians; in the European Union, internal migration has dominated, almost half of Japan's immigrants came from Asia. There has been some migration from South to

South, but South-North migration is very strong due to considerable wage gap, the combination effect to invite families and friends by the existing migrants and slowing down of workforce in developed countries. It has been estimated that in 2005, 11.4 percent of the developed countries population was foreign born, whereas this figure was 6.2 percent in 1980 (World Bank, 2007).

The major beneficiaries of this migration are the migrants themselves and the sending countries. The migrants are not only the source of funds but also potential for change and innovation. Even when the issue of 'brain drain' persists but due to inability of the developing countries to absorb the technically trained, on the whole, international migration has benefitted such countries. Migrants send back remittances amounting to $75 billion annually and the amount is far greater than Overseas Development Assistance of $52 billion. This eases foreign exchange constraints on growth. Opportunity to work in developed countries is a valuable source of skill and experience. About 38 percent of the workforce in Silicon Valley is of Indian origin. This brain drain can be turned into 'brain gain' accompanied by financial resources (Yusuf, 2001).

The most dramatic element of globalization over the past two decades has been the rapid integration of financial markets. The Bretton Woods System, created after the Second World War, rested on the foundation of closed capital accounts and fixed exchange rates. Thus, in contrast to trade and FDI, where gradual liberalization had been initiated, financial globalization was not even on the policy agenda at that time. Thc world lived with a system of separate national financial markets. This began to change in 1973 with the breakdown of Bretton Woods System. But there was no immediate rush to capital account liberalization. This began in the industrialized countries only in the early 1980s, with a subsequent increase in capital flows among them. Since late 1980s there has been a global trend towards financial liberalization. This ranged from relatively simple steps such as the unification of exchange rates and removal of controls over the allocation of credit in the domestic market to full-blown liberalization of the financial sector that included the opening up of capital accounts. Within the developing world, the latter type of reform was initially confined to a group of middle-income countries with a relatively greater range of institutions of financial intermediation that included bond and equity markets. The action in terms of the explosive growth in private financial flows from North to South was concentrated in these "emerging markets". (World Commission on the Social Dimension of Globalization, 2004)

The financial globalization is likely to lead to a more financially interconnected world and a deeper degree of financial integration of developing countries with international financial markets. Arguably, the main benefit of financial globalization of developing countries is the development of their financial system, which involves more complete, deeper, stable, and better-regulated financial markets. A better functioning financial system with more credit fosters economic growth. There are two main channels through which financial globalization promotes financial development. First, financial globalization implies that a new type of capital and more capital is available to developing countries. Among other things, new and more capital allows countries to better smooth consumption, deepens financial markets, and increases the degree of market discipline. Second, financial globalization leads to a better financial infrastructure, which mitigates information asymmetries and, as a consequence, reduces problems such as adverse selection and moral hazard (Schmukler, 2004).

Thus, financial globalization, which refers to increasing global linkages created through cross-border financial flows can help the developing countries in raising their growth rate in a number of ways. By augmenting domestic savings, reducing cost of capital, helping in transfer of technology and in development of domestic financial sectors, it can directly affect the determinants of economic growth. Indirect effects on development include increased production specialization owing to better risk management, improvement in macro-economic policies and institutions, constituting the 'disciplinary effect' of globalization (Prasad *et. al.*, 2003). Thus, financial policy also plays an important role in economic development. According to Ghani (1992) the initial level of financial development is positively associated with a country's subsequent GDP growth rate, after controlling for the effect of the starting value of human capital and investment rate.

Net resource flows to developing countries, consisting of official flows, direct investment, equity investment, bonds and others increased to $230.8 billion in 2001. While some components experienced cyclical fluctuations, foreign direct investment has remained largely independent of the cycles. During the nineties, private flows largely concentrated in middle-income countries, and low-income countries have got a smaller share. However, still FDI produces positive effects through competition and linkage effects. It helps in raising level of technology, improves access to international markets and raises trade flows.

Foreign direct investment (FDI) is an integral part of an open and effective international economic system and a major catalyst to development. Yet, the benefits of FDI do not accrue automatically and evenly across countries, sectors and local communities. National policies and the international investment architecture matter for attracting FDI to a larger number of developing countries and for reaping the full benefits of FDI for development.

Opening to foreign direct investment can also bring important benefits, including knowledge about technologies and markets and an upgrading of the skills of domestic workers. (Isard, 2005)

Empirical evidence has shown that more financially integrated economies grew faster than less integrated ones, though financial integration is not the only source of rapid growth. For example, China and India have grown at a higher rate despite limited financial integration. Therefore, financial integration is not a sufficient condition for faster growth (Prasad *et. al.*, 2003). There is some evidence of a 'threshold effect' in the relationship between financial integration and economic growth. The beneficial effects are more likely to be derived when the developing countries have a certain amount of absorptive capacity. Moreover, in addition to sound macro-economic policies, good governance and institutions play important role in attracting less volatile capital inflows and reduce a country's vulnerability to crises.

Technological innovations in the financial markets and their integration have changed the financial system of the world dramatically. With increasing share of developing countries in trade, the importance of their currencies has increased and some such currencies have been strengthened. Saving and investment rates in these countries have picked up. There is North-South and South-South flow of capital. Private capital flows to developing countries increased from only one percent of GDP in 1990 to 4.5 percent in 1996 and still higher later on. Portfolio flows accounted for large part of capital flows. Foreign direct investment has increased rapidly from $ 32 billion in 1991 to $ 161.5 billion in 2001 and emerged as the largest single source of external financing for developing countries.

Even when technological progress and diffusion were going on before the recent wave of globalization, but the communication revolution, increased training and skills have increased the pace of diffusion, which has played significant role in productivity growth. Internet has boosted the prospects of developing countries for sharing the gains of liberalized and globalized world economy. Information and communication technology benefits have been reaped by the developing countries in a big way, which include stimulation to trade-oriented business, information and technology transfer. The research in many fields, especially in agriculture, has been stimulated which is crucial for the welfare, food security, employment, resource mobilization, foreign exchange earnings and growth. Communication technology offered a better chance of sharing knowledge, drawing researchers in the developing countries to mainstream, providing incentives to them to pursue innovation and deriving commercial benefits from innovation.

It is also widely acknowledged that increased competition in global markets has come about through the combined effect of two underlying factors: policy decisions to reduce national barriers to international economic transactions and the impact of new technology. The current effects of new technology have also given a distinctive character to the process of globalization. The natural barriers of time and space have been vastly reduced. The cost of moving information, people, goods and capital across the globe has fallen dramatically, and global communications are becoming cheap and instantaneous. This has vastly expanded the feasibility of economic transactions across the world. Markets can now be global in scope with expanding range of goods and services. (World Commission on the Social Dimension of Globalization, 2004)

Globalization presents new possibilities for eliminating global poverty. By providing many types of interactions with wealthier people in other countries, globalization can potentially benefit poor countries directly and indirectly through cultural, social, scientific and technological changes, as well as through conventional trade and finance. A faster diffusion of productive ideas, such as shorter time between innovation and adoption of new technologies around the world, might help developing countries catch up much more quickly (Todaro and Smith, 2003).

The potential for good is immense. The growing inter-connectivity among people across the world is nurturing the realization that we are all part of a global community. This nascent sense of inter-dependence, commitment to shared universal values, and solidarity among people across the world can be channelled to build enlightened and democratic global governance in the interests of all. The global market economy has demonstrated great productive capacity. Wisely managed, it can deliver unprecedented material progress, generate more productive and better jobs for all, and contribute significantly to reducing world poverty. (World Commission on the Social Dimension of Globalization, 2004)

The massive increase in global inter-connectivity is affecting people's lives in different ways, some of them predictable and others unforeseen. One important change is an increase in global awareness. People anywhere are now much more aware of events and issues everywhere. This has vastly expanded awareness of global disparities in living standards and life chances, and political and social rights and liberties. For people in the richer countries, the information revolution is helping forge a greater sense of global community and transnational solidarity, as seen in the explosive growth of global coalitions of non State actors around issues of universal concern such as globalization itself, the environment, human rights, humanitarian aid and labour exploitation (World Commission on the Social Dimension of Globalization, 2004).

Globalization also promotes democracy; the link comes from the fact that rural farmers are now able to bye pass the dominant classes and castes by taking their produce directly to the market, thereby loosening the control of these traditionally hegemonic groups. In turn, this can help them on the way to become more independent actors, with democratic aspirations, in the political arena. (Bhagwati, 2004)

Thus, on the whole, globalization has many actual and potential benefits. Better communication mechanisms and lower transportation costs have provided consumers with access to lower-priced goods and a much broader range of products. International capital flows have financed production facilities in countries where labour is relatively abundant and ready to be profitably employed in more productive and remunerative activities. The spread of technological and marketing know-how and other ideas across national borders has also contributed to the more productive employment of local labour force, enabling them to raise their standards of living. At the same time, opportunities for idle or low-wage labour to migrate to countries with relatively low unemployment rates have enabled worker to earn better incomes and acquire new skills while also easing labour shortages in the countries to which they have moved. (Isard, 2005)

Also, globalization has reduced the sense of isolation felt in much of the developing world and has given many people in the developing countries access to knowledge well beyond the reach of even the wealthiest in any country in the seventies or even in eighties. People are most directly affected by globalization through their work and employment. That is how people experience the opportunities and advantages, as well as the risks and exclusions. For the gains from globalization to be widely shared, countries, enterprises and people have to be able to convert global opportunities into jobs and incomes.

DANGERS/PITFALLS OF GLOBALIZATION

As every coin has two sides, similarly, there are both positive and negative aspects of globalization. While globalization is a catalyst for and a consequence of economic development, it is also a messy process that creates significant challenges and problems. When people criticize the effects of globalization, they generally refer not only to economic globalization, but also other types.

Economic globalization is the favoured target of many of the critics of globalization. It is distinct from other aspects of globalization, such as cultural globalization (which is affected by economic globalization) and communications (which is among the factors that cause the deepening of economic globalization) (Bhagwati, 2004).

Concerns have emerged over equality of opportunity and the unequal distribution of benefits of globalization. Many poor countries and poor people in many countries have not been able to take full advantage of the opportunities brought by globalization or participate in its benefits (World Bank, 2006).

A basic step in evaluating the impact of globalization is to look at what has happened to rates of economic growth both globally and across countries. Here it is striking that since 1990 global GDP growth has been slower than in previous decade, the period in which globalization has been most pronounced. At the very least this outcome is at variance with the more optimistic predictions on the growth enhancing impact of globalization. Growth has also been unevenly distributed across countries, among both industrialized and developing countries. In terms of per capita income growth, only 16 developing countries grew at more than 3 per cent per annum between 1985 and 2000. In contrast, 55 developing countries grew at less than 2 per cent per annum, and of these 23 suffered negative growth. At the same time, the income gap between the richest and poorest countries increased significantly (World Commission on the Social Dimension of Globalization, 2004).

Although, there are some good arguments suggesting that trade liberalization may improve the resource allocation in the short term or raise growth rates permanently (and thus be beneficial to the poor), there are a number of other arguments suggesting the opposite. Opening a country's market to foreign firms, for instance, tends to reduce the market power of domestic firms and increase competitive pressures on them, eventually forcing some of them out of business. In the longer run the country may well become more efficient in using its productive resources, thereby enjoying higher growth rates and lower poverty. But in the short-run, inability to compete and the presence of labour market rigidities (segmentation due to minimum wage legislation or wage-setting behaviour by firms or trade unions, as well as imperfect mobility across sectors), may hamper the reallocation of labour between non-tradables and tradables that a reduction in tariff normally entails (Agenor and Aizenman, 1996). As a result, both unemployment and poverty may increase and persist over time.

Similarly, the effects of scale economies and learning-by-doing emphasized in the new theories of trade and growth occur mostly in the production of advanced manufactured products, such as high technology goods. However, if a country is "lagging behind" technologically and has an initial comparative advantage in "non-dynamic" sectors, openness to trade can reduce the growth rate (Matsuyama, 1992). Indeed, exports of many developing countries continue to consist of raw materials (including energy and agricultural products) and relatively low-technology manufactured goods (such as textiles). Even though openness to trade (and capital flow) may help these countries to assimilate technology and production techniques over time (thereby enabling them to shift eventually toward the production of goods and services that are characterized by dynamic factors) there may again be a "transition period" during which globalization may have only a limited effect on growth and poverty. It has also been argued that opening an economy to trade may discourage domestic research and development activities, as the limited supply of skilled labour may be allocated to the production of the manufactured goods.

While it is true that globalization encourages free trade among countries at the international level, there are also negative consequences because some countries try to save their national markets. The main export of poorer countries is usually agricultural goods. It is difficult for these countries to compete with stronger countries that subsidize their own farmers. Because the farmers in the poorer countries cannot compete, they are forced to sell their crops at much lower prices. The critics of globalization accuse western countries of hypocrisy, and the critics are right. The western countries have pushed poor countries to eliminate trade barriers, but kept up their own barriers, preventing developing countries from exporting their agricultural products and so depriving them of desperately needed export income (Stiglitz, 2002).

Many low income countries are concerned about the barriers to broad-based migration to industrialized countries, and the "brain-drain", which undermine efforts to build national capabilities. Migrants from regions are often driven into an illegal economy in countries of destination, leaving them vulnerable to exploitation.

Financial globalization also carries some risks. These risks are more likely to appear in the short-run, when countries open-up. Globalization and resulting free flow of capital may lead to financial crises. The crises in Asia and Russia in 1997-98, Brazil in 1999, Ecuador in 2000, Turkey in 2001, Argentina in 2001 and Uruguay in 2002 are some examples that captured world-wide interest. There are various links between globalization and crises. If the right financial infrastructure is not in place or is not put in place during integration, liberalization followed by capital inflows can debilitate the health of the local financial system. If market fundamentals deteriorate, speculative activities will increase with capital outflows from both domestic and foreign investors. For successful integration, economic fundamentals need to be and remain strong, and local markets need to be properly regulated and supervised. The need for strong fundamentals is the key since, other things being equal, financial globalization tends to intensify a country's sensitivities to foreign shocks. Moreover, international market imperfections, such as herding, panics, and boom-bust cycles, and the fluctuating nature of capital flows can lead to crises and contagion effect, even in countries with good economic fundamentals. Another risk of globalization is the segmentation that it may create between those able to participate in the global financial system and those that need to rely on domestic financial sectors (Schmukler, 2004).

Some new problems are a direct consequence of globalization. In their endeavour to attract direct foreign investment, developing countries compete with each other in 'a race to the bottom', by offering tax holidays, diluting labour laws, repressing trade unions or turning a blind eye to environmental concerns. The rapid integration of international financial markets, combined with the explosive growth in portfolio investment flows and short-term capital movements, has led to a volatility in capital flows and an instability in exchange rates so that the danger of capital flight is ever present (Eatwell and Taylor, 2000).

Financial openness has also, in some cases, led to a misallocation of resources and an increase in the real cost of capital. The misallocation arises when information failures lead foreign lenders to finance unsound investment. The real cost of capital is also increased when governments raise interest rates in order to maintain exchange rate stability. Other side effects of financial openness have been the need to maintain a significantly higher level of foreign exchange reserves and greater vulnerability to the flight of domestic capital.

More fundamentally, financial openness has limited the scope of developing countercyclical macro-economic policy. The reason for this lies in the fact that with financial openness countries have to surrender autonomy over either exchange rate or monetary policy. Given open capital accounts, maintaining a fixed exchange rate implies forgoing the freedom to fix domestic interest rates, while control over the latter can only be regained by allowing the exchange rate to float. In addition, the scope for expansionary fiscal policies is often severely restricted by demands of foreign financiers (World Commission on the Social Dimension of Globalization, 2004).

Moreover, it is now increasingly recognized that the process of globalization entails significant risks and potentially large economic and social costs. Openness to global capital markets has brought greater volatility in domestic financial markets, particularly in countries whose financial systems were weak to begin with and economic policies lacked credibility. Large reversals in short-term capital flows (induced by the volatility of world capital markets) have led to severe financial crises and sharp increases in unemployment and poverty in the short run. Similarly, trade liberalization has led in some countries to reduce demand for unskilled labour and lower real wages in the short-run; combined with a low degree of inter-sectoral labour mobility, job losses and income declines have often translated into higher poverty rates. As a result, there have been growing concerns about the negative effects of globalization, an increasingly polarized debate on the plight of the world's poorest, whether many of the 1.2 billion people who still live on less than $1 a day are sharing the benefits of greater integration among economies or instead are disproportionately hit by short-run crises and economic downturns (Agenor, 2002).

A growing divide between the haves and the have-nots has left increasing numbers in the third world in dire poverty, living on less than a dollar a day. Despite repeated promises of poverty reduction made over the last decade of the twentieth century, the actual number of people living in poverty has actually increased by almost 100 million. This occurred at the same time that total world income actually increased by an average of 2.5 percent annually (Stiglitz, 2002). Thus, Globalization may have created opportunities for a few countries and some people in the developing world, but a very large proportion of countries and people have remained untouched or have been marginalized in the process. Such exclusion has social consequences as some of those deprived have turned to crime, drugs or violence.

Another side-effect of globalization has been a sharp increase in the level of illicit cross-border activities. This has led to increased tax evasion and the rise of multinational crime syndicates engaged in money laundering, trafficking in people and the sex and drug trades. The same factors that facilitated the growth of legitimate cross-border economic transactions have also provided the means for illicit cross-border transactions. The ICT (Information and Communications Technology) revolution has made the cross-border coordination of illicit activities easier, while global financial liberalization has facilitated tax evasion and money laundering. Similarly, the sharp fall in transportation costs and the growth of mass tourism has made the smuggling of people and drugs less costly and more difficult to detect.

Critics of globalization also look at the damage to the planet, in terms of the perceived unsustainable harm done to the biosphere, and the perceived human costs such as increased poverty, inequality and injustice, as the results of globalization.

The opponents of globalization also see the phenomenon as the promotion of corporate interests. They claim that the increasing autonomy and strength of corporate entities shape the political policy of countries to promote their interests further. (Perkins, 2004)

CONCLUSION

Globalization itself is neither good nor bad. It has the power to do enormous good, and for the countries of East Asia, who have embraced globalization under their own terms, at their own pace, it has been of an enormous benefit, in spite of the setback of the 1997 crisis. But in much of the world it has not brought comparable benefits. For many, it seems closer to an unmitigated disaster (Stiglitz, 2002).

However, in this modern world, this is not the time for any nation to survive in isolation. Today, nations have no option but integrate their economies with the world economy. Globalization cannot be washed off despite its many negative implications. Under the circumstances, it is best to understand the pitfalls and cope up with the globalization rather than run away from it.

In fact, either view for or against is incorrect. The only rational view is to accept it as an emerging and powerful global reality, which has a momentum of its own. It has both pluses and minuses like any other major global economic change, i.e. the industrial revolution of the 18th century. Some countries gained, some lost partly because of the prevailing political circumstances.

The globalization process driven by several forces is posing challenges to developing countries. With due attention to their problems, developing countries have to manage the process of globalization with a view to drive maximum benefits while minimizing the risks. It can potentially benefit developing countries directly and indirectly through cultural, social, scientific and technological changes as well as through trade and finance. Developing countries may be able to catch up more quickly and globalization may help in convergence of growth.

Better governance is a must to enlarge the space for national policy to stimulate enterprise development, employment creation, poverty reduction and gender equality. It must reinforce social protection and enhance skills and capabilities. It must support action to overcome inequality and exclusion. It must help each country and community to define its own path of growth and development and achieve its own social and economic goals. Better governance of globalization to ensure sustainable development requires greater coherence between economic and social policies. Good governance at all levels of society—in terms of the rule of law, democracy, human rights and social equity—is essential for a fair and productive process of globalization. It must ensure the public accountability of both the state and private actors, as well as the efficiency of markets.

The naive 'market *versus* state' debate of the 1980s has now been supplanted by the recognition that both, the market and the state, are indispensable for a successful liberalization programme. The major task is to find a proper combination of the two imperfect mechanisms. The public sector has to be reoriented so that it gets out of activities where the state has no comparative advantage (such as hotels, tourism, and production of scooters and tractors) and concentrate on building up social capital in the fields of education, infrastructure, public health, and agricultural support services. (Sikdar, 2002)

In a world of nation state, the governance of globalization is bound up with governance at the national level. To take advantage of the opportunities of globalization and ensure that these are widely and fairly distributed among different groups within nations, there is a need for effective political and legal institutions, strong economic and technological capabilities, and policies which integrate economic and social goals. More generally, well governed countries, whose domestic policies take into account the needs of other countries, will be more effective partners in bringing about a fair and more inclusive process of globalization. This is why the response to globalization can be said to begin at home (World Commission on the Social Dimension of Globalization, 2004).

The issue of global governance also warrants serious attention. Global governance is the system of rules and institutions established by the international community and private actors to manage political, economic and social affairs. Good governance at the global level should enhance values such as freedom, security, diversity, fairness and solidarity. It should also ensure respect for human rights, international rule of law, democracy and participation.

Removing the obstacles to full participation by poor countries and poor people is essential to make globalization more inclusive. For example, subsidies to domestic farmers in high income economies have created formidable barriers for developing economies trying to reach global markets for agricultural products. But there is much that developing countries themselves need to do to make their economies more competitive. Scaling up and increasing the flexibility of official development assistance could assist low-income countries' efforts to attract investment and improve their trade-facilitating infrastructure, whose limitations now restrict poor countries' capacity to take advantage of growing global opportunities (World Bank, 2006).

Globalization is not a zero-sum game that some countries benefit at the cost of the others. All countries can benefit in the process of globalization. But for all countries to be able to reap the benefits of globalization, the international community must continue working to reduce distortions in international trade (cutting agricultural subsidies and trade barriers) that favour developed countries and to create a more fair system. International organizations, such as the World Bank, IMF, WTO; bilateral aid agencies and NGOs should work with developing countries to establish this foundation to help them prepare for global integration. Thus, globalization must be managed so that its fundamentally benign effects are ensured and reinforced. Without this wise management, it is imperiled.

The growth of interdependence among nation-states now means that a broader range of issues affect the countries more strongly than ever before. The growing links between countries through trade, FDI and capital flows mean that changes in economic conditions or policies in major economies have strong spillover effects on the rest of the world. Similarly, new global rules also have a strong impact on the policy options and economic performance of the countries

Thus, globalization demands high quality policy-making both at national and global levels involving good governance. Developing countries across the board have not gained much from increasing integrated world, some of them might have been left behind due to their own structural weaknesses. Government has to steer the economy through proper regulatory policies, management of resources and institutional framework. Developed countries will also have to adopt positive attitude towards the developing countries because in the globalized world, 'poverty anywhere is threat to prosperity everywhere'.

A comprehensive approach towards globalization managed by good policies at country and global level can magnify the effects of growth promoting measures. Openness, together with sound domestic policies and co-operative attitude among countries can unleash full force of economies and technological advances for growth across the board and create win-win situation.

Accepting the global integration as a fact, the urgent task ahead is to make the best use of the opportunities opened up. The task will not be easy, but the situation will have to be squarely faced. (Sikdar, 2002)

It is in this context that the present study has been undertaken so that answers to some of the above mentioned issues can be searched and policies are suggested to make globalization a boon rather than a bane.

3

Review of Literature

To understand the problem precisely and to focus on the rationale of its being undertaken, it becomes urgent to have an idea about the studies conducted so far related directly or indirectly with the problem. The review of these studies provides a broad spectrum of work done in this area and provided basis for the formulation of appropriate objectives and methodology for the present study. What follows is not an exhaustive review of the research done in this vast area of worldwide importance, rather the idea is to highlight in a general way, the type of work done in this direction. A brief review of some important studies which have been conducted, is presented below:

Chenery (1960) established relationships between economic development and industrial structure. A regression model was applied to cross-section data for 51 countries, using per capita income and population as explanatory variables in a log-linear equation; the dependent variables being the shares of primary, industry, and services sectors in GNP. The analysis brought out that the "growth elasticity" for primary sector (agriculture and mining) was 0.494 and the growth elasticity for agriculture alone was 0.474. The growth elasticities for all other sectors were much higher: 1.362 for industry, 1.288 for transport and communications, and 1.066 for other services.

Krishnamurty (1966) analyzed the impact of economic development on population growth in the Indian context for the period 1922 to 1960 by relating birth rate to per capita real income and a time trend. He treated the time trend as a catch-all variable, summarizing all socio-economic trends that pull down the birth rate, to represent such slowly changing factors as urbanization, attitude towards birth control, age at marriage, increasing level of education, etc. Similarly, death rate was treated as a function of per capita real income, government welfare expenditure and a time trend. The variables included in the equation explained about 50 percent of the variation in the birth rate. All the coefficients were significant except that of the time-trend variable. The income coefficient was negative, and its magnitude was (–)0.9290, indicating that a one percent increase in per capita real income, on average, would imply 0.9290 percent decline in the birth rate, given all other factors. In the death rate equation, the income coefficient was negative and was in agreement with both the time-series and cross-section studies. The coefficient was (–)1.7839, implying that a one percent increase in per capita real income, on average, would result in a 1.7839 percent decline in the death rate, given other factors. This negative income coefficient was much higher (quantitatively, the elasticity was about twice) than its counterpart in the birth rate equation. The coefficient of time-trend was also higher in the death rate equation. The author concluded that both birth and death rates had a negative relationship with economic development in India.

Kuznets (1966) while dealing with economic implications of population growth, argued that once the modern demographic pattern is established, it also sets conditions for modern economic growth and may contribute significantly to the rise in economic performance per capita. In his view, population has contributed to a rise in product per capita in several direct ways. However, he cautions that there are also adverse effects of population growth and has suggested that there is a possibility that a lower rate of population growth might have resulted in a higher rate of growth of product per capita. According to him, the decline in death rates has been the more conspicuous trend and the major cause of the acceleration and high level of population increase in modern times. Several aspects of this decline are relevant to economic growth. First, the curve of death rates by age is U-shaped : the rates are high in infancy, drop sharply to a trough in the late teens, and remain low until the second rise which begins at about age 50. Secondly, the death rate is associated with economic conditions. Relating birth rates to economic development, the author reported that fertility and birth rates are affected by economic and related factors. He found a negative association of birth rate with level of income and economic status.

Adelman and Morris (1967) made a quantitative study of development indicators. The purpose of the study was to gain more precise empirical knowledge about the interdependence of economic and non-economic (particularly institutional) aspects of the development process. It was intended to provide 'semi-quantitative' insights into the behaviour of a range of variables which were considered by sociologists and political scientists to play an important role in the early stages of development, and yet which were not usually dealt with systematically because they were difficult to quantify. They classified 74 developing countries according to 41 variables, which were of three types: those for which data could be obtained from published statistics, those for which it was necessary to combine statistical and qualitative elements, and those which were purely qualitative in nature. This use of qualitative indicators in a quantitative study has been one of the innovations in the analysis. They concluded that it was just as reasonable to look at underdevelopment as a social and political phenomenon as it was to analyze it in terms of country differences in economic structure.

Jorgenson (1967) brought out that high income per head is associated with a relatively large proportion to the total population engaged in industry. Low income per head is associated with a predominance of employment in the agricultural sector. The process of economic development might be studied as an increase in income per head or as an increase in the role of industrial activity relative to that in agriculture. He concluded that the industrial sector plays a strategic role in the development of a dual economy with or without disguised unemployment. Industrial output and industrial labour force ultimately come to dominate in the structure of a developed economy as a consequence of the shift in consumer demand from agricultural to industrial products and as a result of the rising proportion of investment demand in total output as income per capita increases. However, supply conditions for the agricultural sector must not be neglected in any analysis of prospects for industrialization. Unless technological progress in agriculture is sufficiently rapid to outpace the growth of population and the force of diminishing returns, the industrial sector may not be economically viable.

Seers (1969) redefined economic development in terms of the reduction or elimination of poverty, inequality and unemployment within the context of growing economy. Seers posed the basic question about the meaning of development in terms of situation of poverty, unemployment, and inequality in the economy. If all three of these have declined from high levels, then beyond doubt this had been a period of development for the country concerned. If one or two of these central problems have been becoming worse especially if all three have, it would be strange to call the result 'development' even if per-capita income doubled. It was argued that development should be perceived as a multi-dimensional process involving reorganization and reorientation of entire economic and social system. In addition to improvement in income and output, it typically involves radical changes in institutional, social and administrative structures as well as in popular attitude and in many cases, even customs and beliefs.

Thirlwall (1972) adopted a production function approach for estimating the impact of population growth on output growth and also on living standards measured in terms of per capita income. He fitted the Cobb-Douglas type production function to a cross-section data drawn from 17 developed and 32 developing countries separately. However, the estimates obtained from cross-section data were averages and represented the individual country's characteristics to the extent that production behaviour was represented by the cross-section model.

Bauer (1973) criticized per-capita income as an index of economic development. The arbitrary nature of the current distinction between developed and underdeveloped countries on the basis of per-capita income is compounded by the fact that per-capita income is in itself a seriously inadequate index of development. This index has resulted in some curious and paradoxical notions which bear on the concept of economic progress, standard of living and also on the widening gap. He further pointed out that better health and longer life expectation often reduce conventionally measured per-capita incomes (compared to what they would have been otherwise), with the paradoxical and indeed perverse result that what is clearly an improvement in people's conditions is represented as deterioration. In his words "in statistics of national income, the birth of a calf represents the increase in the living standards but the birth of a child represents a fall."

Ahluwalia (1974) examined the relationship between the distribution of income and process of development on the basis of cross-section data on income inequality. The study concluded that relative inequality increased in early stages of development. There were intersectoral shifts in the structure of production, expansion in education attainment and skill level of labour force and reduction in rate of growth of population which occurred with development. It was shown by the study that average absolute income of lower percentile group rose with rise in per capita GNP, although slower than for upper income groups.

Hovert (1974) tested whether there existed a relationship between the rate of growth and the level of economic development, if it did, then, what was it like, and what was an appropriate theoretical explanation of such a relationship if it existed. The author tested the hypothesis that countries passed through three successive phases of development. The initial phase is of stationary or slow growth; then a phase when the growth rate increased and finally a phase of decreasing growth. He took into consideration two overlapping ten year periods, i.e. 1953-63 and 1958-68. Since the regression coefficients turned out to be significant at 0.1 per cent level, it might be taken that the hypothesis was confirmed. One of the consequences of established regularity was that the gap was widening between the least developed and other countries, but the countries at the intermediate level of development were catching up.

Chenery and Syrquin (1975) provided a comprehensive description of the structural changes that accompany the growth of developing countries and analyzed their inter-relations. They employed a combination of cross section and time series analysis, and by comparing inter-country and inter-temporal patterns, responded to several important questions left unanswered in previous studies, notably those concerning the stability of the observed patterns and the nature of time trends. To achieve broad coverage of various features of development, they selected 27 variables included in I.B.R.D. economic and social data bank, for a large number of countries. These variables described 10 basic processes of accumulation, resource allocation and income distribution. Analysis of these processes suggested the 'stylized facts' of development that could be used in testing theoretical hypothesis.

Kindleberger and Herrick (1977) stated that economic development is generally defined to include improvements in material welfare, especially for persons with the lowest incomes; the eradication of mass poverty with its correlates of illiteracy, disease and early death; changes in the composition of inputs and outputs that generally include shifts in the underlying structure of production away from agricultural towards industrial activities; the organization of the economy in such a way that productive employment is general among working age population rather than the situation of a privileged minority and the correspondingly greater participation of broadly-based groups in making decisions about the directions, economic and otherwise, in which they should move to improve their welfare.

Khalaf (1979) attempted to provide limited empirical evidence on the nature of relationship between country size and rates of economic growth and levels of economic development and on the possible effects of trade concentration and dependence on trade in this relationship. The author suggested that there was no significant relationship between country size and economic growth, and that neither the dependence on trade of small countries, nor their commodity or geographic export concentration were necessarily important factors in economic growth and development. The implications of this study are obvious. If small countries, on account of their size, have high dependence on trade and export concentration, then neither their dependence on trade, nor their export concentration are likely to be important factors in development and growth. The results could also mean that attempts by small countries to diversify their exports and to reduce their degree of dependence on trade need not have any significant impact on their development and growth.

Morris (1979) developed a physical quality of life index using three indicators viz. life expectancy at age one, infant mortality and literacy which was of the form of a simple composite index of development. For each indicator, the performance of individual countries was rated on a scale of 1 to 100, where 1 represented the "worst" performance by any country and 100 the 'best performance'. For life-expectancy, the upper limit of 100 has been assigned to 77 years (achieved by Sweden in 1973) and lower limit of 1 has been assigned on 28 years (the life expectancy in Guinea Bissau in 1950). Similarly, for infant mortality, the upper limit was set at 9 per 1000 (achieved by Sweden in 1973) and the lower limit at 229 per 1000 (Gabon, 1950). Literacy rates, being measured as percentages were in the range of 1 to 100 and provided their own direct scale. Once a country's performance in life-expectancy, infant mortality, and literacy was rated on the scale of 1 to 100, the composite index (PQLI) for the country was calculated by averaging the three ratings, giving equal weights to each. Morris examined international patterns and made international comparisons among countries and concluded that there was no automatic link between per capita income and even the barest element of human well-being.

Larson and Wilford (1980) in their study of PQLI on three indicators—life expectancy, infant mortality and literacy—established that PQLI was systematically related to GNP/C, especially when atypical countries were eliminated from the sample. They also suggested that, on *a priori* basis, the components used in the construction of the PQLI were even more ambiguous than GNP/C when used as a welfare measure. Finally, they argued that the arbitrary weighting and narrow selection of components included in the PQLI contributed to the construction of an indicator which was statistically unsound.

Majumdar (1982) explained the multi-dimensional nature of development involving changes in the pace and pattern of population growth, the determinants of the rate of accretion in the physical well-being per-capita, improvement in the health of the population as reflected in the rise in life expectancy at birth, increase in literacy rates, and structural changes away from agriculture in terms of employment etc. The study focused on the conceptual limitations of the national income accounting system, based on the price index theory, on interpersonal comparisons of economic well-being. The study also looked into the problems of using the national income data as measure of relative productivity and economic welfare at international level. The relative merits of per-capita income based on purchasing power parity *vis-à-vis* exchange rate based per-capita income were examined. While studying the composite index (PQLI), incorporating demographic indicators like life expectancy at birth, birth rates and literacy rates and proportion on non-agricultural workers, the study concluded that temporal variations in PQLI had occurred in consonance with changes in the rates of growth of per capita income in most of the countries analyzed, even though they were not linearly related in the short run. The study concluded that the judicious use of the national income statistics and the composite index (PQLI) would be better indicators of performance of underdeveloped economies rather than the use of either in isolation. This type of approach would be better suited to explain the dynamics of development operative in any nation of the world.

Goncalves and Richtering (1987) analyzed empirically the apparent positive correlation between export and output growth rates on the basis of rank correlation tests, regression and cluster analysis. They took a sample of 70 developing countries. Three indicators were used, namely the annual average growth rate of total export volume at 1975 prices, the average ratio of exports to GDP and the increment in export-GDP ratio. The analysis showed that although at the aggregate level there might exist a positive statistical rank correlation between the growth rates of export and GDP, this was no so evident when other indicators of export performance were taken into account. Indeed, the mixed evidence only reflected the over-simplification and ahistoricism involved in bivariate test of the relation between export performance and output growth. The results of cluster analysis showed that the regression coefficients of GDP growth on exports for any cluster were not statistically significant. Also, for the clusters characterized by a high output performance, the difference between export growth rates was not remarkable, whereas the difference between export growth rates was enormous. The cluster of countries characterized by a poor export and output performance consisted mostly of economies of small size, having low level of capital accumulation, great structural problems, and a high degree of dependence and vulnerability *vis-à-vis* the world economy.

Hogendorn (1987), while examining various aspects of economic development, described growth as an increase in output or income and development as structural, institutional and qualitative changes, alongwith increase in output or income, that expand a country's capabilities. Development most often means growth as well, but growth need not mean development. He rejected the idea that a single measure like national product or national income was an adequate measure of development. No doubt, these are important, but development is a process of structural change in the way goods and services are produced and the way people live. He defined development as the process through which over a long time period the real per-capita income (output) of a country rises with the understanding that not just a few elite, but the general masses are the beneficiary of the increase. Explaining further, he pointed out that the rise in income (output), if it is to be termed development, must be accompanied by changes in basic conditions, including improved diets, better health, lower infant mortality rates, better clothing and housing, rising literacy and an improved physical and cultural environment. Not just national product, but the content of the national product is important. Type of goods produced (whether capital goods and/or consumer goods), product quality, leisure, durable goods, psychic concerns, etc. are important factors. The author also examined the PCI (PPP) and PQLI as alternative measures of economic development. While examining the development gap, he pointed out that absolute gap between developed and underdeveloped countries was not likely to decline.

Rana and Dowling (1988) examined the effect of foreign capital on growth of Asian developing countries and found that foreign capital flows made a positive contribution to the growth of these countries. While foreign direct investment contributed to growth both by augmenting resources available for capital formation and by improving investment efficiency, foreign aid contributed only by aiding in capital formation. The study also found that export performance, growth of the labour force and domestic saving rate also contributed favourably to growth. In relative terms, foreign private investment and export performance contributed more than aid, supporting the North's position on self-reliant approaches for developing countries. Also, the growth of the labour force and higher domestic saving contributed more than foreign capital flows. The study concluded that based on relative productivity, Asian developing countries should attempt to attract foreign private investment (including long-term commercial credit), improve their export performance, and rely relatively less on aid. In this context, the North's emphasis on self-help procedures based on trade and exchange liberalization and policies to attract foreign private investment were of particular relevance.

Shahi (1989) examined the association between product per capita and production shares of the major sectors: agriculture, industry and services. He took a sample of 75 countries and classified them into four groups: low income developing economies (LIDEs), middle income (MIDEs), high income (HIDEs) and industrial economies (IEs). He found that neither product per capita represented the 'complex of forces' nor it significantly affected the sector shares. Furthermore, product per capita was not affected by changes in sector shares. He reported that there was no consistent and unidirectional association between production per capita and the changing magnitudes of sector shares. The postulated association between product per capita and sector shares could at best be meaningful in the case of the industrialized economies.

Ahmed (1990) made an attempt to examine the effects of inflow of foreign capital on the growth of output, domestic saving, imports and productive structure in Bangladesh economy. For this, simultaneous equation model was applied using time-series data for period 1960-61 and 1979-80. It was found that foreign capital inflow was conducive for economic growth. Foreign capital inflow promoted economic growth by relieving constraints to growth. Capital inflow also changed the production structure of the economy, resulting in changes in the composition of gross domestic product, exports and imports.

Zind (1990) analyzed the absolute and comparative gains registered over the last two decades by 85 less developed countries and 19 more developed countries by using 18 indicators. The study measured three dimensions of development process: demographic, socio-economic and productivity. In this study, less developed countries were divided into groups on the basis of per capita income, geographical location and population size. Overall analysis suggested that the developmental efforts of the last two decades were successful. However, the effort was fairly successful in the socio-demographic field but failed in the income-productivity field, particularly in the view of the widening income gap between more developed and less developed countries. The richer group registered the largest gains in all the fields while the results were exactly the opposite for the poor countries. This suggested that gains are correlated with the initial development level.

Barro (1991) examined the economic growth in a cross section of 98 countries during the period 1960-85 and observed that the growth rate of real per capita GDP was positively related to initial human capital proxied by 1960 school enrolment rates and negatively related to the initial (1980) level of real per capita GDP. Countries with higher human capital also had lower fertility rates and higher ratios of physical investment to GDP. He concluded that growth was inversely related to the share of public investment and growth rates were positively related to the measures of political stability and inversely related to a proxy of market distortions.

Kakwani (1991) undertook a study concerning the measurement of growth rates of various broad economic indicators and then finding out the relationship between growth rates and changes in welfare. These growth rates were computed by fitting a linear trend line using ordinary least square method. The empirical results showed that a large number of countries were victims of the global recession in

1980s. The overall relative growth performance of all developing countries changed significantly between the 1970-79 and 1980-87 periods. According to the study, the low income countries registered a substantial improvement in their relative growth performance. Further, the study found that although the relative growth performance of the middle-income countries deteriorated considerably in the 1980s, they still managed to improve their relative welfare levels better than the low-income countries. In the Central and South African regions, the growth rates deteriorated in twenty-one out of twenty-two countries between 1970-79 and 1980-87 periods, but the actual drop in welfare occurred in only in nine countries.

Bhardwaj and Jamile (1992) attempted to study various aspects of economic development in terms of levels of economic development with the help of a cross-sectional analysis of developing countries. The results showed that higher level of economic development was associated with a lower share of the agricultural sector in GDP and higher shares of secondary and tertiary sectors. Further, developing countries were characterized by a positive relationship between the level of development on the one hand and urbanization, exports ratio to GDP, investment and savings rate on the other. The level of development was inversely associated with the ratio of consumption to GDP. The regression analysis in all cases showed a significant influence of GDP per capita on all the variables studied. The non-agricultural sector's shares in GDP had a positive relationship with urbanization but a negative relationship with the savings rate. In particular, the services sector's growth seemed to have a dampening influence on the savings rate. Also, higher level of development was associated with lower indebtedness although investment exports and consumption which tend to rise with development did not reveal a negative effect on indebtedness.

Ghani (1992) examined the role of financial policy in development. The study examined the relationship between the policy and development of financial markets in some fifty developing countries. It provided evidence that the initial level of financial development was positively associated with a country's later growth rate of gross domestic product. According to the study, a country which started with a more developed financial system tended to grow faster because it was able to improve the efficiency of resource use and was able to transform a given amount of inputs into a larger amount of output. Given the initial level of financial development and human capital stock, subsequent growth rate was found to be significantly and negatively related to the initial level of per-capita gross domestic product. This was consistent with the convergence hypothesis of neo-classical growth models. The study concluded that policy reforms that fostered financial development also had a positive and significant effect on the rate of growth of real gross domestic product.

Baffes and Shah (1993) examined the composition of public spending and its implications for economic growth. The objective of this study was to examine the relationship between different components of public investment and the rate of economic growth. In the study, a translog production model was estimated, by expressing per capita gross domestic product as a function of following five types of labour and capital stocks: labor, private capital, infrastructure capital, human resource development capital and military capital. From a sample of 25 countries which covered 1965-84 time periods, with the exception of four cases, the production function of all the countries exhibited increasing returns to scale. The highest output elasticity was with respect to human resource development capital followed by private capital and labor. Infrastructure capital exhibited low output elasticity while military capital had negative output elasticity in slightly more than half of the cases considered. This suggested that reshaping public expenditure priorities in favour of human resource development capital and away from military spending would provide a positive stimulus for the growth of the world economy.

Kawai (1994) statistically verified whether or not trade policy had a significant impact on economic growth diversity in Asia and Latin America. He examined this impact by comparing total factor productivities (TFP) between countries and between points of time using comparable long-term data, and by analyzing policy changes over time and country, using unified trade policy indices. He reported that capital accumulation and productivity change were important in explaining the diversity of growth patterns among developing countries. Secondly, difference in trade policy was an important factor in explaining the disparities in growth rate of developing countries. Thirdly, trade policy could work positively or negatively on productivity. The study concluded that though export promotion policies certainly worked positively for productivity, import substitution policies and liberalization of FDI could work positively or negatively depending on the country it was applied to as well as the stage of that country's development. Effective trade policy differed from country to country in accordance with its stage of development.

King and Levin (1994) tried to find out if research and policy advice should be guided by a modem version of capital fundamentalism, in which capital and investment were viewed as primary determinants of economic development and long run growth. According to the study, increasing investment was the best way to raise future output and it was the basic idea for the theory of "capital fundamentalism". The study found that although the capital-output ratio varied positively with the level of per-capita income, there was little support for the view that capital fundamentalism should guide the agenda for research and policy advice. Taking a broad sample of one hundred five countries, it was found that differences in capital-per-person explained a little of the differences in output-per-person across countries. The ratio of investment to gross domestic product was strongly and robustly associated with economic growth. The study concluded that economic growth caused increase in investment and savings rather than increase in investment and savings causing economic growth.

Dhillon (1995) examined the relationship of economic development with structural and demographic changes in the light of experience of countries for the period 1960-86. The study of relationship between growth rate of GDP and level of development in case of all countries, suggested that no significant relationship existed between the two. It was also found that development gap was not bridging even within the groups. There was not even a single low income, middle income and upper middle income country for which gap was bridging with USA as the target and even for the developed countries, development gap was not bridging. The study confirmed the hypothesis that structural changes and demographic changes were closely related and economic development, structural changes and demographic changes have a well-defined pattern of change.

Otsubo (1996) reviewed trends and developments in world trade, and investigated the elements involved in the accelerated integration of world trade in the past decade. Focusing on the changing strategies and role of low and middle income countries, the author explored the conditions and policy initiatives which made it easier for countries to benefit from global trade and capital flows. The author concluded that world trade relative to world income has grown more in the 1990s than in the 1970s or 1980s, mainly because of three factors: the de-synchronization of business cycles in Japan, Europe, and the United States; the expanded role in world trade of developing countries, especially of East Asia and Latin America; and the transfer of purchasing power (in the form of international capital flows) that supported heightened import demand among developing countries. The trend toward global integration, measured as the ratio of trade to output, accelerated sharply in the mid-1980s, with a reversal in the once-slowed trend toward trade integration for OECD countries. A wave of liberalization among low and middle income countries resulted in an upward kink in their trade/output ratio in the mid-1980s, representing a shift from an inward-oriented development strategy to an outward-oriented one. The author opined that the balanced integration—with export and import capacities expanding sustainably—could be achieved only through prudent, complementary domestic and border policies that encouraged long-term productive investment in the export sector.

Solimano (1999) reviewed opportunities opened by globalization to developing countries and also identified the dilemmas and tensions posed by it. He reported that the main opportunities of globalization for developing countries lay in the potential for wealth-creation through export led-growth and the benefits of expanded international trade of goods, services; access to new technologies, ideas, institutional designs in the global market place. Globalization created the potential of rapid overall output growth, increasing natural wealth and contributing to improve living standards in developing countries. However, globalization also brought serious problems and tensions that need to be managed in appropriate ways. Global business cycles give rise to considerable macro-economic volatility at the national level. The severe macro/financial crisis in the era of globalization often led to increase in poverty and social tensions that could be politically destabilizing. The study also discussed the challenge for global financial institutions (the Bretton Woods Institutions) of coping with globalization.

Mohanasundaram (2000) analyzed globalization in respect of trade and private capital inflows to developing countries. The study showed that with globalization, exports from developing increased after 1990, i.e. their rate of increase was found higher than that of advanced countries. Similarly, the imports into developing countries had also seen a phenomenal growth during the same period. Both these have increased the volume of world trade. The liberalization measures taken at the domestic front as well as at the external front by the developing countries, from eighties onwards resulted in increasing private capital flows to them. The net private capital flows into all the developing countries taken together, significantly increased during 1994-96; from 142.1 billion dollars in 1994 to 219.6 billion dollars in 1996. The developing countries of Asia were continuously getting private capital flows in the form of direct foreign investment till 1997. The study showed that the immediate consequence of rapid growth in world trade and foreign investment flows was the unprecedented strengthening of world competition.

Yusuf (2001) reported that a comprehensive approach towards globalization, managed and abetted by good policies, could magnify the effects of growth promoting measures. He opined that low income countries would need time to raise domestic savings ratios and allocate funds via financial markets. FDI and portfolio flows as well as inputs from migrants could provide the capital, some of the technology and the stimulus to deepen domestic financial markets. Openness, together with neutral domestic policies and the scaling back of regulatory constraints on domestic business activities could unleash the full force of agglomeration economies and networking externalities, inducing the emergence of industrial clusters in metropolitan regions. Openness was reported to be the surest way for low income countries to tap into the technologies that would galvanize agriculture which is the economic center of their economies. The author suggested that globalization was not a panacea. It could increase many countries' susceptibility to shocks. But reversing globalization, even if it could be done, would be an enormous setback. Embracing globalization piecemeal and keeping in place an excess of regulations would be highly inefficient. He suggested embracing all the key elements of globalization together, while sequencing the pace of integration in areas such as finance and trade.

Pietro and Sawhney (2002) studied the relationship between exports and economic growth. This study also estimated the impact of direct foreign investment on economic growth of less developed economies and also the process by which it exerted its influence on changes in economic growth as development proceeded. The study found that as development proceeded, both externalities and foreign investment became more important for economic growth, causing a positive synergistic interaction between the two sectors. For developing countries, foreign investment became more growth inducing at higher levels of development than at lower level, as both direct and indirect effects of foreign investment on economic growth improved as development proceeded. The study also found that with economic development, exports became more important for economic growth and also all external interactions became more positive for growth as development unfolded.

Santos-Paulino (2002) examined whether trade related measures affected import growth in developing countries or not. He analyzed the impact of the reduction of tariff and non-tariff barriers on the imports of 22 selected developing countries, utilizing dynamic panel data techniques. Domestic income and relative prices were found to be significant determinants of import growth. In addition, the results indicated that import duties reduced import growth, but the effect varied according to the region and the type of trade policy regime existing in the country. The results also showed that the elimination of trade policy distortions has a strong, positive impact on import growth. Also, the income and price elasticities were higher as a result of trade policy reform.

Sikdar (2002) examined the twin phenomena of liberalization and globalization alongwith complex economic issues thrown up by them. According to him, expanding international trade was just one of many manifestations of growing economic integration; others were mobility of factors of production and exchange of assets. The global transaction of foreign exchange had reached incredible levels. He reported four principal factors that caused the current wave of globalization. First, increased pace of technological innovation during the last decade, which shortened the economic life cycle of processes and products. Second, IT revolution, which made easier to control and manage the production facilities scattered over several countries. Third, communication and transportation facilities, which facilitated MNCs to fine-tune their value chain. Fourth, the collapse of socialism, which forced the countries from developing world to move out of planning and regulation, and built market-friendly, outward-oriented economic structures. He opined that countries with strong governments and at a more advanced stage of social development (with respect to social security, health and education, etc.) would be better able to derive benefits from global integration and to withstand its harmful consequences. The author suggested that the countries should definitely integrate more with the world since isolation is no longer an option, but the process should be very carefully regulated. The government should get out of non-viable activities in which private enterprise has comparative advantage and concentrate on improving efficiency, transparency, and the building up of social capital, which includes safety nets for the underprivileged.

Stiglitz (2002) analyzed the 'discontents' of globalization even though globalization was not an inherently evil concept. However, it is the management of globalization by international institutions such as International Monetary Fund (IMF), World Bank and World Trade Organization (WTO) that has produced 'discontents' particularly for developing countries. He stated that international trade has helped many economies to grow more quickly than they would have otherwise done without joining global market. Globalization has allowed people to live longer, have better standards of living and increased the access to knowledge. But the three main institutions that govern globalization, i.e. IMF, World Bank and WTO, used the 'Washington Consensus' as their blueprint for policymaking. The Washington Consensus cites three pillars that should be present in economies to be able to assimilate into global market—fiscal austerity, privatization and market liberalization. The IMF provides funds only if countries engage in policies like cutting deficits, raising taxes, or raising interest rates that lead to contraction of economy and these three pillars produce adverse effects on developing countries if there is a lack of proper management of globalization. He reported that IMF has failed in its mission of promoting global stability, development and guiding the transition of countries from communism to a market economy. He suggested that the international institutions that govern globalization should be reformed, and there should be better governance of international financial institutions with greater transparency in their decision-making, so that there is sustainable growth and fruits of this growth are more equitably shared.

Prasad et. al. (2003) examined the effects of financial globalization on developing countries and reviewed the potential and actual benefit-risk trade-offs associated with financial globalization. According to them, financial integration might be associated with higher consumption volatility. Therefore, it might be worthwhile for developing countries to experiment with different paces and strategies in pursuing financial integration. Most of the countries that initiated financial integration had continued along this path despite temporary setbacks. This observation was consistent with the notion that the indirect benefits of financial integration could be quite important. They opined that it might not be essential for a country to develop a full set of sound institutions matching the best practices in the world before embarking on financial integration. Doing so might strain the capacity of the country. An intermediate and more practical approach could be to focus on making progress on the core indicators—transparency, control on corruption, the rule of law, and financial supervisory capacity. The IMF and the World Bank—through financial sector assessment programs and among other ways—helped promulgate codes and standards on best practices for financial supervision and transparency, so that countries could implement the needed changes, supported by technical assistance.

Alfaro et. al. (2004) examined the links among foreign direct investment (FDI), financial markets and economic growth. The study looked into role of local financial markets and also the link between foreign direct investment and growth. Using cross-country data from 1975 to 1995, the study showed that foreign direct investment alone played an ambiguous role in contributing to economic growth. The countries with better financial systems could exploit foreign direct investment more efficiently. The link between foreign direct investment and growth was causal, where foreign direct investment promoted growth through financial markets. The result of this study suggested that countries should weigh the cost of policies aimed at attracting foreign direct investment *versus* those that seek to improve local conditions. Better local conditions not only attract foreign companies but also allow host economies to maximize the benefits of foreign investments.

Bhagwati (2004) examined the impact of globalization on growth, labour, poor, women and culture. According to him, the argument that globalization has benefited the poor has centered on a two-step argument: that trade enhances economic growth, and that growth reduces poverty. The growth spurred by globalization has not only expanded the pie but has done so in a way that is 'socially benign' and globalization possessed a 'human face'. Also, globalization has beneficial effects on an array of social issues like child labour, women's rights, democracy, wage and labour standards. He stated that restriction of trade often was the chief cause of domestic monopolies. Freer trade produced enhanced competition and gains therefrom. He further argued that while it was almost impossible to prevent illegal immigration, the governments must find a way to integrate the migrants into society so that they maximized the economic benefits. He also advocated spreading migrants all over the country so that the wages in one region were not affected. According to him, the world badly needs enlightened immigration policies and best practices to be spread and codified. He suggested World Migration Organization to juxtapose each nation's entry, exit and residence policies toward migrants. He cautioned the countries wishing to globalize by emphasizing the need of institutions and processes to come to the assistance if there was an unexpected change in the global markets. He pointed out that in many cases, globalization was blamed for whatever went wrong within a country. But, that this was a political deflection used by corrupt and ineffective political leaders. Instead of implementing more effective domestic and international policies, many government leaders preferred to blame all ills on globalization, which indirectly meant on the U.S. He suggested that globalization must be managed so that its fundamentally benign effects are ensured and reinforced. The management would be better and more effective if the governments, international institutions, corporations and intellectuals who celebrate and reinforce globalization joined hands with the non-governmental organizations. He opined that by focusing so much on purported evils of globalization, the opportunities to focus on accelerating its achievements while coping with its downslides are missed.

Rogoff et. al. (2004) studied. the impact of financial globalization on growth and volatility in developing countries. The study provided a comprehensive assessment of empirical evidence about the impact. The results suggested that it was difficult to establish a robust causal relationship between financial integration and economic growth. Furthermore, there was little evidence that developing countries had been consistently successful in using financial integration to stabilize fluctuations in consumption growth. However, this study also found that financial globalization could be beneficial under the right circumstances. Empirically, good institutions and quality of governance were crucial in helping developing countries derive the benefits of globalization. Similarly, macro-economic stability appeared to be an important prerequisite for ensuring financial globalization to be beneficial for developing countries. Finally, countries that employed relatively flexible exchange rate regimes and succeeded in maintaining fiscal discipline were more likely to enjoy the potential growth and stabilization benefits of financial globalization.

World Commission on Social Dimension of Globalization (2004) opined that the benefits of globalization could be extended to more people and better shared between and within countries. The Commission suggested focusing on people, democratic as well as effective state, sustainable development, productive as well as equitable markets, and fair rules of global economy with deeper partnerships of international organizations. The nascent sense of interdependence, commitment to shared universal values, and solidarity among people across the world could be channeled to build enlightened and democratic global governance in the interest of all. Wisely managed, globalization could deliver the unprecedented material progress, generate more productive and better jobs for all, and contribute significantly to reduce global poverty. According to the Commission, to share the benefits of globalization at national level, there should be good political governance, an effective state that ensures high and stable economic growth, and strong representative organizations of workers and employers. At the global level, global rules and policies on trade and finance must allow space for policy autonomy in developing countries. Fair rules for trade and capital flows were needed to be complemented by fair rules for the cross-border movement of people. The multilateral trading system should substantially reduce unfair barriers to allow market access for goods in which developing countries have comparative advantage. In this context, the interests of least developed countries should be safeguarded through special and differential treatment to nurture their export potential. Also, international financial system should be made supportive of sustainable global growth. Cross-border financial flows have grown massively but the system was unstable, prone to crises and largely bypass the poor and capital scarce countries. In this context, the Commission recommended that developing countries should be permitted to adopt a cautious and gradual approach to capital account liberalization and more socially sensitive sequencing of adjustment measures in response to crises. The Commission suggested increasing representation of developing countries in the decision making bodies i.e. UN, WTO, IMF and World Bank. Also, a 'Globalization Policy Forum' should be organized by the

UN and its specialized agencies to review the social impact of globalization.

Das (2005) examined the role of trade and technology in the growth process. According to him, trade and growth may be linked via technology; i.e. (a) Openness leads to technological upgradation; and (b) technological progress leads to growth. However, these relationships need not be automatic. He concluded that a developing country, which is labour-abundant, could utilize FDI and labour-intensive technologies for employment generation. In terms of this growth paradigm, employment generation and its income-effects would be demand-creating. These internal or domestic sources of growth impulses lead to expansion in economic activities in other sectors of the economy. This itself might contribute to technological capability building efforts. These outcomes, combined with the creation of patenting infrastructure and mechanisms to commercialize technologies could together provide an impetus to the technological diffusion process. Also, there could be further improvements in the export competitiveness of products with the help of technological modernization in different sectors. To the extend exports are a component of GDP, they would generate economic growth via income expansions. Finally, growth in turn would further boost employment generation if labour-intensive technologies of production are used. This completes the virtuous circle. The study highlighted the importance of trade and technological capability in achieving economic growth.

Chow (2006) studied the nature and implications of globalization in China's economic development since 1978. He discovered the four aspects of the flows of goods, capital, technology/information and of people to and from China. After examining the facts of globalization for China he concluded that the open-door policy first advanced by Deng Xioping when China had a very different ideology has been essential in the modernization of China. The open-door policy has allowed globalization and economic development to take place. The flow of goods, capital, technology and people to and from China has been essentially beneficial to both China and its partners in the globalization process although there have been short-run harmful effects on some of them. Understanding the nature and economic implications of China's open-door policy would enable us to appreciate some of the important forces at work which would propel China's future economic growth and determine the role of China in the global economic community.

Nayyar (2006) analyzed the prospects for development in a changed international context, where globalization has diminished the policy space so essential for countries that are latecomers to development. The main theme was that, to use the available policy space for development, it was necessary to redesign strategies by introducing correctives and to rethink development by incorporating different perspectives, if development was to bring about an improvement in the well-being of people. In redesigning strategies, some obvious correctives emerged from an understanding of theory and a study of experience that recognized not only the diversity but also the complexity of development. In rethinking development, it was imperative to recognize the importance of initial conditions, the significance of institutions, the relevance of politics in economics and the critical role of good governance. The study opined that even if difficult, there was also a clear need to create more policy space for national development, by reshaping the rules of the game in the world economy and contemplating some governance of globalization.

Roe et. al. (2006) focused on developing countries in the context of the world economy and examined the effects of globalization on income levels and a country's rate of economic growth. According to them, persistently poor countries could gain from globalization but trade and institutional reforms were required. Since poor countries were largely exporters of primary commodities, access to developed country agricultural markets seemed crucial. Market access would appear to help create the conditions for institutional reform, but surely this was not sufficient in itself and trade reforms in poor countries were required for development. They concluded that (1) Institutional change was induced by the potential for economic gain, and thus the incentive for change followed the emergence of economic opportunities, and (2) these economic opportunities could be enhanced by agricultural trade reform in advanced countries that open markets particularly for those countries faced with persistent levels of low growth in per capita income.

Otherwise, there might not be compelling reasons to expect these societies to naturally speed up their gravitation to better institutions.

Stiglitz (2006) opined that the globalization has the potential to bring enormous benefits to both the developing and the developed countries, but it has failed to live up to the expectations. He believed that problem was not with globalization itself but the way the globalization has been managed. The rules of the game have been largely set by the advanced industrial countries and they have shaped globalization to further their own interests. According to him, the current model of globalization would not work. It has five key flaws: the rules of the game are unfair, and designed to benefit rich countries and corporations; globalization advances material values over other values such as concern for the environment; global trade rules have undermined the sovereignty of poor countries; globalization has not benefited the developing as well as the developed world, there are losers in both; and the American model forced on the poor has caused damage and resentment in the developing countries. He argued that globalization is like "a pact with the devil", but this is not how it has to be. The author suggested for the reform of global financial institutions; the IMF and the World Bank. He suggested changes in the voting system at the IMF and the World Bank by giving more weight to developing countries, increasing transparency and accountability in these financial institutions. Besides reforms in international institutions, the author also suggested the reform of trade agreements and intellectual property laws to make them better able to respond to the growing disparity between the richest and poorest countries.

Rassekh (2007) examined whether the effect of international trade on income growth depended on the economy's level of development, and whether trade was more beneficial to lower income economies. The paper derived implications regarding international income disparities. The standard deviation of the logarithm of per worker income of the sample of 128 economies in 1960 stood at 0.96 and rose modestly to 1.06 in 1985. The estimates suggested that trade might have moderated the increase in the standard deviation over the period 1960-1985. The paper found that trade favoured lower income economies.

Bhargava (2008) analyzed GDP growth rates, poverty measures and inequality using aggregate panel data of developing countries for the period 1990-2000. Issues of globalization were investigated by analyzing the differential effects of the countries' exports and imports and by postulating trans-logarithmic models that allow for non-linear effects of literacy levels and measures of openness. The main findings were that literacy rates affected growth rates in a quadratic manner and countries with higher literacy rates were more likely to benefit from globalization. Second, the model for growth rates showed non-linear and differential effects of the export/GDP and import/GDP ratios. Third, the models indicated that population health indicators such as life expectancy were important predictors of GDP growth rates. Fourth, models for poverty measures showed that poverty was not directly affected by globalization indicators. Finally, the model for Gini-coefficients indicated significant effects of 'medium' and 'high' skilled labour work force, with higher proportions of high-skilled labour implying greater inequality. Since the diffusion of technical knowledge to developing countries and availability of educated labour force were critical ingredients for economic growth, short-run increases in inequality due to globalization might be inevitable. Overall, developing countries needed to invest additional resources in education and health for creating skilled labour force to enjoy greater benefits of globalization.

Data Base and Methodology

The present study entitled "Globalization and Economic Development: Experience of Developing Countries" aims to examine the relationship of Globalization and Economic Development and its correlates at four points of time, i.e. in early eighties, early nineties, early 2K and in the recent past and also to construct alternative measures of economic development. As such the study required secondary data, which were collected mainly from various World Bank publications such as World Tables, World Development Indicators, World Development Indicators (CD version), World Development Report, World Development Report (CD version), UNCTAD's Handbook of Statistics and UNDP's Human Development Report, etc. Attempt was made to collect data for maximum number of developing countries and for maximum number of variables depending upon the availability since 1980. The number of countries varied between 66 and 113 in case of each variable depending upon the availability of data. The number of countries for which data were available increased since 1980. The technique of Interpolation and Extrapolation was used in a few cases for some variables where data for some years were not available.

The study covered the period of 1980 to 2004 (the latest year for which data were available). Keeping in view the long time-period and number of countries, the data was collected at four points of time viz. 1980, 1990, 2000 and 2004. Countries were categorized as developing countries on the basis of World Bank's grouping of countries.

To carry out the objectives of the study, a number of economic, social, demographic and globalization-related variables, as mentioned below, have been used :

1. Agriculture value-added (% of GDP)
2. Agriculture average annual growth rate (%)
3. Industry value-added (% of GDP)
4. Industry average annual growth rate (%)
5. Services value-added (% of GDP)
6. Services average annual growth rate (%)
7. GDP average annual growth rate (%)
8. GNI per capita, (current US $)
9. GNI per capita, PPP (current international $ reflecting purchasing power)
10. Private consumption expenditure (% of GDP)
11. Gross domestic savings (% of GDP)
12. Energy use per capita (kg of oil equivalent)
13. Fuel + ores and metal exports (% of merchandise exports) (Merchandise exports are the f.o.b. (free on board) value of goods provided to the rest of the world, (value in U.S. Dollars))
14. Food + agricultural raw material exports (% of merchandise exports)
15. Manufactures exports (% of merchandise exports)
16. Birth rate, crude (per 1,000 people)
17. Death rate, crude (per 1,000 people)
18. Infant mortality rate (per 1,000 live births)
19. Life expectancy at birth (years)
20. School enrolment, primary (% net)
21. School enrolment, secondary (% net)
22. Adult Literacy Rate (%)
23. Percentage of population of working age (15-64 yrs.)
24. Employment in agriculture (% of total employment)
25. Employment in industry (% of total employment)

26. Employment in services (% of total employment)
27. Urban population (% of total)
28. Daily calorie supply (per capita)
29. Number of Physicians (per 1,000 people) (Number)
30. International migration stock (% of population)
31. Gross private capital flows (% of GDP)
32. Foreign direct investment, net inflows (% of GDP) (It is the sum of equity capital, reinvestment of earnings, and other short-term and long-term capital, as shown in the balance of payments. This series shows net inflows in the reporting economy and is divided by the value of GDP)
33. Foreign direct investment, net outflows (% of GDP) (These are the net outflows of investment from the reporting economy to the rest of the world)
34. Gross capital formation (% of GDP)
35. Exports of goods and services (% of GDP)
36. Imports of goods and services (% of GDP)
37. Degree of openness (exports + imports) % to GDP
38. Export volume, average annual growth rate (%)
39. Import volume, average annual growth rate (%)
40. Merchandise trade (% of GDP)
41. Trade in services (% of GDP)
42. Total debt service (% of GNI)

METHODOLOGY

In order to meet the specified objectives of the study, several statistical techniques, which were applied to analyze the data, are discussed below:

Tabular Analysis

Simple as well as two-way tables alongwith ratios and percentages, etc. were used to analyze the data.

Chi-Square Test

Technique of Chi-Square Test has been applied to know the nature as well as significance of association between level of economic development and various economic, social and demographic indicators. Tables showing two-way classification of countries with respect to level of economic development and various economic, social and demographic variables, were prepared for each of the years 1980, 1990, 2000 and 2004. Chi-Square values were calculated using the following formula:

$$\chi^2 = \frac{\sum (O-E)^2}{E}$$

where O = observed frequency
E = expected frequency

Values of χ^2 were calculated and compared with the tabular values at 5 percent level of significance to know the significance of association between level of economic development and various economic, social and demographic variables. While preparing the two-way tables for Chi-Square test, efforts were made to prepare class-intervals in such a way that the table forms more or less normal distribution and the frequency is not concentrated too much in a single cell. However, if the theoretical (expected) frequency in a cell was less than 5, pooling of the columns was done and degrees of freedom were adjusted accordingly.

Two-way Tables were prepared for each of the years viz. 1980, 1990, 2000 and 2004 and correspondingly χ^2 values were calculated, however, for the sake of brevity, tables are given in the thesis only for the year 2004 and the calculated χ^2 values for the remaining years have been given below the tables so as to compare the change in significance of association over time.

Correlation Analysis

The relationship between various economic, social and demographic variables has been studied through Karl Pearson's co-efficient of correlation. Its significance has been tested by applying student's 't-statistic' using the following formula:

$$t_{n-2} = \frac{r\sqrt{n-2}}{\sqrt{1-r^2}}$$

where n is the number of paired observations, r is the co-efficient of correlation between various economic, social and demographic variables in a specific year. Calculated value of 't' has been compared with the tabular value of 't' for n-2 degree of freedom at 0.01 and 0.05 percent level of significance for two-tailed test.

Rank Correlation Analysis

Countries were ranked in different time periods, i.e. 1980, 1990, 2000 and 2004; on the basis of different measures of economic development like GNI per capita, GNI PPP, PQLI and Composite Index (CINDEX). This was done by estimating Spearman's Rank Correlation Coefficient between different measures of economic development.

$$\text{Spearman's Rank Correlation Coefficient} = 1 = \frac{6\sum D^2}{n(n^2-1)}$$

where D is the difference between the ranks and 'n' is the number of ranks.

Factor Analysis

As economic development is a multi-dimensional phenomenon, a single indicator cannot reflect it. Thus, effort was made to develop a composite index of development by applying Factor Analysis. To make the number of variables manageable, out of total 42 variables, 22 variables having higher partial correlation with GNI per capita were selected.

To examine the contribution of the different variables in economic development, Factor Analysis was used. In Factor Analysis, a given set of n variables is grouped into p number of groups called 'Factors' which are less in number than the set of original variables. The variables within a group (Factor) are of the same nature or are complementary with respect to the phenomenon under study but between two groups 'Factors' variables are independent. Thus factors F_i and F_j are orthogonal.

The data was first normalized using Nagar-Basu (2002) methodology. The selected variables were normalized by subtracting the minimum value of the particular variable from its actual value and dividing it by the range, which is the difference between the maximum and minimum value of the selected variables. The formula is given below:

$$Z_{ij} = \frac{Actual\ \ Value_{ij} - Minimun\ \ Value_{ik}}{Maximum\ \ Value_{ik} - Minimum\ \ Value_{ik}}$$

where, Z_{ij} = Normalized value of ith variable for j^{th} country;
i = variable;
j = country;
k = specific value.

The technique of Factor Analysis, as used in the present study, is given as under:

$$X = LF + U$$

where X is vector of all the original variables.

$$X' = [X_1, X_2, X_3, \ldots\ldots\ldots. X_n]$$

F is vector of 'Factors' derived

$$F' = [F_1, F_2, F_3, \ldots\ldots\ldots. F_p]$$

U is vector of error terms

$$U' = [E_1, E_2, E_3, \ldots\ldots\ldots. E_n]$$

and X', F' and U' are the respective transposes.

L is matrix of Factor Loading (Loading Coefficient Matrix)

$$L = \begin{bmatrix} a_{11} & a_{12} & a_{13} & a_{14} \ldots\ldots\ldots\ldots a_{1p} \\ a_{21} & a_{22} & a_{23} & a_{24} \ldots\ldots\ldots\ldots a_{2p} \\ a_{31} & a_{32} & a_{33} & a_{34} \ldots\ldots\ldots\ldots a_{3p} \\ . & . & & . \\ . & . & . & . \\ a_{n1} & a_{n2}. & .a_{n3} & a_{n4} \ldots\ldots\ldots\ldots a_{np} \end{bmatrix}$$

The coefficient (Factor Loading) a_{ij} belongs to i^{th} variable and j^{th} factor which is similar to simple correlation coefficient and shows the extent to which variable X_i is related to F_j Factor. "A salient loading is one which is sufficiently high to assume that a relationship exists between the variable and the Factor. In addition, it usually means that relationship is high enough so that the variable can aid in interpreting the factor and *vice-versa.*" (Gorsuch, 1974)

The sum of the square of factor loadings of X_i original variables under the derived p Factors is called the communalities (C_i) for X_i variables.

$$(a_{i1})^2 + (a_{i2})^2 + (a_{i3})^2 + \ldots\ldots\ldots\ldots + (a_{ip})^2 = (C_i)^2$$

Communality in Factor Analysis is something like R^2 in the Regression Analysis and it shows the extent to which the derived factors explain the ith variables. Derived communality value generally should be larger (more than 70 percent) to be sure that each variable has been explained well. By definition, the communality of a variable is that proportion of its variance which can be accounted for the common factors (Lindeman *et. al.*, 1980).

The Principal Component Analysis (Factor Analysis) produces components (Factors) in descending order of their importance and factor loadings which explain the relative importance of different variables in explaining variance in the phenomenon. Some studies using 'Factor Analysis' adopted 'First Principal Component' as guiding principle for determining individual indicator weights. In the present study, all the 'Principal Components' (Factors derived) are taken into account to determine relative weights of selected variables so as to reflect maximum possible variations in the economic development. The method for determining the relative weights for the variables is explained below:

$$W_i = F_{ik}\lambda_k$$

where,

W_i = Weight of ith variable

F_{ik} = Factor loading of ith variable and k^{th} factor which reflects the highest correlation between variable (X_i) and factor (F_k)

λ_k = variation explained by k^{th} factor

The weights for the variable determined by applying above mentioned technique are in accordance with the contribution made by the variable in the inter country variations.

Composite Index

The statistical technique employed to develop the weighted composite index involves finding out the 'Principal Components' of the groups consisting of these selected 22 variables and derive the implicit weights based thereon. The composite index is then constructed by combining various indicators whose implicit weights are already determined through the technique of 'Principal Component Analysis' (Hagood, (1943), Aldeman & Morris, 1967)).

$$\text{Composite Index for ith country} = \frac{\sum W_i Z_{ij}}{\sum W_i}$$

where, Z_{ij} = Normalized value of the ith variable for the jth country

W_i = Weight of ith variable

Bridging of Gap

To examine whether the development gap is bridging or not, a test was applied following Hogendorn (1987). The absolute gap in income would increase whenever the ratio of GNI per capita of the target country to country in question is greater than inverse ratio of their growth rates, i.e.

$$\frac{Y_1}{Y_2} > \frac{r_2}{r_1}$$

where Y_1 = GNI per capita of the target country

Y_2 = GNI per capita of the follower country

r_1 = Growth rate of GDP of target country

r_2 = Growth rate of GDP of follower country

Regression Analysis

Linear regression equations were fitted by regressing dependent variable on each of the independent variables separately as well as jointly (multiple regression).

$$Y = a_0 + b_i X_i + u$$

where, Y is dependent variable

X_i is independent variable

U is the disturbance term

The statistical significance of estimates of b_i was examined by applying t-test and r^2/R^2 was computed to see the percentage variations in the dependent variable explained by a particular independent variable, or all the independent variables jointly.

Step-wise (Step-up) Regression Analysis was carried out on the basis of correlation coefficients of independent variables with the dependent variable. At the first step, the variable with highest correlation was considered. In the subsequent steps, the variables were added on the basis of correlation with the dependent variable, after checking for the problem of multicollinearity.

The polynomial regression analysis was also carried out in the following form:

$$Y = a_0 + b_1 X + u$$
$$Y = a_0 + b_1 X + b_2 X^2 + u$$
$$Y = a_0 + b_1 X + b_2 X^2 + b_3 X^3 + u$$

where X is independent variable, X^2 and X^3 are the square and cube of this independent variable and u is the disturbance term. However, the linear form turned out to be the best fit in all cases and results (graphs) have been given accordingly.

PQLI

GNP per capita is the most widely accepted single measure of general economic performance within and among countries but it is not easy to show how output is distributed among people and groups within countries. Moreover, it is not certain that the output of a society so distributed, is clearly related to the quality of life results. The Physical Quality of Life Index is an index showing how benefits ("welfare") are distributed and reflected in quality of life (Morris and Michelle, 1982).

PQLI was constructed using the methodology given by Morris and Michelle (1982). The three indicators used in the PQLI are life expectancy at age one, infant mortality rate and literacy rate. For each indicator, the performance of individual countries is placed on a scale of 0 to 100, where 0 represents an absolutely defined "worst" performance and 100 represents an absolutely defined "best" performance. Once performance for each indicator is scaled to this common measure, a composite index is calculated by averaging the three indicators, giving equal weights to each of them. The resulting Physical Quality of Life Index thus also is scaled 0 to 100 (Morris and Michelle, 1982).

The formula for constructing PQLI is:

$$PQLI = \frac{(LI + IMI + LEI)}{3}$$

where,

PQLI = Physical Quality of Life Index
LI = Literacy Index
IMI = Infant Mortality Index
LEI = Life Expectancy Index

Creating the 0-100 scale for literacy, of course, poses no problem. Using the proportion of the population 15 years and older who are literate, the index is identical with the adult literacy rate. The scaling of the other indicators is not simple.

Infant mortality, being expressed as the number of infant deaths per thousand live births, could lend itself to a similar solution. The worst conceivable situation (=0) would be one in which every child died within the first year; the best (=100) would be one in which no child died during that period.

The formula for calculating Infant Mortality Index is:

$$IMI_i = \frac{Maximum\, IMR_t - IMR_i}{(Maximum\, IMR_t - Minimum\, IMR_t)/100}$$

where,

IMI_i = Infant mortality index of country i.
IMR_i = Infant mortality rate of country i.
Maximum IMR_t = Highest infant mortality rate in the year t.
Minimum IMR_t = Lowest infant mortality rate in the year t.

Life expectancy is the number of years a newborn infant would live if prevailing patterns of mortality at the time of his/

her birth were to stay the same throughout his/ her life. But PQLI uses life expectancy at age one in order to avoid double-counting of the infant mortality rate. The data of life expectancy at birth was converted to life expectancy at age one by using the following formula:

$$e^1 = \frac{e^0 - 1 + q^0\left(1 - k^0\right)}{1 - q^0}$$

where,

e^1 = Life expectancy at age one
e^0 = Life expectancy at birth
q^0 = Infant mortality rate
k^0 = Average survival period (0.2)

Then, Life Expectancy Index was calculated by using the following formula:

$$LEI_i = \frac{e_i^1 - Minimum\ e_t^1}{\left(\left(Maximum\ e_t^1\right) - Minimum\ e_t^1\right) / 100}$$

where,

LEI_i = Life expectancy Index of country i.
e_t^1 = Life expectancy at age one of country i.
Minimum e_t^1 = Lowest life expectancy at age one in the year t.
Maximum e_t^1 = Highest life expectancy at age one in the year t.

Coefficient of Variation

In order to examine the nature of change in the degree of disparity in various indicators, coefficient of variation (C.V.) as measure of convergence/divergence was used.

$$\text{Coefficient of Variation (C.V.)} = \frac{\sigma}{\overline{\overline{X}}} \times 100$$

where, $\sigma = \sqrt{\frac{\sum fx^2}{N}}$

$$x = (X - \bar{X})$$

Chow Test

Chow Test was applied to test the stability of regression parameters over time. The test was applied using methodology given by Gujarati (2004). Those variables were selected for this analysis whose correlation coefficients were high and significant with GDP growth rate. GDP growth rate was taken as dependent variable (Y) alongwith gross capital formation (% of GDP) (X_1), urban population (% of total) (X_2), GNI per capita PPP (X_3), services value added (% of GDP) (X_4) and manufacture exports (% of merchandise exports) (X_5) as independent variables.

For checking stability of regression parameters over time, i.e. 1980 and 1990, following regression equations were obtained:

For 1980;

$$Y_1 = \lambda_1 + \lambda_2X_1 + \lambda_3X_2 + \lambda_4X_3 + \lambda_5X_4 + \lambda_6X_5 + u_1$$
$$n_1 = \text{No. of observations} \quad \text{(Eq. 1)}$$

For 1990;

$$Y_2 = \gamma_1 + \gamma_2X_1 + \gamma_3X_2 + \gamma_4X_3 + \gamma_5X_4 + \gamma_6X_5 + u_2$$
$$n_2 = \text{No. of observations} \quad \text{(Eq. 2)}$$

Pooled for 1980-90;

$$Y_3 = \alpha_1 + \alpha_2X_1 + \alpha_3X_2 + \alpha_4X_3 + \alpha_5X_4 + \alpha_6X_5 + u_3$$
$$n_3 = (n_1+n_2) \quad \text{(Eq. 3)}$$

The Regressions (Eqs. 1 and 2) assume that the regressions in the two time periods are different, i.e. instability in regression parameters. The Regression (Eq. 3) which is pooled regression, assumes that there is no difference between the two time periods, i.e. stability in regression parameters. The u's represent error terms and n's represent the number of observations.

The RSS (residual sum of squares) were obtained for the three equations, i.e. RSS_1 for equation 1, RSS_2 for equation 2 and RSS_3 for equation 3. Since the two equations (Eqs. 1 and 2) are independent, RSS_1 and RSS_2 can be added to obtain RSS_{UR} (unrestricted residual sum of squares) :

$$RSS_{UR} = RSS_1 + RSS_2 \qquad df = (n_1 + n_2 - 2k)$$

The RSS_3 is called RSS_R (restricted residual sum of squares):

$$RSS_R = RSS_3 \qquad df = (n_1 + n_2 - k)$$

The basic logic behind Chow Test is that if there is stability in regression parameters (i.e. Regression Eq. 1 and Eq. 2 are essentially the same) then the RSS_R and RSS_{UR} should not be statistically different. Therefore, we work out the following ratio:

$$F = \frac{(RSS_R - RSS_{UR})/k}{(RSS_{UR})/(n_1 + n_2 - 2k)} \sim F_{[k,(n_1+n_2-2k)]}$$

We check the hypothesis;

H_o = Regression parameters are Stable
H_1 = Regression parameters are Instable

For $v_1 = k$ (k is number of parameters)
$v_2 = n_1 + n_2 - 2k$

If calculated value of F > tabulated value of F for v_1 and v_2 degrees of freedom, then H_o is rejected and we say that regression parameters are unstable.

On same pattern, stability was examined for the periods 1990-2000 and 1980-2000 also.

The results were interpreted accordingly.

Economic Growth and Structural Changes

Economic development involves structural changes in the composition of output, employment, consumption, trade and other related aspects. Structural changes imply the transition from a traditional agricultural society to a modern industrial economy involving a radical transformation of existing institutions, social attitudes, and motivations. Such structural changes lead to more employment opportunities, higher labour productivity, larger stock of capital, exploitation of new resources and improvements in technology. Thus, economic development has been stated to be equal to economic growth plus structural changes.

Economic growth is generally measured in terms of rising per capita income and structural changes accompany economic development along with rising per capita income. Measurement of structural changes helps to examine the sources of economic growth, which have significant implications for future rate and pattern of economic growth and development. Thus, it is pertinent to examine the relationship of economic growth and structural indicators in the developing countries, especially during the globalization period.

The present chapter attempts to study the relationship between economic growth (level of per capita income) and structural indicators in the developing countries. The growth has been measured in terms of per capita income. The developing countries have been divided into 3 categories; low income countries, lower-middle income countries and upper-middle income countries, as classified by World Bank (2006) on the basis of gross national income per capita.

The present study is carried out at four points of time and therefore relationship between level of growth and various structural indicators has been examined at these four points of time i.e. 1980, 1990, 2000 and 2004. As, the effect of globalization strengthened since early nineties, the analysis of later periods' data will help to examine the impact of globalization on the relationship between level of economic growth and various structural indicators.

Analysis of each of the indicators is taken up one by one to study the nature of association of these variables with level of economic growth. For the sake of brevity, the tables have been given for the year 2004 only along with values worked out for previous years, i.e. 1980, 1990 and 2000 under the table. The purpose is to see whether the association has changed over time or not.

LEVEL OF GROWTH AND SHARE OF AGRICULTURE IN GDP

With economic development share of agriculture in GDP is expected to decline over time. This association between level of economic growth and share of agriculture in GDP is examined in Table 5.1

The table shows the two-way classification of countries with respect to level of growth and share of agriculture in GDP in the year 2004. There were 34 countries with share of agriculture in GDP as 25 percent and above, of which 31 countries were low income countries and 3 were lower-middle income countries. Out of 51 countries with share of agriculture in GDP between 10 to 25 percent, 17 countries were low income countries, 30 were lower-middle income countries and only 4 were upper-middle income countries. Similarly, there were 28 countries having share of agriculture in GDP below 10 percent, out of these, only one was low income country, 4 were lower-middle income countries and 23 were upper-middle income countries.

Viewed from another angle, out of 49 low income countries, only one had share of agriculture in GDP below 10 percent, 17 had it between 10 to 25 percent and 31 had the share as 25 percent or above. In case, of 37 lower middle income countries, 3 countries had 25 percent or above, 30 had between 10 to 25 percent and 4 countries had below 10 percent share of agriculture in GDP. Similarly, out of 27 lower middle income countries, 4 had between 10 to 25 percent and 23 countries had below 10 percent share of agriculture in GDP.

TABLE 5.1
Level of Growth and Share of Agriculture in GDP (%) (2004)

Level of Growth	*Share of agriculture*			
	Below 10	*10-25*	*25 or Above*	*Total R_i's*
Low	1	17	31	49
Lower Middle	4	30	3	37
Upper Middle	23	4	0	27
Total C_j's	28	51	34	113

Tabular value at 5 percent level at 4 d.f. = 9.488
Calculated χ^2_{2004} – 102.164
(No. of countries = 113)
Calculated χ^2_{2000} = 76.961
(No. of countries = 102)
Calculated χ^2_{1990} = 82.000
(No. of countries = 82)
Calculated χ^2_{1980} = 62.097
(No. of countries = 66)

Chi-square value was calculated to be 102.164 and was significant at 5 percent level, indicating that the two variables were significantly associated with each other. The distribution of countries in the table showed that the two variables were negatively associated. Thus, at higher level of economic development, the share of agriculture in GDP declined even in case of developing countries. The association between the two variables was significant and negative throughout the period of study, i.e. 1980, 1990, 2000 and 2004, and appears to have strengthened over time with the strengthening of globalization.

The results of simple regression (Table 5.31) showed that the regression coefficient was negative and significant, indicating that economic growth (per capita income) negatively and significantly affected the share of agriculture in GDP of the developing countries.

LEVEL OF GROWTH AND AVERAGE ANNUAL GROWTH RATE OF AGRICULTURE

With economic development, agriculture is expected to grow at a slower rate as compared to other sectors. The relationship between level of economic growth and growth rate of agriculture is examined in Table 5.2.

TABLE 5.2
Level of Growth and Average Annual Growth Rate of Agriculture (%) (2000-2004)

Level of growth	*Growth rate of agriculture*			
	Below 2	*2–5*	*5 or Above*	*Total R_i's*
Low	19	17	13	49
Lower Middle	7	17	13	37
Upper Middle	12	11	4	27
Total C_j's	38	45	30	113

Tabular value at 5 percent level at 4 d.f. = 9.488
Calculated $\chi^2_{2000\text{-}2004} = 6.811$
(No. of countries = 113)
Calculated $\chi^2_{1990\text{-}2000} = 68.728$
(No. of countries = 102)
Calculated $\chi^2_{1980\text{-}1990} = 41.785$
(No. of countries = 82)

The table shows the two-way classification of countries with respect to level of growth and average annual growth rate of agriculture during the period 2000-04. There were 30 countries with average annual growth rate of agriculture as 5 percent and above, of which 13 countries were low income countries, another 13 were lower middle income countries and only 4 were upper-middle income countries. Out of 45 countries with average annual growth rate of agriculture between 2 to 5 percent, 17 countries were low income countries, another 17 were lower middle income countries and 11 were upper-middle income countries. There were 38 countries having average annual growth rate of agriculture below 2 percent, and out of these, 19 were low income countries, 7 were lower-middle income countries and 12 were upper-middle income countries.

Chi-square value was calculated to be 6.811 and was non-significant at 5 percent level, indicating that the two variables were not associated with each other. However, the association between the two variables was significant during the period 1980-90 and 1990-2000. During these periods, the two variables were positively associated.

The results of simple regression (Table 5.31) showed that the regression coefficient was negative and non significant, indicating that economic growth (rise in per capita income) has not affected the growth rate of agriculture of the developing countries.

LEVEL OF GROWTH AND SHARE OF INDUSTRY IN GDP

With economic development, industrialization takes place and the share of industry in GDP increases. The relationship between level of economic growth and share of industry in GDP is examined in Table 5.3.

The table shows the two-way classification of countries with respect to level of growth and share of industry in GDP in the year 2004. There were 33 countries with share of industry as 35 percent and above, of which 8 countries were low income countries, 15 were lower-middle income countries and 10 were upper-middle income countries. Out of 44 countries with share of industry in GDP between 25 to 35 percent, 13 countries were low income countries, 19 were lower-middle income countries and 12 were upper-middle income countries. There were 36 countries having share of industry in GDP below 25 percent, and out of these, 28 were low income countries, 3 were lower-middle income countries and 5 were upper-middle income countries.

Table 5.3
Level of Growth and Share of Industry in GDP (%) (2004)

Level of growth	*Share of industry*			
	Below 25	*25-35*	*35 or Above*	*Total R_i's*
Low	28	13	8	49
Lower Middle	3	19	15	37
Upper Middle	5	12	10	27
Total C_j's	36	44	33	113

Tabular value at 5 percent level at 4 d.f. = 9.488
Calculated χ^2_{2004} = 26.482
(No. of countries = 113)
Calculated χ^2_{2000} = 61.528
(No. of countries = 102)
Calculated χ^2_{1990} = 54.424
(No. of countries = 82)
Calculated χ^2_{1980} = 45.257
(No. of countries = 66)

Chi-square value was calculated to be 26.482 and was significant at 5 percent level, indicating that the two variables were significantly associated with each other. The distribution of countries in the table showed that the two variables were positively associated. Thus, at higher level of economic development, the share of industry in GDP increased. The association between the two variables was significant and positive throughout the period of the study, i.e. 1980, 1990, 2000 and 2004. The association strengthened upto the year 2000 and appears to have weakened later on, perhaps due to the reason that share of industry did not improve much with rise in per capita income after 2000.

The results of simple regression (Table 5.31) showed that the regression coefficient was positive and significant, indicating that economic growth (per capita income) positively and significantly affected the share of industry in GDP of the developing countries.

LEVEL OF GROWTH AND AVERAGE ANNUAL GROWTH RATE OF INDUSTRY

With economic development, industry is expected to grow at a higher rate since industry attracts more investment in the development process. In Table 5.4, the relationship between level of growth and average annual growth rate of industry is examined.

TABLE 5.4
Level of Growth and Average Annual Growth Rate of Industry (%) (2000-2004)

Level of growth	*Growth rate of industry*			
	Below 2	*2-7*	*7 or Above*	*Total R_i's*
Low	11	24	14	49
Lower Middle	5	20	12	37
Upper Middle	7	15	5	27
Total C_j's	23	59	31	113

Tabular value at 5 percent level at 4 d.f. = 9.488
Calculated $\chi^2_{2000\text{-}2004}$ = 2.690
(No. of countries = 113)
Calculated $\chi^2_{1990\text{-}2000}$ = 51.552
(No. of countries = 102)
Calculated $\chi^2_{1980\text{-}1990}$ = 48.219
(No. of countries = 82)

The table shows the two-way classification of countries with respect to level of growth and average annual growth rate of industry during the period 2000-04. There were 31 countries with average annual growth rate of industry as 7 percent and above, of which 14 countries were low income countries, 12 were lower-middle income countries and only 5 were upper-middle income countries. Out of 59 countries with average annual growth rate of industry between 2 to 7 percent, 24 countries were low income countries, 20 were lower-middle income countries and 15 were upper-middle income countries. There were 23 countries having average annual growth rate of industry below 2 percent, and out of these, 11 were low income countries, 5 were lower-middle income countries and 7 were upper-middle income countries.

Chi-square value was calculated to be 2.690 and was non-significant at 5 percent level, indicating that the two variables were not associated with each other. However, the association between the two variables was significant during the period 1980-90 and 1990-2000. During these periods, the two variables were positively associated.

The results of simple regression (Table 5.31) showed that the regression coefficient was negative and non-significant, indicating that economic growth (per capita income) has not affected the growth rate of industry of the developing countries.

LEVEL OF GROWTH AND SHARE OF SERVICES IN GDP

In the process of economic development, structural changes involve rapid development of services sector and consequently the share of this sector in GDP increases. In Table 5.5, the relationship between level of growth and share of services in GDP is examined.

The table shows the two-way classification of countries with respect to level of growth and share of services in GDP in the year 2004. There were 26 countries with share of services as 60 percent and above, of which only 2 countries were low income countries, 6 were lower-middle income countries and 18 were upper-middle income countries. Out of 62 countries with share of services in GDP between 40 to 60 percent, 26 countries were low income countries, 28 were lower-middle income countries and 8 were upper-middle income countries. There were 25 countries having share of services in GDP below 40 percent, and out of these, 21 were low income countries, 3 were lower-middle income countries and only one was upper middle income country.

TABLE 5.5
Level of Growth and Share of Services in GDP (%) (2004)

Level of growth	*Share of services*			
	Below 40	*40-60*	*60 or Above*	*Total R_i's*
Low	21	26	2	49
Lower Middle	3	28	6	37
Upper Middle	1	8	18	27
Total C_j's	25	62	26	113

Tabular value at 5 percent level at 4 d.f. = 9.488
Calculated χ^2_{2004} = 53.768
(No. of countries = 113)
Calculated χ^2_{2000} = 45.773
(No. of countries = 102)
Calculated χ^2_{1990} = 24.797
(No. of countries = 82)
Calculated χ^2_{1980} = 22.440
(No. of countries = 66)

Chi-square value was calculated to be 53.768 and was significant at 5 percent level, indicating that the two variables were significantly associated with each other. The distribution of countries in the table showed that the two variables were positively associated. Thus, with economic development, the share of services in GDP increased. The association between the two variables was positive and significant throughout the period of the study, i.e. 1980, 1990, 2000 and 2004. The association between the two variables strengthened throughout the period of study.

The results of simple regression (Table 5.31) showed that the regression coefficient was positive and significant, indicating that economic growth (per capita income) positively and significantly affected the share of services in GDP of the developing countries.

LEVEL OF GROWTH AND AVERAGE ANNUAL GROWTH RATE OF SERVICES

On the pattern of industry, services sector is also expected

TABLE 5.6
Level of Growth and Average Annual Growth Rate of Services (%) (2000-04)

Level of growth	*Growth rate of services*			
	Below 3	*3-6*	*6 or Above*	*Total R_i's*
Low	19	18	12	49
Lower Middle	9	19	9	37
Upper Middle	9	13	5	27
Total C_j's	37	50	26	113

Tabular value at 5 percent level at 4 d.f. = 9.488
Calculated $\chi^2_{2000\text{-}04} = 2.799$
(No. of countries = 113)
Calculated $\chi^2_{1990\text{-}2000} = 74.449$
(No. of countries = 102)
Calculated $\chi^2_{1980\text{-}1990} = 78.117$
(No. of countries = 82)

to grow at a faster rate with economic development in an economy. In Table 5.6, the relationship between level of growth and average annual growth rate in services is examined.

Table 5.6 shows the two-way classification of countries with respect to level of growth and average annual growth rate of services during the period 2000-04. There were 26 countries with average annual growth rate of services as 6 percent and above, of which 12 countries were low income countries, 9 were lower-middle income countries and only 5 were upper-middle income countries. Out of 50 countries with average annual growth rate of services between 3 to 6 percent, 18 countries were low income countries, 19 were lower-middle income countries and 13 were upper-middle income countries. There were 37 countries having average annual growth rate of services below 3 percent, and out of these, 19 were low income countries, 9 were lower-middle income countries and another 9 were upper-middle income countries.

Chi-square value was calculated to be 2.799 and was non-significant at 5 percent level, indicating that the two variables were not associated with each other. However, the association between the two variables was significant during the period 1980-90 and 1990-2000. During these periods, the two variables were positively associated.

The results of simple regression (Table 5.31) showed that the regression coefficient was positive and non significant, indicating that economic growth (per capita income) has not affected the growth rate of services of the developing countries during 2000-04.

LEVEL OF GROWTH AND AVERAGE ANNUAL GROWTH RATE OF GDP

Growth rate of GDP is an important measure of economic growth. A higher growth rate of GDP indicates an increasing productive capacity of the economy and rapid increase in production of goods and services.

Table 5.7 shows the two-way classification of countries with respect to level of growth and average annual growth rate of GDP during the period 2000-04. There were 26 countries with average annual growth rate of GDP as 6 percent and above, of which 15 countries were low income countries, 9 were lower-middle income countries and only 5 were upper-middle income countries. Out of 52 countries with average annual growth rate

TABLE 5.7
Level of Growth and Average Annual Growth Rate of GDP (%) (2000-04)

Level of growth	*Growth rate of GDP*			
	Below 3	*3-6*	*6 or Above*	*Total R_i's*
Low	15	22	12	49
Lower Middle	11	17	9	37
Upper Middle	9	13	5	27
Total C_j's	35	52	26	113

Tabular value at 5 percent level at 4 d.f. = 9.488
Calculated $\chi^2_{2000-2004}$ = 0.420
(No. of countries = 113)
Calculated $\chi^2_{1990-2000}$ = 68.728
(No. of countries = 102)
Calculated $\chi^2_{1980-1990}$ = 64.307
(No. of countries = 82)

of GDP between 3 to 6 percent, 22 countries were low income countries, 17 were lower-middle income countries and 13 were upper-middle income countries. There were 35 countries having average annual growth rate of GDP below 3 percent, and out of these, 15 were low income countries, 11 were lower-middle income countries and 9 were upper-middle income countries.

Chi-square value was calculated to be 0.420 and was non-significant at 5 percent level, indicating that the two variables were not associated with each other. However, the association between the two variables was significant during the period 1990-2000 and 1980-90. During these periods, the two variables were positively associated.

The results of simple regression (Table 5.31) showed that the regression coefficient was negative and non-significant, indicating that economic growth (per capita income) has not affected the growth rate of GDP of the developing countries. This may also indicate some trend towards convergence during the period 2000-04.

LEVEL OF GROWTH AND GNI PER CAPITA (PPP)

Table 5.8 shows the two-way classification of countries with respect to level of growth and GNI per capita (PPP) in the year 2004. There were 31 countries with GNI per capita (PPP) as $ 7000 and above, of which only 2 countries were low income countries, 7 were lower-middle income countries and 22 were upper-middle income countries. Out of 46 countries with GNI per capita (PPP) between $ 2000 to $ 7000, 12 countries were low income countries, 29 were lower-middle income countries and 5 were upper-middle income countries. There were 36 countries having GNI per capita (PPP) below $ 2000, and out of these, 35 were low income countries and only one was lower-middle income country.

Chi-square value was calculated to be 101.355 and was significant at 5 percent level, indicating that the two variables were significantly associated with each other. The distribution of countries in the table showed that the two variables were positively associated. The association between the two variables was significant throughout the period of the study, i.e. 1980, 1990, 2000 and 2004. Thus, even when GNI per capita (PPP) is considered a better measure of level of living, it is largely associated with GNI per capita (US$).

The results of simple regression (Table 5.31) showed that the regression coefficient was positive and significant, indicating that economic growth (per capita income) positively and significantly affected the GNI per capita PPP of the developing countries, which means that most of the developing countries having higher GNI per capita (US$) also had higher GNI per capita PPP.

TABLE 5.8
Level of Growth and GNI Per Capita PPP (International $) (2004)

Level of growth	*GNI per capita PPP*			
	Below 2000	*2000-7000*	*7000 or Above*	*Total R_i's*
Low	35	12	2	49
Lower Middle	1	29	7	37
Upper Middle	0	5	22	27
Total C_j's	36	46	31	113

Tabular value at 5 percent level at 4 d.f. = 9.488
Calculated χ^2_{2004} = 101.355
(No. of countries = 113)
Calculated χ^2_{2000} = 66.011
(No. of countries = 102)
Calculated χ^2_{1990} = 74.404
(No. of countries = 82)
Calculated χ^2_{1980} = 58.422
(No. of countries = 66)

LEVEL OF GROWTH AND PRIVATE CONSUMPTION EXPENDITURE (% OF GDP)

The relationship between level of growth and private consumption as percentage of GDP is examined in the Table 5.9.

The table shows the two-way classification of countries with respect to level of growth and private consumption expenditure-GDP ratio in the year 2004. There were 28 countries with private consumption expenditure-GDP ratio as 80 percent and above, of which 21 countries were low income countries, 6 were lower-middle income countries and only one was upper-middle income countries. Out of 56 countries with private consumption expenditure-GDP ratio between 60 to 80 percent, 22 countries were low income countries, 20 were lower-middle income countries and 14 were upper-middle income countries. There were 29 countries having private consumption expenditure-GDP ratio below 60 percent, and out of these, 6 were low income countries, 11 were lower-middle income countries and 12 were upper-middle income countries.

Table 5.9
Level of Growth and Private Consumption Expenditure (% of GDP) (2004)

Level of growth	*Private consumption*			
	Below 60	*60-80*	*80 or Above*	*Total R_i's*
Low	6	22	21	49
Lower Middle	11	20	6	37
Upper Middle	12	14	1	27
Total C_j's	29	56	28	113

Tabular value at 5 percent level at 4 d.f. = 9.488
Calculated χ^2_{2004} = 20.179
(No. of countries = 113)
Calculated χ^2_{2000} = 49.993
(No. of countries = 102)
Calculated χ^2_{1990} = 45.404
(No. of countries = 82)
Calculated χ^2_{1980} = 34.868
(No. of countries = 66)

Chi-square value was calculated to be 20.179 and was significant at 5 percent level, indicating that the two variables were significantly associated with each other. The distribution of countries in the table showed that the two variables were negatively associated. Thus, with economic development, the share of private consumption in GDP falls. The association between the two variables was negative and significant throughout the period of the study, i.e. 1980, 1990, 2000 and 2004. When share of private consumption in GDP falls, of private savings and investment rises, which leads to rapid development. The association between economic development and private consumption expenditure strengthened upto the year 2000 but somewhat weakened later on.

The results of simple regression (Table 5.31) showed that the regression coefficient was negative and significant, indicating that economic growth (per capita income) negatively and significantly affected the private consumption expenditure of the developing countries.

LEVEL OF GROWTH AND GROSS DOMESTIC SAVINGS (% OF GDP)

An increase in the level of savings in the economy reflects increased capacity of the people to save which generally results from increased per capita income. Thus, increased rate of gross

TABLE 5.10
Level of Growth and Gross Domestic Savings (% of GDP) (2004)

Level of growth	*Gross domestic savings*			
	Below 15	*15-25*	*25 or Above*	*Total R_i's*
Low	27	15	7	49
Lower Middle	6	19	12	37
Upper Middle	4	15	8	27
Total C_j's	37	49	27	113

Tabular value at 5 percent level at 4 d.f. = 9.488
Calculated χ^2_{2004} = 19.919
(No. of countries = 113)
Calculated χ^2_{2000} = 83.824
(No. of countries = 102)
Calculated χ^2_{1990} = 51.280
(No. of countries = 82)
Calculated χ^2_{1980} = 42.472
(No. of countries = 66)

domestic savings is an important indicator of development. A higher level of savings is necessary since it makes possible more investment and further development of the economy. The relationship between level of growth and gross domestic savings as percentage of GDP is examined in Table 5.10

The table shows the two-way classification of countries with respect to level of growth and gross domestic savings (% of GDP) in the year 2004. There were 27 countries with gross domestic savings (% of GDP) as 25 percent and above, of which 7 countries were low income countries and 12 were lower-middle income countries and 8 were upper-middle income countries. Out of 49 countries with gross domestic savings (% of GDP) between 15 to 25 percent, 15 countries were low income countries, 19 were lower-middle income countries and 15 were upper-middle income countries. There were 37 countries having gross domestic savings (% of GDP) below 15 percent, and out of these, 27 were low income countries, 6 were lower-middle income countries and 4 were upper-middle income countries.

Chi-square value was calculated to be 19.919 and was significant at 5 percent level, indicating that the two variables were significantly associated with each other. The distribution of countries in the table showed that the two variables were positively associated. The association between the two variables was significant throughout the period of study i.e. 1980, 1990, 2000 and 2004. Again, the association strengthened upto the year 2000, but somewhat weakened later on.

The results of simple regression (Table 5.31) showed that the regression coefficient was positive and significant, indicating that economic growth (per capita income) positively and significantly affected the gross domestic savings of the developing countries.

LEVEL OF GROWTH AND GROSS CAPITAL FORMATION (% OF GDP)

Table 5.11 shows the two-way classification of countries with respect to level of growth and gross capital formation-GDP ratio in the year 2004. There were 47 countries with gross capital formation-GDP ratio as 24 percent and above, of which 16 countries were low income countries, 20 were lower-middle income countries and 11 were upper-middle income countries. Out of 44 countries with gross capital formation-GDP ratio between 18 to 24 percent, 18 countries were low income countries, 12 were lower-middle income countries and 14 were upper-middle income countries. There were 22 countries having gross capital formation-GDP ratio below 18 percent, and out of these, 15 were low income countries, 5 were lower-middle income countries and 2 were upper-middle income countries.

TABLE 5.11
Level of Growth and Gross Capital Formation (% of GDP) (2004)

Level of Growth	*Gross capital formation*			
	Below 18	*18-24*	*24 or Above*	*Total R_i's*
Low	15	18	16	49
Lower Middle	5	12	20	37
Upper Middle	2	14	11	27
Total C_j's	22	44	47	113

Tabular value at 5 percent level at 4 d.f. = 9.488
Calculated χ^2_{2004} = 9.764
(No. of countries = 113)
Calculated χ^2_{2000} = 77.462
(No. of countries = 102)
Calculated χ^2_{1990} = 69.489
(No. of countries = 82)
Calculated χ^2_{1980} = 55.000
(No. of countries = 66)

Chi-square value was calculated to be 9.764 and was significant at 5 percent level, indicating that the two variables were significantly associated with each other. The distribution of countries in the table showed that the two variables were positively associated. The association between the two variables was significant and positive throughout the period of the study, i.e. 1980, 1990, 2000 and 2004.

The results of simple regression (Table 5.31) showed that the regression coefficient was positive and non-significant, indicating that economic growth (per capita income) has not significantly affected the gross capital formation of the developing countries.

LEVEL OF GROWTH AND ENERGY USE PER CAPITA

Table 5.12 shows the two-way classification of countries with respect to level of growth and energy use per capita (kg of oil equivalent) in the year 2004. There were 25 countries with energy use per capita (kg. of oil equivalent) as 1500 kg and above, of which 6 countries were lower-middle income countries and 19 were upper middle income countries. Out of 49 countries with energy use per capita between 500 to 1500 kg of oil equivalent, 15 countries were low income countries, 27 were lower-middle income countries and 7 were upper-middle income countries. There were 39 countries having energy use

TABLE 5.12
Level of Growth and Energy Use Per Capita (kg. of oil equivalent) (2004)

Level of Growth	*Energy use per capita*			
	Below 500	*500-1500*	*1500 or Above*	*Total R_i's*
Low	34	15	0	49
Lower Middle	4	27	6	37
Upper Middle	1	7	19	27
Total C_j's	39	49	25	113

Tabular value at 5 percent level at 4 d.f. = 9.488
Calculated χ^2_{2004} = 81.759
(No. of countries = 113)
Calculated χ^2_{2000} = 70.326
(No. of countries = 102)
Calculated χ^2_{1990} = 67.806
(No. of countries = 82)
Calculated χ^2_{1980} = 49.194
(No. of countries = 66)

per capita below 500 kg of oil equivalent, and out of these, 34 were low income countries, 4 were lower-middle income countries and only one was upper-middle income country.

Chi-square value was calculated to be 81.759 and was significant at 5 percent level, indicating that the two variables were significantly associated with each other. The distribution of countries in the table showed that the two variables were positively associated. The association between the two variables was significant throughout the period of the study, i.e. 1980, 1990, 2000 and 2004. The association between the two variables strengthened throughout the period of study.

The results of simple regression (Table 5.12) showed that the regression coefficient was positive and significant, indicating that economic growth (per capita income) positively and significantly affected the energy use per capita of the developing countries.

LEVEL OF GROWTH AND SHARE OF FUEL, ORES AND METAL EXPORTS IN MERCHANDISE EXPORTS

Trade plays very important role in economic development. It also increases knowledge and experience which are essential for economic development. Table 5.13 shows the two-way classification of countries with respect to level of growth and share of fuel, ores and metal exports in merchandise exports in the year 2004.

Table shows that there were 33 countries with share of fuel, ores and metal exports in merchandise exports as 35 percent and above, of which 16 countries were low income countries, 11 were lower-middle income countries and 6 were upper middle income countries. Out of 51 countries with share of fuel, ores and metal exports in merchandise exports between 5 to 35 percent, 15 countries were low income countries, 19 were lower-middle income countries and 17 were upper-middle income countries. There were 29 countries having share of fuel, ores and metal exports in merchandise exports below 5 percent, and out of these, 18 were low income countries, 7 were lower-middle income countries and 4 were upper-middle income countries.

Chi-square value was calculated to be 9.396 and was non-significant at 5 percent level, indicating that the two variables

TABLE 5.13
Level of Growth and Share of Fuel, Ores and Metal Exports in Merchandise Exports (%) (2004)

Level of growth	*Share of fuel, ores, metals*			
	Below 5	*5-35*	*35 or Above*	*Total R_i's*
Low	18	15	16	49
Lower Middle	7	19	11	37
Upper Middle	4	17	6	27
Total C_j's	29	51	33	113

Tabular value at 5 percent level at 4 d.f. = 9.488
Calculated χ^2_{2004} = 9.396
(No. of countries = 113)
Calculated χ^2_{2000} = 60.317
(No. of countries = 102)
Calculated χ^2_{1990} = 51.839
(No. of countries = 82)
Calculated χ^2_{1980} = 47.850
(No. of countries = 66)

had no association with each other. However, the association between the two variables was significant during 1980, 1990 and 2000. During these periods, these two variables were positively associated. With economic growth, share of fuel, ores and metal exports in merchandise exports is expected to decline. However, as the study relates to only developing countries, the positive relation between economic growth and share of fuel, ores and metal exports in merchandise exports may not be termed as contradictory.

The results of simple regression (Table 5.31) showed that the regression coefficient was negative and non-significant, indicating that economic growth (per capita income) has not affected the share of fuel, ore and metal exports in merchandise exports of the developing countries in the year 2004.

LEVEL OF GROWTH AND SHARE OF FOOD AND AGRICULTURAL RAW MATERIAL EXPORTS IN MERCHANDISE EXPORTS

The composition of exports changes from primary goods to

manufactured goods and within manufactured goods from consumer goods to capital goods. Thus, with economic development, the share of primary commodities in exports of a country generally decreases.

Table 5.14 shows the two-way classification of countries with respect to level of growth and share of food and agricultural raw material exports in merchandise exports in 2004. There were 22 countries with share of food and agricultural raw material exports in merchandise exports as 60 percent and above, of which 16 countries were low income countries, 4 were lower-middle income countries and 2 were upper-middle income countries. Out of 52 countries with share of food and agricultural raw material exports in merchandise exports between 15 to 60 percent, 22 countries were low income countries, 20 were lower-middle income countries and 10 were upper-middle income countries. There were 39 countries having share of food and agricultural raw material exports in merchandise exports below 15 percent, and out of these, 11 were low income countries, 13 were lower-middle income countries and 15 were upper-middle income countries.

TABLE 5.14
Level of Growth and Share of Food and Agriculture Raw Material Exports in Merchandise Exports (%) (2004)

Level of Growth	*Share of Food and Agri. Raw-material*			
	Below 15	*15-60*	*60 or Above*	*Total R_i's*
Low	11	22	16	49
Lower Middle	13	20	4	37
Upper Middle	15	10	2	27
Total C_j's	39	52	22	113

Tabular value at 5 percent level at 4 d.f. = 9.488
Calculated χ^2_{2004} = 14.357
(No. of countries = 113)
Calculated χ^2_{2000} = 66.011
(No. of countries = 102)
Calculated χ^2_{1990} = 50.964
(No. of countries = 82)
Calculated χ^2_{1980} = 55.587
(No. of countries = 66)

Chi-square value was calculated to be 14.357 and was significant at 5 percent level, indicating that the two variables were significantly associated with each other. The distribution of countries in the table showed that the two variables were negatively associated. The association between the two variables was negative and significant during 1980, 1990 and 2000 also.

The results of simple regression (Table 5.31) showed that the regression coefficient was negative and significant, indicating that economic growth (per capita income) negatively and significantly affected the share of primary exports in merchandise exports of the developing countries.

LEVEL OF GROWTH AND SHARE OF MANUFACTURE EXPORTS IN MERCHANDISE EXPORTS

With economic development, the share of manufacture exports in merchandise exports generally increases. The relationship between level of growth and share of manufacture exports in merchandise exports is examined in Table 5.15.

The table shows the two-way classification of countries with respect to level of growth and share of manufacture exports in merchandise exports in 2004. There were 45 countries with share of manufacture exports in merchandise exports as 50 percent and above, of which 8 countries were low income countries, 19 were lower middle income countries and 18 were upper-middle income countries. Out of 50 countries with share of manufacture exports in merchandise exports between 10 to 50 percent, 28 countries were low income countries, 14 were lower-middle income countries and 8 were upper-middle income countries. There were 18 countries having share of manufacture exports in merchandise exports below 10 percent, and out of these, 13 were low income countries, 4 were lower-middle income countries and only one was upper-middle income country.

Chi-square value was calculated to be 21.530 (after merging first two columns) and was significant at 5 percent level, indicating that the two variables were significantly associated with each other. The distribution of countries in the table showed that the two variables were positively associated.

TABLE 5.15
Level of Growth and Share of Manufacture Exports in Merchandise Exports (%) (2004)

Level of growth	*Share of manufactured exports*			
	Below 10	*10-50*	*50 or Above*	*Total R_i's*
Low	13	28	8	49
Lower Middle	4	14	19	37
Upper Middle	1	8	18	27
Total C_j's	18	50	45	113

Tabular value at 5 percent level at 4 d.f. = 9.488
Tabular value at 5 percent level at 2 d.f. = 5.991
Calculated χ^2_{2004} = 21.530
(No. of countries = 113)
Calculated χ^2_{2000} = 74.230
(No. of countries = 102)
Calculated χ^2_{1990} = 43.795
(No. of countries = 82)
Calculated χ^2_{1980} = 44.142
(No. of countries = 66)

The association between the two variables was significant during the period of the study i.e. 1980, 1990, 2000 and 2004. During these periods, the two variables were positively associated.

The results of simple regression (Table 5.31) showed that the regression coefficient was positive and significant, indicating that economic growth (per capita income) positively and significantly affected the manufacture exports in merchandise exports of the developing countries.

LEVEL OF GROWTH AND EXPORTS-GDP RATIO

Generally, with economic development, the percentage of exports to GDP increases and globalization appears to have further strengthened this association. The relationship between level of growth and exports-GDP ratio is examined in Table 5.16.

Table 5.16
Level of Growth and Exports of Goods and Services (% of GDP) (2004)

Level of growth	*Exports of goods & services*			
	Below 25	*25-50*	*50 or Above*	*Total R_i's*
Low	20	21	8	49
Lower Middle	5	21	11	37
Upper Middle	1	14	12	27
Total C_j's	26	56	31	113

Tabular value at 5 percent level at 4 d.f. = 9.488
Calculated χ^2_{2004} = 18.558
(No. of countries = 113)
Calculated χ^2_{2000} = 58.377
(No. of countries = 102)
Calculated χ^2_{1990} = 78.104
(No. of countries = 82)
Calculated χ^2_{1980} = 52.349
(No. of countries = 66)

The Table 5.16 shows the two-way classification of countries with respect to level of growth and exports-GDP ratio in 2004. There were 31 countries with exports GDP ratio as 50 percent and above, of which 8 countries were low income countries, 11 were lower-middle income countries and 12 were upper-middle income countries. Out of 56 countries with exports-GDP ratio between 25 to 50 percent, 21 countries were low income countries, another 21 were lower-middle income countries and 14 were upper-middle income countries. There were 26 countries having exports-GDP ratio below 25 percent, and out of these, 20 were low income countries, 5 were lower-middle income countries and only one was upper-middle income country.

Chi-square value was calculated to be 18.558 and was significant at 5 percent level, indicating that the two variables were significantly associated with each other. The distribution of countries in the table showed that the two variables were positively associated. Thus, with economic development, the export-GDP ratio increases. The association between the two variables was significant and positive during all the years of study, i.e. 1980, 1990, 2000 and 2004.

The results of simple regression (Table 5.31) showed that the regression coefficient was positive and significant, indicating that economic growth (per capita income) positively and significantly affected the exports GDP ratio of the developing countries.

LEVEL OF GROWTH AND IMPORTS-GDP RATIO

Table 5.17 shows the two-way classification of countries with respect to level of growth and imports-GDP ratio in 2004. There were 32 countries with imports GDP ratio as 55 percent and above, of which 10 countries were low income countries, another 10 were lower-middle income countries and 12 were upper-middle income countries. Out of 52 countries with imports-GDP ratio between 30 to 55 percent, 23 countries were low income countries, 19 were lower-middle income countries and 10 were upper-middle income countries. There were 29 countries having imports-GDP ratio below 30 percent, and out of these, 16 were low income countries, 8 were lower-middle income countries and 5 were upper-middle income countries.

TABLE 5.17

Level of Growth and Imports of Goods and Services (% of GDP) (2004)

Level of growth	*Imports of goods & services*			
	Below 30	*30-55*	*55 or Above*	*Total R_i's*
Low	16	23	10	49
Lower Middle	8	19	10	37
Upper Middle	5	10	12	27
Total C_j's	29	52	32	113

Tabular value at 5 percent level at 4 d.f. = 9.488

Calculated χ^2_{2004} = 6.000

(No. of countries = 113)

Calculated χ^2_{2000} = 77.462

(No. of countries = 102)

Calculated χ^2_{1990} = 82.000

(No. of countries = 82)

Calculated χ^2_{1980} = 52.257

(No. of countries = 66)

Chi-square value was calculated to be 6.000 and was non-significant at 5 percent level, indicating that the two variables had no association with each other. However, the association between the two variables was significant during 1980, 1990 and 2000. During these periods, the two variables were positively associated.

The results of simple regression (Table 5.31) showed that the regression coefficient was positive and non significant, indicating that economic growth (per capita income) has not affected the imports GDP ratio of the developing countries in the year 2004.

LEVEL OF GROWTH AND DEGREE OF OPENNESS (TRADE-GDP RATIO)

Table 5.18 shows the two-way classification of countries with respect to level of growth and degree of openness, i.e. trade-GDP ratio in 2004. There were 34 countries with degree of

TABLE 5.18
Level of Growth and Degree of Openness (Exports+Imports % of GDP) (2004)

Level of growth	*Degree of openness*			
	Below 50	*50-100*	*100 or Above*	*Total R_i's*
Low	16	25	8	49
Lower Middle	4	21	12	37
Upper Middle	1	12	14	27
Total C_j's	21	58	34	113

Tabular value at 5 percent level at 4 d.f. = 9.488
Calculated χ^2_{2004} = 17.504
(No. of countries = 113)
Calculated χ^2_{2000} = 51.098
(No. of countries = 102)
Calculated χ^2_{1990} = 62.007
(No. of countries = 82)
Calculated χ^2_{1980} = 40.590
(No. of countries = 66)

openness as 100 percent and above, of which 8 countries were low income countries, 12 were lower-middle income countries and 14 were upper-middle income countries. Out of 58 countries with degree of openness between 50 to 100 percent, 25 countries were low income countries, 21 were lower middle income countries and 12 were upper-middle income countries. There were 21 countries having degree of openness below 50 percent, and out of these, 16 were low income countries, 4 were lower-middle income countries and only one was upper-middle income country.

Chi-square value was calculated to be 17.504 and was significant at 5 percent level, indicating that the two variables were significantly associated with each other..The distribution of countries in the table showed that the level of growth and degree of openness were positively associated. The association between the two variables was significant and positive during 1980, 1990 and 2000 also.

The results of simple regression (Table 5.31) showed that the regression coefficient was positive and significant, indicating that economic growth (per capita income) positively and significantly affected the degree of openness of the developing countries.

LEVEL OF GROWTH AND AVERAGE ANNUAL GROWTH RATE OF EXPORT VOLUME

Table 5.19 shows the two-way classification of developing countries with respect to level of growth and average annual growth rate of export volume during the period 2000-04. There were 46 countries with average annual growth rate of export volume as 14 percent and above, of which 19 countries were low income countries, 17 were lower-middle income countries and 10 were upper-middle income countries. Out of 33 countries with average annual growth rate of export volume between 7 to 14 percent, 17 countries were low income countries, another 9 were lower-middle income countries and 7 were upper-middle income countries. There were 34 countries having average annual growth rate of export volume below 7 percent, and out of these, 13 were low income countries, 11 were lower-middle income countries and 10 were upper-middle income countries.

Chi-square value was calculated to be 1.931 and was non-significant at 5 percent level, indicating that the two variables were not associated with each other. However, the association between the two variables was significant during the period 1980-90 and 1990-2000. During these periods, the two variables were positively associated.

The results of simple regression (Table 5.31) showed that the regression coefficient was negative and non significant, indicating that economic growth (per capita income) has not affected the growth of export volume of the developing countries. It appears that by the year 2000, exports have grown rapidly and the growth rate has tapered off later on.

TABLE 5.19
Level of Growth and Average Annual Growth Rate of Export Volume (%)
(2000-04)

.Level of growth	*Growth rate of export vol.*			
	Below 7	*7-14*	*14 or Above*	*Total R_i's*
Low	13	17	19	49
Lower Middle	11	9	17	37
Upper Middle	10	7	10	27
Total C_i's	34	33	46	113

Tabular value at 5 percent level at 4 d.f. = 9.488
Calculated $\chi^2_{2000\text{-}2004} = 1.931$
(No. of countries = 113)
Calculated $\chi^2_{1990\text{-}2000} = 94.301$
(No. of countries = 102)
Calculated $\chi^2_{1980\text{-}1990} = 26.704$
(No. of countries = 82)

LEVEL OF GROWTH AND AVERAGE ANNUAL GROWTH RATE OF IMPORT VOLUME

Table 5.20 shows the two-way classification of countries with respect to level of growth and average annual growth rate of import volume during the period 2000-04. There were 41 countries with average annual growth rate of import volume as

TABLE 5.20

Level of Growth and Average Annual Growth Rate of Import Volume (%) (2000-04)

Level of growth	*Growth rate of Import vol.*			
	Below 7	*7-14*	*14 or Above*	*Total R_i's*
Low	14	16	19	49
Lower Middle	11	13	13	37
Upper Middle	10	8	9	27
Total C_j's	35	37	41	113

Tabular value at 5 percent level at 4 d.f. = 9.488
Calculated $\chi^2_{2000\text{-}2004}$ = 0.737
(No. of countries = 113)
Calculated $\chi^2_{1990\text{-}2000}$ = 98.074
(No. of countries = 102)
Calculated $\chi^2_{1980\text{-}1990}$ = 15.400
(No. of countries = 82)

14 percent and above, of which 19 countries were low income countries, another 13 were lower-middle income countries and 9 were upper middle income countries. Out of 37 countries with average annual growth rate of import volume between 7 to 14 percent, 16 countries were low income countries, 13 were lower middle income countries and 8 were upper-middle income countries. There were 35 countries having average annual growth rate of import volume below 7 percent, and out of these, 14 were low income countries, 11 were lower-middle income countries and 10 were upper-middle income countries.

Chi-square value was calculated to be 0.737 and was non-significant at 5 percent level, indicating that the two variables were not associated with each other. However, the association between the two variables was significant during the period 1980-90 and 1990-2000. During these periods, the two variables were positively associated.

The results of simple regression (Table 5.31) showed that the regression coefficient was negative and non-significant, indicating that economic growth (per capita income) has not affected the growth of import volume of the developing countries in 2004. The reason may be similar as in case of exports growth.

LEVEL OF GROWTH AND MERCHANDISE TRADE-GDP RATIO

The relationship between level of growth and merchandise trade-GDP ratio is examined in Table 5.21. Table shows the two-way classification of countries with respect to level of growth and merchandise trade-GDP ratio in the year 2004. There were 47 countries with merchandise trade-GDP ratio as 70 percent and above, of which 15 countries were low income countries, 17 were lower-middle income countries and 15 were upper-middle income countries. Out of 41 countries with merchandise trade-GDP ratio between 40 to 70 percent, 17 countries were low income countries, 14 were lower-middle income countries and 10 were upper-middle income countries. There were 25 countries having merchandise trade-GDP ratio below 40 percent, and out of these, 17 were low income countries, 6 were lower-middle income countries and only 2 were upper-middle income countries.

TABLE 5.21

Level of Growth and Merchandise Trade-GDP Ratio (2004)

Level of growth	*Merchandise trade*			
	Below 40	*40-70*	*70 or Above*	*Total R_i's*
Low	17	17	15	49
Lower Middle	6	14	17	37
Upper Middle	2	10	15	27
Total C_j's	25	41	47	113

Tabular value at 5 percent level at 4 d.f. = 9.488
Calculated χ^2_{2004} = 9.643
(No. of countries = 113)
Calculated χ^2_{2000} = 54.010
(No. of countries = 102)
Calculated χ^2_{1990} = 67.752
(No. of countries = 82)
Calculated χ^2_{1980} = 40.239
(No. of countries = 66)

Chi-square value was calculated to be 9.643 and was significant at 5 percent level, indicating that the two variables were significantly associated with each other. The distribution of countries in the table showed that the two variables were positively associated. The association between the two variables was significant and positive throughout the period of the study, i.e. 1980, 1990, 2000 and 2004.

The results of simple regression (Table 5.31) showed that the regression coefficient was positive and significant, indicating that economic growth (per capita income) positively and significantly affected the merchandise trade GDP ratio of the developing countries.

LEVEL OF GROWTH AND TRADE IN SERVICES-GDP RATIO

Table 5.22 shows the two-way classification of countries with respect to level of growth and trade in services-GDP ratio in the year 2004. There were 27 countries with trade in services-GDP ratio as 24 percent and above, of which 10 countries were

TABLE 5.22

Level of Growth and Trade in Services-GDP Ratio (2004)

Level of Growth	*Trade in services*			
	Below 12	*12-24*	*24 or Above*	*Total R_i's*
Low	12	27	10	49
Lower Middle	11	16	10	37
Upper Middle	8	12	7	27
Total C_j's	31	55	27	113

Tabular value at 5 percent level at 4 d.f. = 9.488
Calculated $\chi^2_{2004} = 1.461$
(No. of countries = 113)
Calculated $\chi^2_{2000} = 94.661$
(No. of countries = 102)
Calculated $\chi^2_{1990} = 67.784$
(No. of countries = 82)
Calculated $\chi^2_{1980} = 66.000$
(No. of countries = 66)

low income countries, another 10 were lower-middle income countries and 7 were upper-middle income countries. Out of 55 countries with trade in services-GDP ratio between 12 to 24 percent, 27 countries were low income countries, 16 were lower-middle income countries and 12 were upper-middle income countries. There were 31 countries having trade in services-GDP ratio below 12 percent, and out of these, 12 were low income countries, 11 were lower-middle income countries and 8 were upper-middle income countries.

Chi-square value was calculated to be 1.461 and was non-significant at 5 percent level, indicating that the two variables had no association with each other. However, the association between the two variables was significant during 1980, 1990 and 2000. During these periods, the two variables were positively associated.

The results of simple regression (Table 5.31) showed that the regression coefficient was positive and non significant, indicating that economic growth (per capita income) has not

TABLE 5.23

Level of Growth and Gross Private Capital Flows-GDP Ratio (2004)

Level of growth	*Gross private Capital flows*			
	Below 7	*7 -14*	*14 or Above*	*Total R_i's*
Low	24	14	11	49
Lower Middle	11	18	8	37
Upper Middle	2	4	21	27
Total C_j's	37	36	40	113

Tabular value at 5 percent level at 4 d.f. = 9.488

Calculated χ^2_{2004} = 33.247

(No. of countries = 113)

Calculated χ^2_{2000} = 66.970

(No. of countries = 102)

Calculated χ^2_{1990} = 60.766

(No. of countries = 82)

Calculated χ^2_{1980} = 39.600

(No. of countries = 66)

affected the trade in services-GDP ratio of the developing countries in 2004.

LEVEL OF GROWTH AND GROSS PRIVATE CAPITAL FLOWS-GDP RATIO

In the era of globalization, the economies are more integrated than before, leading to increased capital flows. In Table 5.23, the relationship between level of growth and gross private capital flows as percentage of GDP is examined.

Table 5.23 shows the two-way classification of countries with respect to level of growth and gross private capital flows as percentage of GDP in the year 2004. There were 40 countries with gross private capital flows as 14 percent and above, of which 11 countries were low income countries, 8 were lower-middle income countries and 21 were upper-middle income countries. Out of 36 countries with gross private capital flows between 7 to 14 percent, 14 countries were low income countries, another 18 were lower-middle income countries and 4 were upper-middle income countries. There were 37 countries having gross private capital flows below 7 percent, and out of these, 24 were low income countries, 11 were lower-middle income countries and only 2 were upper-middle income countries.

Chi-square value was calculated to be 33.247 and was significant at 5 percent level, indicating that the two variables were significantly associated with each other. The distribution of countries in the table showed that the two variables were positively associated. The association between the two variables was significant and positive throughout the period of the study, i.e. 1980, 1990, 2000 and 2004.

The results of simple regression (Table 5.31) showed that the regression coefficient was positive and significant, indicating that economic growth (per capita income) positively and significantly affected the gross private capital flows of the developing countries.

LEVEL OF GROWTH AND FDI NET INFLOWS-GDP RATIO

Table 5.24 shows the two-way classification of countries

Table 5.24
Level of Growth and Net Inflows of Foreign Direct Investment-GDP Ratio (2004)

Level of Growth	*Net inflows of FDI*			
	Below 0.1	*0.1-1.3*	*1.3 or Above*	*Total R_i's*
Low	6	16	27	49
Lower Middle	0	10	27	37
Upper Middle	1	4	22	27
Total C_j's	7	30	76	113

Tabular value at 5 percent level at 4 d.f. = 9.488
Tabular value at 5 percent level at 2 d.f. = 5.991
Calculated $\chi^2_{2004} = 6.317$
(No. of countries = 113)
Calculated $\chi^2_{2000} = 65.462$
(No. of countries = 102)
Calculated $\chi^2_{1990} = 70.705$
(No. of countries = 82)
Calculated $\chi^2_{1980} = 36.960$
(No. of countries = 66)

with respect to level of growth and FDI net inflows as percentage of GDP in the year 2004. There were 32 countries with FDI net inflows as 1.3 percent and above, of which 27 countries were low income countries, another 27 were lower-middle income countries and 22 were upper-middle income countries. Out of 30 countries with FDI net inflows between 0.1 to 1.3 percent, 16 countries were low income countries, 10 were lower-middle income countries and 4 were upper-middle income countries. There were 7 countries having FDI net inflows below 0.1 percent, and out of these, 6 were low income countries and only one was upper-middle income country.

Chi-square value was calculated (after merging first two columns) to be 6.317 and was significant at 5 percent level at 2 d.f., indicating that the two variables were significantly associated with each other. The distribution of countries in the table showed that the two variables were positively associated.

The association between the two variables was significant and positive throughout the period of the study, i.e. 1980, 1990, 2000 and 2004.

The results of simple regression (Table 5.31) showed that the regression coefficient was positive and non significant, indicating that economic growth (per capita income) has not significantly affected the FDI net inflows GDP ratio of the developing countries in 2004.

LEVEL OF GROWTH AND FDI NET OUTFLOWS-GDP RATIO

In Table 5.25, the relationship between level of growth and net outflows of foreign direct investment as percentage of GDP is examined.

Table shows the two-way classification of countries with

TABLE 5.25
Level of Growth and Net Outflows of Foreign Direct Investment-GDP Ratio (2004)

Level of Growth	*Net outflows of FDI*			
	Below 0.0 (Negative)	*0.0-0.2*	*0.2 or Above*	*Total R_i's*
Low	1	40	8	49
Lower Middle	3	26	8	37
Upper Middle	2	5	20	27
Total C_j's	6	71	36	113

Tabular value at 5 percent level at 4 d.f. = 9.488
Tabular value at 5 percent level at 2 d.f. = 5.991
Calculated χ^2_{2004} = 29.330
(No. of countries = 113)
Calculated χ^2_{2000} = 65.734
(No. of countries = 102)
Calculated χ^2_{1990} = 56.611
(No. of countries = 82)
Calculated χ^2_{1980} = 68.424
(No. of countries = 66)

respect to level of growth and FDI net outflows as percentage of GDP in the year 2004. There were 36 countries with FDI net outflows as 0.2 percent and above, of which 8 countries were low income countries, another 8 were lower-middle income countries and 20 were upper-middle income countries. Out of 71 countries with FDI net outflows between 0.0 to 0.2 percent, 40 countries were low income countries, 26 were lower-middle income countries and only 5 were upper-middle income countries. There were 6 countries having FDI net outflows below 0.0 percent, and out of these, only 1 was low income country, 3 were lower-middle income countries and 2 were upper middle income countries.

Chi-square value was calculated (after merging first two columns) to be 29.330 and was significant at 5 percent level, indicating that the two variables were significantly associated with each other. The association between the two variables was significant during the period of study, i.e. 1980, 1990, 2000 and 2004. During these periods, the two variables were positively associated.

The results of simple regression (Table 5.31) showed that the regression coefficient was positive and non significant, indicating that economic growth (per capita income) has not affected the FDI net outflows GDP ratio of the developing countries.

LEVEL OF GROWTH AND TOTAL DEBT SERVICE-GNI RATIO

Table 5.26 shows the two-way classification of countries with respect to level of growth and total debt service-GNI ratio in the year 2004. There were 36 countries with total debt service-GNI ratio as 7 percent and above, of which 8 countries were low income countries, 11 were lower-middle income countries and 17 were upper middle income countries. Out of 48 countries with total debt service GNI ratio between 2 to 7 percent, 20 countries were low income countries, another 20 were lower middle income countries and 8 were upper middle income countries. There were 29 countries having total debt service-GNI ratio below 2 percent, and out of these, 21 countries were low

TABLE 5.26
Level of Growth and Total Debt Service (% of GNI) (2004)

Level of Growth	*Total debt service*			
	Below 2	*2-7*	*7 or Above*	*Total R_i's*
Low	21	20	8	49
Lower-Middle	6	20	11	37
Upper-Middle	2	8	17	27
Total C_j's	29	48	36	113

Tabular value at 5 percent level at 4 d.f. = 9.488
Calculated χ^2_{2004} = 24.648
(No. of countries = 113)
Calculated χ^2_{2000} = 65.463
(No. of countries = 102)
Calculated χ^2_{1990} = 56.784
(No. of countries = 82)
Calculated χ^2_{1980} = 34.682
(No. of countries = 66)

income counties, 6 were lower-middle income countries and only 2 were upper-middle income countries.

Chi-square value was calculated to be 24.648 and was significant at 5 percent level, indicating that the two variables were significantly associated with each other. The distribution of countries in the table showed that the two variables were positively associated. The association between the two variables was significant and positive throughout the period of study i.e. 1980, 1990, 2000 and 2004. Thus, at higher level of economic development, the debt service of the developing countries increased. This may highlight the role of external debt in economic development of developing countries.

The results of simple regression (Table 5.31) showed that the regression coefficient was positive and significant, indicating that economic growth (per capita income) positively and significantly affected the total debt service GNI ratio of the developing countries.

LEVEL OF GROWTH AND DAILY CALORIE SUPPLY PER CAPITA

Table 5.27 shows the two-way classification of countries with respect to level of growth and daily calorie supply per capita in the year 2004. There were 34 countries with daily calorie supply per capita as 2700 and above, of which only 2 countries were low income countries, 16 were lower-middle income countries and another 16 were upper-middle income countries. Out of 45 countries with daily calorie supply per capita between 2200 to 2700, 18 countries were low income countries, 19 were lower-middle income countries and 8 were upper-middle income countries. There were 34 countries having daily calorie supply per capita below 2200, and out of these, 29 countries were low-income countries, only 2 were lower middle income countries and 3 were upper-middle income countries.

Chi-square value was calculated to be 47.345 and was significant at 5 percent level, indicating that the two variables were significantly associated with each other. The distribution of

TABLE 5.27
Level of Growth and Daily Calorie Supply (Per Capita) (2004)

Level of growth	*Daily calorie supply*			
	Below 2200	*2200-2700*	*2700 or Above*	*Total R_i's*
Low	29	18	2	49
Lower Middle	2	19	16	37
Upper Middle	3	8	16	27
Total C_j's	34	45	34	113

Tabular value at 5 percent level at 4 d.f. = 9.488
Calculated χ^2_{2004} = 47.345
(No. of countries = 113)
Calculated χ^2_{2000} = 62.039
(No. of countries = 102)
Calculated χ^2_{1990} = 42.690
(No. of countries = 82)
Calculated χ^2_{1980} = 42.265
(No. of countries = 66)

countries in the table showed that the two variables were positively associated. The association between the two variables was significant and positive throughout the period of study, i.e. 1980, 1990, 2000 and 2004.

The results of simple regression (Table 5.31) showed that the regression coefficient was positive and significant, indicating that economic growth (per capita income) positively and significantly affected the daily calorie supply per capita of the developing countries.

LEVEL OF GROWTH AND EMPLOYMENT IN AGRICULTURE (% OF TOTAL EMPLOYMENT)

With economic development in an economy, the share of agricultural sector in total employment generally declines and that of other sectors increases. The relationship between level of growth and percentage of employment in agricultural sector is examined in Table 5.28

Table shows the two-way classification of countries with respect to level of growth and employment in agriculture in the year 2004. There were 31 countries with employment in agriculture as 60 percent and above, of which 29 countries were low income countries and only 2 were lower-middle income countries. Out of 44 countries with employment in agriculture between 20 to 60 percent, 18 countries were low income countries, 24 were lower-middle income countries and only 2 were upper-middle income countries. There were 38 countries having employment in agriculture below 20 percent, and out of these, only 2 countries were low income counties, 11 were lower-middle income countries and 25 were upper-middle income countries.

Chi-square value was calculated to be 86.102 and was significant at 5 percent level, indicating that the two variables were significantly associated with each other. The distribution of countries in the table showed that the two variables were negatively associated. Thus, at higher level of development, the percentage of employment in the agricultural sector decreased. The association between the two variables was significant and negative throughout the period of study, i.e.1980, 1990, 2000 and 2004, and appears to have strengthened over time.

TABLE 5.28
Level of Growth and Employment in Agriculture (% of Total Employment) (2004)

Level of Growth	*Employment in agriculture*			
	Below 20	*20-60*	*60 or Above*	*Total R_i's*
Low	2	18	29	49
Lower Middle	11	24	2	37
Upper Middle	25	2	0	27
Total C_j's	38	44	31	113

Tabular value at 5 percent level at 4 d.f. = 9.488
Calculated χ^2_{2004} = 86.102
(No. of countries = 113)
Calculated χ^2_{2000} = 77.477
(No. of countries = 102)
Calculated χ^2_{1990} = 65.228
(No. of countries = 82)
Calculated χ^2_{1980} = 52.261
(No. of countries = 66)

The results of simple regression (Table 5.31) showed that the regression coefficient was negative and significant, indicating that economic growth (per capita income) negatively and significantly affected the employment in agricultural sector of the developing countries.

LEVEL OF GROWTH AND EMPLOYMENT IN INDUSTRY (% OF TOTAL EMPLOYMENT)

The percentage of employment in industry generally increases with economic development. Table 5.29 shows the relationship between level of growth and employment in industry.

The table ,shows the two-way classification of countries with respect to level of growth and employment in industry in the year 2004. There were 31 countries with employment in industry as 24 percent and above, of which 4 countries were low income countries, 12 were lower-middle income countries and

15 were upper-middle income countries. Out of 46 countries with employment in industry between 12 to 24 percent, 16 countries were low income countries, 19 were lower-middle income countries and 11 were upper-middle income countries. There were 36 countries having employment in industry below 12 percent, and out of these, 29 countries were low income countries, 6 were lower-middle income countries and only one was upper-middle income country.

TABLE 5.29
Level of Growth and Employment in Industry (% of Total Employment) (2004)

Level of growth	*Employment in industry*			
	Below 12	*12-24*	*24 or Above*	*Total R_i's*
Low	29	16	4	49
Lower Middle	6	19	12	37
Upper Middle	1	11	15	27
Total C_j's	36	46	31	113

Tabular value at 5 percent level at 4 d.f. = 9.488
Calculated χ^2_{2004} = 37.608
(No. of countries = 113)
Calculated χ^2_{2000} = 64.890
(No. of countries = 102)
Calculated χ^2_{1990} = 59.969
(No. of countries = 82)
Calculated χ^2_{1980} = 40.404
(No. of countries = 66)

Chi-square value was calculated to be 37.608 and was significant at 5 percent level, indicating that the two variables were significantly associated with each other. The distribution of countries in the table showed that the two variables were positively associated. Thus, at higher level of development, the percentage of employment increased in the industrial sector. The association between the two variables was significant and positive throughout the period of study, i.e. 1980, 1990, 2000 and 2004.

The results of simple regression (Table 5.31) showed that the regression coefficient was positive and significant, indicating that economic growth (per capita income) positively and significantly affected the employment in industrial sector of the developing countries.

LEVEL OF GROWTH AND EMPLOYMENT IN SERVICES (% OF TOTAL EMPLOYMENT)

As in case of industry, the percentage of employment in services sector also increases with improvement in level of economic development. Table 5.30 shows the two-way classification of countries with respect to level of growth and employment in services in the year 2004. There were 37 countries with employment in services as 55 percent and above, of which only 2 countries were low income countries, 12 were lower-middle income countries and 23 were upper-middle income countries. Out of 52 countries with employment in

TABLE 5.30
Level of Growth and Employment in Services (% of Total Employment) (2004)

Level of growth	*Employment in services*			
	Below 25	*25-55*	*55 or Above*	*Total R_i's*
Low	22	25	2	49
Lower Middle	2	23	12	37
Upper Middle	0	4	23	27
Total C_j's	24	52	37	113

Tabular value at 5 percent level at 4 d.f. = 9.488
Calculated χ^2_{2004} = 66.063
(No. of countries = 113)
Calculated χ^2_{2000} = 58.296
(No. of countries = 102)
Calculated χ^2_{1990} = 45.489
(No. of countries = 82)
Calculated χ^2_{1980} = 33.733
(No. of countries = 66)

services between 25 to 55 percent, 25 countries were low income countries, 23 were lower-middle income countries and only 4 were upper-middle income countries. There were 24 countries having employment in services below 25 percent, and out of these, 22 countries were low income counties and only 2 were lower-middle income countries.

Chi-square value was calculated to be 66.063 and was significant at 5 percent level, indicating that the two variables were significantly associated with each other. The distribution of countries in the table showed that the two variables were positively associated. Thus, at higher level of development, the percentage of employment increased in the services sector. The association between the two variables was significant and positive during the entire period of study, i.e. 1980, 1990, 2000 and 2004, and appears to have strengthened over time.

The results of simple regression (Table 5.31) showed that the regression coefficient was positive and significant, indicating that economic growth (per capita income) positively and significantly affected the employment in services sector of the developing countries.

Thus, majority of structural indicators, discussed in this chapter, showed significant association with level of development of developing countries, especially during 1980 to 2000.

Globalization emerged mainly during the early nineties. To examine the extent of globalization, the trade related variables were examined over time (Appendix 5.1). It was seen that the share of manufacture exports in merchandise exports increased over time especially during 1990-2004 period. On the other hand, the share of food and agriculture raw material in merchandise exports decreased. Thus, with globalization, the exports of primary goods decreased and the share of manufactured exports increased showing that the developing countries also started exporting manufactured goods, but earlier these countries exported mainly the primary goods.

In the developing countries, the exposure to international trade picked up in 1990s, coinciding with their movement towards trade liberalization. It was also seen that the average annual growth rate of export volume and import volume was positively associated with level of economic growth during the

TABLE 5.31

Regression Results of Structural Variables with GNI Per Capita as Independent Variable (2004)

Sl. No.	Dependent Variable	Constant	Reg. Coeff. of GNI per capita	r^2	F-ratio
(1)	(2)	(3)	(4)	(5)	6)
1.	Agriculture Value Added (% of GDP)	29.154 (20.777)	-0.004* (-9.505)	0.448	90.341
2.	Agriculture average annual growth rate (%)	3.412 (7.369)	-0.002 (-1.268)	0.014	1.606
3.	Industry Value Added (% of GDP)	27.274 (19.234)	0.001* (3.211)	0.084	10.31
4.	Industry average annual growth rate (%)	4.448 (7.708)	-0.0001 (-0.020)	0.001	0.001
5.	Services Value Added (% of GDP)	43.245 (31.964)	0.003* (6.675)	0.286	44.548
6.	Services average annual growth rate (%)	3.748 (7.574)	0.0009 (0.585)	0.003	0.342
7.	GDP average annual growth rate (%)	4.142 (10.351)	-0.0003 (-0.264)	0.006	0.069
8.	GNI per capita PPP	1765.256 (6.642)	1.609* (18.891)	0.762	356.882
9.	Private Consumption Expenditure (% of GDP)	76.150 (43.193)	-0.003* (-4.986)	0.183	24.862

10.	Gross Domestic Savings (% of GDP)	16.06 (11.576)	0.001* (2.508)	0.053	6.29
11.	Gross capital formation (% of GDP)	21.563 (24.864)	0.004 (1.427)	0.018	2.036
12.	Energy use per capita (kg of oil equivalent)	235.288 (2.155)	0.381* (10.912)	0.517	119.072
13.	Fuel, ore and metal exports (% of merchandise exports)	29.553 (7.726)	-0.0007 (-0.588)	0.003	0.346
14.	Food and agricultural raw material exports (% of merchandise exports)	40.276 (12.558)	-0.004* (-4.191)	0.136	17.561
15.	Manufacture exports (% of merchandise exports)	29.896 (8.518)	0.005* (4.436)	0.15	19.678
16.	Exports of goods and services (% of GDP)	32.615 (13.448)	0.003* (4.158)	0.134	17.288
17.	Imports of goods and services (% of GDP)	42.852 (16.499)	0.002 (1.781)	0.027	3.17
18.	Degree of openness (exports+imports) % of GDP	75.358 (16.025)	0.005* (3.152)	0.082	9.932
19.	Export volume average annual growth rate (%)	14.618 (8.260)	-0.005 (-0.801)	0.005	0.641
20.	Import volume average annual growth rate (%)	13.003 (10.838)	-0.001 (-0.377)	0.001	0.142
21.	Merchandise trade (% of GDP)	63.643 (13.532)	0.003* (2.104)	0.038	4.426

(Contd.)

TABLE 5.31 (Contd.)

(1)	(2)	(3)	(4)	(5)	6)
22.	Trade in services (% of GDP)	16.948 (12.325)	0.007 (1.743)	0.027	3.038
23.	Gross private capital flows (% of GDP)	10.284 (6.342)	0.002* (3.470)	0.097	12.037
24.	Employment in agriculture (% of total employment)	54.338 (23.256)	-0.007* (-10.190)	0.483	103.836
25.	Employment in industry (% of total employment)	13.874 (11.640)	0.002* (6.230)	0.26	38.814
26.	Employment in services (% of total employment)	32.632 (16.927)	0.005* (8.697)	0.405	75.638
27.	Daily calorie supply (per capita)	2313.409 (43.650)	0.087* (5.178)	0.194	26.82
28.	Foreign direct investment, net inflows (% of GDP)	3.622 (5.745)	0.001 (0.098)	0.0001	0.009
29.	Foreign direct investment, net outflows (% of GDP)	0.225 (1.209)	0.0003 (0.650)	0.004	0.422
30.	Total debt service (% of GNI)	3.871 (7.154)	0.0008* (4.918)	0.178	24.187

Note : Figures in parentheses are t-values.
* Regression coefficient significant at 5 percent level.

period 1990-2000 which clearly showed the positive impact of globalization in developing countries. The export-GDP ratio and degree of openness were positively associated with level of economic growth. This showed that due to increased openness and major reductions in barriers to international trade, globalization has opened the door for export-led growth.

The trade in services increased at higher levels of economic growth especially during the period of 1990s. At lower levels of economic growth, the developing countries lagged behind in services sector and there was predominance of agricultural sector. With globalization, the MNCs became more active and increased their area of operations. As a result, there was a boost in services sector. Thus, services sector of developing countries developed more due to globalization.

The emergence of global production systems that drove the increasing financial flows, created new opportunities for growth and industrialization in developing countries. The growth of these production systems has been most pronounced in the high-tech industries (electronic and semi-conductors, etc.) and in labour-intensive consumer goods (textiles, garments and footwear, etc.). It is also becoming significant in the service sector where technological advances have made it possible to supply services such as software development, financial services and call centers from different countries around the globe. The high-tech industries have experienced the fastest growth and now constitute the largest single component of the manufactured exports of developing countries.

The gross private capital flows and total debt service also showed positive association with level of economic growth. The changes in trade, FDI and financial flows have increasingly become part of a new systemic whole. An underlying common factor is that all these elements necessarily evolved in the context of increasing economic openness and the growing influence of global market forces.

The analysis of various structural indicators in the chapter also confirmed that structural changes go along with economic development. Share of agriculture and level of growth were negatively associated showing that at higher levels of per capita income, the share of agriculture in GDP of developing countries declined. On the other hand, share of industry and services were positively associated with level of growth. Thus, structural changes took place even within the developing countries and share of agricultural sector in GDP declined whereas that of industry and services sectors increased.

The sectoral shifts in labour force also took place with time in the developing countries. Employment in agriculture and level of growth were negatively associated. On the other hand, employment in industry and services both were positively associated with level of growth. This shows that with economic growth, the labour force shifted from agricultural sector to industrial and services sectors, confirming that structural changes have been taking place in employment in developing countries.

GNI per capita (PPP), energy use per capita and daily calorie supply per capita were positively associated with level of economic development.

It can be concluded from this chapter that, on the whole, there was positive impact of globalization on the relationship of economic development and structural indicators. This impact in terms of accompanying structural changes was more pronounced during 1990 and 2000 and appears to have tapered off later on in case of some of the structural variables.

Economic Growth and Demographic Changes

Economic development involves not only change in structure of output and employment but also an improvement in the quality of life of people. It essentially affects living standards which have strong bearing on demographic aspects.

For decades, economists and social thinkers have debated about the influence of population change on economic growth and vice-versa. Three alternative positions intensify this debate: Whether population growth (1) restricts, (2) promotes or (3) is independent of economic growth. Proponents of each explanation can find evidence to support their cases. All of these explanations, however, focus on population size, and other demographic indicators such as birth rate, death rate, infant mortality rate, life expectancy at birth, adult literacy rate, availability of physicians, level of education and migration of people, etc. It is also believed that economic growth affects, and is in turn, affected by demographic indicators. Thus, it is pertinent to examine the relationship of economic growth and demographic indicators. Globalization has also bearing on the relationship as the awareness about living standards, health and education, etc. has improved much due to integration of the economies.

The present chapter attempts to study the relationship, if any, between economic growth and demographic indicators of developing countries. The developing countries have been divided into 3 categories; low income countries, lower-middle income countries and upper-middle income countries, as classified by World Bank (2006) on the basis of gross national income per capita.

The analysis has been carried out at four points of time and therefore relationship between level of growth and various demographic indicators has been examined at these four points of time, i.e. 1980, 1990, 2000 and 2004. Tabular analysis, Chi-square test and simple regression have been used to determine the nature, degree and extent of relationship between the level of growth and various demographic indicators.

LEVEL OF GROWTH AND BIRTH RATE (PER 1000 PEOPLE)

As economic development takes place, birth rate in an economy is likely to decrease. Alternatively, a declining birth rate is generally a sign of development while a higher birth rate is a sign of underdevelopment.

Table 6.1 shows the two-way classification of countries with respect to level of growth and birth rate (per 1000 people) in the year 2004. There were 22 countries with birth rate as 40 and above, of which 21 countries were low income countries and only one country was lower-middle income country. Out of 54 countries with birth rate between 20 to 40, there were 26 low income countries, 21 lower-middle income countries and 7 upper-middle income countries. There were 37 countries having birth rate below 20, and out of these, only 2 countries were low income countries, 15 were lower-middle income countries and 20 were upper-middle income countries.

Chi-square value was calculated to be 55.041 and was significant at 5 percent level, indicating that the two variables were significantly associated with each other. The distribution of countries in the table showed that the two variables were negatively associated. Thus, birth rate declined at higher levels

TABLE 6.1
Level of Growth and Birth Rate (Per 1000 People) (2004)

Level of Growth	*Birth rate*			
	Below 20	*20-40*	*40 or Above*	*Total R_i's*
Low	2	26	21	49
Lower Middle	15	21	1	37
Upper Middle	20	7	0	27
Total C_j's	37	54	22	113

Tabular value at 5 percent level at 4 d.f. = 9.488
Calculated $\chi^2_{2004} = 55.041$
(No. of countries = 113)
Calculated $\chi^2_{2000} = 46.93$
(No. of countries = 102)
Calculated $\chi^2_{1990} = 74.359$
(No. of countries = 82)
Calculated $\chi^2_{1980} = 58.438$
(No. of countries = 66)

of economic growth. The association between the two variables was significant and negative throughout the period of study, i.e. 1980, 1990, 2000 and 2004.

The results of simple regression (Table 6.12) showed that the regression coefficient was negative and significant, indicating that economic growth (per capita income) negatively and significantly affected the birth rate of the developing countries.

LEVEL OF GROWTH AND DEATH RATE (PER 1000 PEOPLE)

As economic development takes place in an economy, the death rate declines due to improved medical facilities. Hence, a low death rate is a sign of economic development. The relationship between level of growth and death rate is shown in Table 6.2.

The table shows the two-way classification of countries with respect to level of growth and death rate (per 1000 people) in the year 2004. There were 34 countries with death rate as 14 and above, of which 25 countries were low income countries, 5 were lower-middle income countries and 4 countries were upper-middle income countries. Out of 46 countries with death rate between 7 to 14, there were 22 low income countries, 10 lower-middle income countries and 14 upper-middle income countries. There were 33 countries having death rate below 7, and out of these, only 2 countries were low income counties, 22 were lower-middle income countries and 9 were upper-middle income countries.

TABLE 6.2
Level of Growth and Death Rate (Per 1000 People) (2004)

Level of Growth	*Death rate*			
	Below 7	*7-14*	*14 or Above*	*Total R_i's*
Low	2	22	25	49
Lower Middle	22	10	5	37
Upper Middle	9	14	4	27
Total C_j's	33	46	34	113

Tabular value at 5 percent level at 4 d.f. = 9.488
Calculated χ^2_{2004} = 37.688
(No. of countries = 113)
Calculated χ^2_{2000} = 53.108
(No. of countries = 102)
Calculated χ^2_{1990} = 35.082
(No. of countries = 82)
Calculated χ^2_{1980} = 29.796
(No. of countries = 66)

Chi-square value was calculated to be 37.688 and was significant at 5 percent level, indicating that the two variables were significantly associated with each other. The distribution of countries in the table showed that the two variables were negatively associated. The association between the two variables was negative and significant throughout the period of study i.e. 1980, 1990, 2000 and 2004.

The results of simple regression (Table 6.12) showed that the regression coefficient was negative and significant, indicating that economic growth (per capita income) negatively and significantly affected the death rate of the developing countries.

LEVEL OF GROWTH AND INFANT MORTALITY RATE

With economic development, infant mortality rate declines in the economy. Alternatively, a high infant mortality rate shows underdevelopment in the economy. In Table 6.3, the relationship between level of growth and infant mortality rate is examined.

TABLE 6.3
Level of Growth and Infant Mortality Rate
(Per 1000 Live Births)
(2004)

Level of growth	*Infant mortality rate*			
	Below 25	*25-100*	*100 or Above*	*Total R_i's*
Low	2	29	18	49
Lower Middle	16	19	2	37
Upper Middle	22	5	0	27
Total C_j's	40	53	20	113

Tabular value at 5 percent level at 4 d.f. = 9.488
Tabular value at 5 percent level at 2 d.f. = 5.991
Calculated χ^2_{2004} = 47.084
(No. of countries = 113)
Calculated χ^2_{2000} = 45.637
(No. of countries = 102)
Calculated χ^2_{1990} = 46.331
(No. of countries = 82)
Calculated χ^2_{1980} = 48.974
(No. of countries = 66)

Table shows the two-way classification of countries with respect to level of growth and infant mortality rate (per 1000 live births) in the year 2004. There were 20 countries with infant mortality rate as 100 and above, of which 18 countries were low income countries and only 2 were lower-middle income countries. Out of 53 countries with infant mortality rate between 25 to 100, there were 29 low income countries, 19 lower-middle income countries and 5 upper-middle income countries. There were 40 countries having infant mortality rate below 25, and out of these, 2 countries were low income countries, 16 were lower-middle income countries and 22 were upper-middle income countries.

Chi-square value was calculated (after merging the last two columns) to be 47.084 and was significant at 5 percent level, indicating that the two variables were significantly associated with each other. The distribution of countries in the table showed that the two variables were negatively associated. Thus, at higher levels of economic growth, the infant mortality rate declined. The association between the two variables was negative and significant during the entire period of study i.e. 1980, 1990, 2000 and 2004.

The results of simple regression (Table 6.12) showed that the regression coefficient was negative and significant, indicating that economic growth (per capita income) negatively and significantly affected the infant mortality rate of the developing countries.

LEVEL OF GROWTH AND LIFE EXPECTANCY AT BIRTH

A high life expectancy, in a sense, shows improved medical and other facilities in an economy that are available for the people due to economic development. Life expectancy generally increases with economic development in an economy.

Table 6.4 shows the two-way classification of countries with respect to level of growth and life expectancy at birth in the year 2004. There were 11 countries with life expectancy at birth as 75 years and above, of which only one country was lower-middle income country and 10 countries were upper-middle income countries. Out of 67 countries with life expectancy at birth between 55 to 75 years, there were 20 low income countries, 33 lower-middle income countries and 14 upper-middle income countries. There were 35 countries having life expectancy at birth below 55 years, and out of these, 29 countries were low income countries, 3 were lower-middle income countries and another 3 were upper-middle income countries.

TABLE 6.4

Level of Growth and Life Expectancy at Birth (Yrs.) (2004)

Level of Growth	*Life expectancy at birth*			
	Below 55	*55-75*	*75 or Above*	*Total R_i's*
Low	29	20	0	49
Lower Middle	3	33	1	37
Upper Middle	3	14	10	27
Total C_j's	35	67	11	113

Tabular value at 5 percent level at 4 d.f. = 9.488
Tabular value at 5 percent level at 2 d.f. = 5.991
Calculated χ^2_{2004} = 32.310
(No. of countries = 113)
Calculated χ^2_{2000} = 55.992
(No. of countries = 102)
Calculated χ^2_{1990} = 41.154
(No. of countries = 82)
Calculated χ^2_{1980} = 38.077
(No. of countries = 66)

Chi-square value was calculated (after merging the last two columns) to be 32.310 and was significant at 5 percent level, indicating that the two variables were significantly associated with each other. The distribution of countries in the table showed that the two variables were positively associated. Thus, life expectancy at birth increased at higher levels of economic growth. The association between the two variables was positive and significant during the period of study, i.e. 1980, 1990, 2000 and 2004.

The results of simple regression (Table 6.12) showed that the regression coefficient was positive and significant, indicating that economic growth (per capita income) positively and significantly affected the life expectancy at birth of the developing countries.

LEVEL OF GROWTH AND NUMBER OF PHYSICIANS (PER 1000 PEOPLE)

Physicians are defined as graduates of any faculty or

school of medicine who are working in the country in any medical field, practice, teaching or research (World Bank, 2006). It is expected that with economic development, availability of physicians per thousand persons increases.

Table 6.5 shows the two-way classification of countries with respect to level of growth and number of physicians (per 1000 people) in the year 2004. There were 26 countries with number of physicians as 2.0 and above, of which 5 countries were low income countries, 9 were lower-middle income countries and 12 countries were upper-middle income countries. Out of 48 countries with number of physicians between 0.5 to 2.0, there were 10 low income countries, 24 lower-middle income countries and 14 upper-middle income countries. There were 39 countries having number of physicians below 0.5, and out of these, 34 countries were low income counties, 4 were lower-middle income countries and only one was upper-middle income country.

Chi-square value was calculated to be 50.170 and was significant at 5 percent level, indicating that the two variables

TABLE 6.5
Level of Growth and Number of Physicians (per 1000 People) (2004)

Level of Growth	*Number of Physicians*			
	Below 0.5	*0.5-2.0*	*2.0 or Above*	*Total R_i's*
Low	34	10	5	49
Lower Middle	4	24	9	37
Upper Middle	1	14	12	27
Total C_j's	39	48	26	113

Tabular value at 5 percent level at 4 d.f. = 9.488
Calculated $\chi^2_{2004} = 50.170$
(No. of countries = 113)
Calculated $\chi^2_{2000} = 77.462$
(No. of countries = 102)
Calculated $\chi^2_{1990} = 78.068$
(No. of countries = 82)
Calculated $\chi^2_{1980} = 51.480$
(No. of countries = 66)

were significantly associated with each other. The distribution of countries in the table showed that the two variables were positively associated. The association between the two variables was positive and significant during all the period of study i.e. 1980, 1990, 2000 and 2004.

The results of simple regression (Table 6.12) showed that the regression coefficient was positive and significant, indicating that economic growth (per capita income) positively and significantly affected the number of physicians in the developing countries.

LEVEL OF GROWTH AND ADULT LITERACY RATE

Adult literacy rate is the percentage of adults, who can with understanding, read and write a short, simple statement about their everyday life. It is the literacy rate among people aged 15 and older. With economic development, literacy level is likely to improve. The relationship between level of growth and adult literacy rate is examined in Table 6.6.

TABLE 6.6
Level of Growth and Adult Literacy Rate (%) (2004)

Level of Growth	*Adult literacy rate*			
	Below 50	*50-90*	*90 or Above*	*Total R_i's*
Low	16	27	6	49
Lower Middle	2	17	18	37
Upper Middle	1	8	18	27
Total C_j's	19	52	42	113

Tabular value at 5 percent level at 4 d.f. = 9.488
Tabular value at 5 percent level at 2 d.f. = 5.991
Calculated χ^2_{2004} = 25.140
(No. of countries = 113)
Calculated χ^2_{2000} = 56.654
(No. of countries = 102)
Calculated χ^2_{1990} = 43.221
(No. of countries = 82)
Calculated χ^2_{1980} = 36.422
(No. of countries = 66)

The table shows the two-way classification of countries with respect to level of growth and adult literacy rate in the year 2004. There were 42 countries with adult literacy rate as 90 percent and above, of which 6 countries were low income countries, 18 were lower-middle income countries and another 18 countries were upper-middle income countries. Out of 52 countries with adult literacy rate between 50 to 90 percent, there were 27 low income countries, 17 lower-middle income countries and 8 upper-middle income countries. There were 19 countries having adult literacy rate below 50 percent, and out of these, 16 countries were low income countries, 2 were lower-middle income countries and only one was upper-middle income country.

Chi-square value was calculated (after merging the first two columns) to be 25.140 and was significant at 5 percent level, indicating that the two variables were significantly associated with each other. The distribution of countries in the table showed that the two variables were positively associated. The association between the two variables was positive and significant during the entire period of study, i.e. 1980, 1990, 2000 and 2004.

The results of simple regression (Table 6.12) showed that the regression coefficient was positive and significant, indicating that economic growth (per capita income) positively and significantly affected the adult literacy rate of the developing countries.

LEVEL OF GROWTH AND PRIMARY SCHOOL ENROLLMENT

Primary education provides children with basic reading, writing, and mathematical skills along with an elementary understanding of such subjects as history, geography, natural science, social science, art and music (World Bank, 2006). Primary school enrollment ratio shows the level of primary education in an economy. With economic development, this ratio is also likely to increase due to increase in educational facilities. In Table 6.7, the relationship between level of growth and primary school enrollment is examined.

Table 6.7 shows the two-way classification of countries with respect to level of growth and primary school enrollment ratio in the year 2004. There were 27 countries with primary school enrollment ratio as 95 and above, of which 5 countries were low income countries, 14 were lower-middle income countries and 8 countries were upper-middle income countries. Out of 51 countries with primary school enrollment ratio between 80 to 95, there were 13 low income countries, 20 lower-middle income countries and 18 upper-middle income countries. There were 35 countries having primary school enrollment ratio below 80, and out of these, 31 countries were low income counties, 3 were lower-middle income countries and only one was upper-middle income country.

TABLE 6.7
Level of Growth and Primary School Enrollment (% Net) (2004)

Level of Growth	*Primary school enrollment*			
	Below 80	*80-95*	*95 or Above*	*Total R_i's*
Low	31	13	5	49
Lower Middle	3	20	14	37
Upper Middle	1	18	8	27
Total C_j's	35	51	27	113

Tabular value at 5 percent level at 4 d.f. = 9.488
Calculated χ^2_{2004} = 43.634
(No. of countries = 113)
Calculated χ^2_{2000} = 63.383
(No. of countries = 102)
Calculated χ^2_{1990} = 35.506
(No. of countries = 82)

Chi-square value was calculated to be 43.634 and was significant at 5 percent level, indicating that the two variables were significantly associated with each other. The distribution of countries in the table showed that the two variables were positively associated. The association between the two variables was positive and significant during 1990, 2000 and 2004. For the year 1980, the Chi-square could not be calculated due to non-availability of data.

The results of simple regression (Table 6.12) showed that the regression coefficient was positive and significant, indicating that economic growth (per capita income) positively and significantly affected the primary school enrollment ratio of the developing countries.

LEVEL OF GROWTH AND SECONDARY SCHOOL ENROLLMENT

Similarly, secondary school enrollment ratio shows the level of secondary education in an economy. With economic development, this ratio is also expected to increase, and therefore, it is an indicator of economic development.

TABLE 6.8
Level of Growth and Secondary School Enrollment (% Net) (2004)

Level of Growth	*Secondary school enrollment*			
	Below 40	*40-80*	*80 or Above*	*Total R_i's*
Low	35	12	2	49
Lower Middle	6	22	9	37
Upper Middle	2	14	11	27
Total C_j's	43	48	22	113

Tabular value at 5 percent level at 4 d.f. = 9.488
Calculated $\chi^2_{2004} = 45.129$
(No. of countries = 113)
Calculated $\chi^2_{2000} = 66.011$
(No. of countries = 102)
Calculated $\chi^2_{1990} = 33.462$
(No. of countries = 82)

Table 6.8 shows the two-way classification of countries with respect to level of growth and secondary school enrollment ratio in the year 2004. There were 22 countries with secondary school enrollment ratio as 80 and above, of which only 2 countries were low income countries, 9 were lower-middle income countries and 11 countries were upper-middle income countries. Out of 48 countries with secondary school enrollment ratio between 40 to 80, there were 12 low income countries, 22 lower-middle income countries and 14 upper-middle income countries. There were 43 countries having secondary school enrollment ratio below 40, and out of these, 35 countries were low income counties, 6 were lower-middle income countries and only 2 were upper-middle income countries.

Chi-square value was calculated to be 45.129 and was significant at 5 percent level, indicating that the two variables were significantly associated with each other. The distribution of countries in the table showed that the two variables were positively associated. The association between the two variables was positive and significant during 1990, 2000 and 2004. For the year 1980, the Chi-square could not be calculated due to non-availability of data.

The results of simple regression (Table 6.12) showed that the regression coefficient was positive and significant, indicating that economic growth (per capita income) positively and significantly affected the secondary school enrollment ratio of the developing countries.

LEVEL OF GROWTH AND PERCENTAGE OF POPULATION OF WORKING AGE (15-64 YRS.)

The developing countries are in varying stages of a demographic transition from high to low rates of mortality and fertility. This transition produces a "boom" generation that is gradually working its way through each nation's age structure. As the boom generation enters working age (15-64 years) there is the opportunity to unleash an economic growth spurt, provided the right kinds of policies are in place to ensure that extra workers are productively employed. Thus, a higher percentage of working population is a good sign and conducive for development since it also indicates lower percentage of dependent population in the economy.

Table 6.9 shows the two-way classification of countries with respect to level of growth and population of working age (15-64 years) in the year 2004. There were 33 countries with population of working age (15-64 years) as 65 percent and above, of which only 2 countries were low income countries, 17 were lower-middle income countries and 14 countries were upper-middle income countries. Out of 46 countries with population of working age (15-64 years) between 55 to 65 percent, there were 18 low income countries, 16 lower-middle income countries and 12 upper-middle income countries. There were 34 countries having population of working age (15-64 years) below 55 percent, and out of these, 29 countries were low income countries, 4 were lower-middle income countries and only one was upper-middle income country.

TABLE 6.9

Level of Growth and Percentage of Population of Working Age (15-64 Yrs.) (2004)

Level of Growth	*Population of working age*			
	Below 55	*55-65*	*65 or Above*	*Total R_i's*
Low	29	18	2	49
Lower Middle	4	16	17	37
Upper Middle	1	12	14	27
Total C_j's	34	46	33	113

Tabular value at 5 percent level at 4 d.f. = 9.488
Calculated χ^2_{2004} = 43.827
(No. of countries = 113)
Calculated χ^2_{2000} = 53.680
(No. of countries = 102)
Calculated χ^2_{1990} = 82.000
(No. of countries = 82)
Calculated χ^2_{1980} = 45.257
(No. of countries = 66)

Chi-square value was calculated to be 43.827 and was significant at 5 percent level, indicating that the two variables were significantly associated with each other. The distribution of countries in the table showed that the two variables were positively associated. The association between the two variables was positive and significant throughout the period of study, i.e. 1980, 1990, 2000 and 2004.

The results of simple regression (Table 6.12) showed that the regression coefficient was positive and significant, indicating that economic growth (per capita income) positively and significantly affected the population of working age of the developing countries.

LEVEL OF GROWTH AND URBAN POPULATION (% OF TOTAL)

Urbanization generally goes hand in hand with the process of economic growth. This is so because the accompanying increase in industrial activity acts as an impetus to concentration of population in towns and cities where there are economies of agglomeration. Thus, as the sectoral composition of the economy changes towards the secondary and tertiary sectors and as economic growth takes place, urbanization has a tendency to grow (Bhardwaj and Jamile, 1992). The relationship between level of growth and urban population is examined in Table 6.10

The table shows the two-way classification of countries with respect to level of growth and urban population ratio in the year 2004. There were 36 countries with urban population ratio as 60 percent and above, of which only one country was low income country, 16 were lower-middle income countries and 19 countries were upper-middle income countries. Out of 48 countries with urban population ratio between 35 to 60 percent, there were 23 low income countries, 17 lower-middle income countries and 8 upper-middle income countries. There were 29 countries having urban population ratio below 35 percent, and out of these, 25 countries were low income countries and only 4 were lower-middle income countries.

Chi-square value was calculated to be 51.519 and was significant at 5 percent level, indicating that the two variables were significantly associated with each other. The distribution of countries in the table showed that the two variables were positively associated. The association between the two variables was positive and significant during the entire period of study, i.e. 1980, 1990, 2000 and 2004.

TABLE 6.10
Level of Growth and Urban Population (% of Total) (2004)

Level of Growth	*Urban Population*			
	Below 35	*35-60*	*60 or Above*	*Total R_i's*
Low	25	23	1	49
Lower Middle	4	17	16	37
Upper Middle	0	8	19	27
Total C_j's	29	48	36	113

Tabular value at 5 percent level at 4 d.f. = 9.488
Calculated χ^2_{2004} = 51.519
(No. of countries = 113)
Calculated χ^2_{2000} = 64.047
(No. of countries = 102)
Calculated χ^2_{1990} = 53.971
(No. of countries = 82)
Calculated χ^2_{1980} = 41.368
(No. of countries = 66)

The results of simple regression (Table 6.12) showed that the regression coefficient was positive and significant, indicating that economic growth (per capita income) positively and significantly affected the urban population of the developing countries.

LEVEL OF GROWTH AND INTERNATIONAL MIGRATION STOCK (% OF POPULATION)

Movement of people through migration is a significant part of international integration. Migrants contribute to the economies of both their host country and their country of origin. Migration stock is defined as the number of people born in a country other than that in which they live (World Bank, 2006).

Table 6.11 shows the two-way classification of countries with respect to level of growth and international migration stock (% of population) in the year 2004. There were 32 countries with international migration stock as 4 percent and above, of which 11 countries were low income countries, 9 were lower-middle income countries and 12 countries were upper-middle income countries. Out of 47 countries with international migration stock between 1 to 4 percent, 23 were low income countries, 11 lower-middle income countries and 13 upper-middle income countries. There were 34 countries having international migration stock below 1 percent, and out of these, 15 countries were low income counties, 17 were lower-middle income countries and only 2 were upper-middle income countries.

TABLE 6.11
Level of Growth and International Migration Stock (% of Population) (2004)

Level of Growth	*International migration stock*			
	Below 1	*1-4*	*4 or Above*	*Total R_i's*
Low	15	23	11	49
Lower Middle	17	11	9	37
Upper Middle	2	13	12	27
Total C_j's	34	47	32	113

Tabular value at 5 percent level at 4 d.f. = 9.488
Calculated χ^2_{2004} = 12.864
(No. of countries = 113)
Calculated χ^2_{2000} = 58.023
(No. of countries = 102)
Calculated χ^2_{1990} = 56.015
(No. of countries = 82)
Calculated χ^2_{1980} = 42.472
(No. of countries = 66)

Chi-square value was calculated to be 12.864 and was significant at 5 percent level, indicating that the two variables were significantly associated with each other. The distribution of countries in the table showed that the two variables were positively associated. The association between the two variables was positive and significant throughout the period of study, i.e. 1980, 1990, 2000 and 2004.

The results of simple regression (Table 6.12) showed that the regression coefficient was positive and significant, indicating that economic growth (per capita income) positively and

Table 6.12
Regression Results of Demographic Variables with GNI Per Capita as Independent Variable (2004)

Sl. No.	Dependent Variable	Constant	Reg. Coeff. of GNI per capita	r^2	F-ratio
1.	Birth rate (per 1000 people)	33.966	-0.004* (28.050)	0.404 (-8.682)	75.373
2.	Death rate (per 1000 people)	12.878 (18.124)	-0.0007* (-3.292)	0.088	10.838
3.	Infant mortality rate (per 1000 live births)	78.398 (19.080)	-0.011* (-8.619)	0.401	74.288
4.	Life expectancy at birth (years)	55.054 (41.517)	0.003* (7.113)	0.313	50.591
5.	Physicians (per 1000 people)	0.725 (5.198)	0.0002* (5.514)	0.215	30.408
6.	Adult literacy rate (%)	65.541 (26.642)	0.004* (5.583)	0.219	31.174
7.	School enrollment, primary (% net)	76.525 (40.203)	0.003* (4.671)	0.164	21.817
8.	School enrollment, secondary (% net)	39.598 (14.506)	0.006* (7.413)	0.331	54.958
9.	Percentage of population of working age (15-64 years)	56.372 (71.597)	0.002* (6.115)	0.251	37.391
10.	Urban population (% of total)	36.82 (18.665)	0.006* (8.875)	0.415	78.768
11.	International migration stock (% of population)	2.648 (3.378)	0.0008* (3.314)	0.09	10.984

Note : Figures in parentheses are t-values.
* Regression coefficient significant at 5 percent level.

significantly affected the international migration stock of the developing countries.

Thus, majority of demographic indicators discussed in this chapter showed significant association with level of growth of the developing countries. The analysis of various indicators in the chapter confirmed that economic growth has an impact on the demographic indicators.

Life expectancy at birth and number of physicians showed positive association with level of economic growth, indicating that these increased with improved levels of economic growth in the developing countries. It may be largely due to improved medical facilities at higher levels of economic growth.

A low death rate and infant mortality rate is a sign of economic development. The birth rate, death rate and infant mortality rate were negatively associated with level of economic growth. Birth rate, death rate and infant mortality rate also declined with economic growth due to increased medical and other facilities in the developing countries. The relationship between demographic changes and economic growth has assumed added importance in recent years because of emerging demographic trends in the developing world. At varying rates, developing countries have been undergoing a demographic transition, from high to low rates of mortality and fertility. This transition is producing a "boom" period of working age proportion of population.

Also, the population of working age and level of growth were positively associated showing that higher proportion of working age population may lead to still higher level of economic growth in future as the added productivity of the working age population may produce a demographic dividend.

Urban population and international migration stock showed positive association with level of growth. With economic development, sectoral changes take place and labour shifts from agricultural sector to industrial and services sectors. The industries and services sector generally develop in urban areas, thus workers shift from rural areas to the urban areas and settle there. Similarly, skilled workers prefer to shift to developed countries as they find more employment opportunities and higher wages there. Due to globalization, this trend is increasing in developing countries and it was strengthened mainly in 1990s.

Adult literacy rate, primary school enrolment ratio and secondary school enrollment ratio were also positively and significantly associated with level of economic growth throughout the period of study. This shows that with economic growth, the literacy rate increased in the developing world due to increased educational facilities. Due to the impact of globalization the youth go in for higher studies in order to get jobs in MNCs as they require educated and skilled persons.

Also, due to the sectoral changes with economic development, demand of educated persons increases in services sector.

Thus, it can be concluded from this chapter that globalization and economic growth has a positive effect on health related and other demographic variables.

Factors in Economic Development : An Empirical Investigation

In this chapter, an attempt has been made to find out factors in economic development of developing countries by applying different techniques, including Factor Analysis. Different measures have been used to measure the economic development and to find the impact of globalization on economic development of developing countries by using the data for the years 1980, 1990, 2000 and 2004. As economic development is a multi-dimensional process and a single indicator cannot appropriately express economic development, a composite index has been constructed to measure economic development. The number of countries, for which data were available in respect of various indicators, increased from 66 in 1980 to 82 in 1990, 102 in 2000 and 113 in 2004. However, for comparison purposes, in this chapter 66 common countries have been included in the analysis for which data were available at all the four points of time. The ranking of countries has been compared in respect of level of development based on composite index, GNI per capita, GNI per capita PPP and PQLI. An attempt has also been made to examine whether there occurred any change in the ranking of countries with the use of different measures of development or not.

CORRELATION MATRICES

Keeping in view that economic development is a multi-dimensional phenomenon, 22 important variables were selected out of the 42 variables on the basis of partial correlation analysis, as per details given in Chapter IV. The variables selected included the following:

1. Gross National Income PPP per capita (X_1)
2. Gross National Income per capita (X_2)
3. Share of industry in GDP (%) (X_3)
4. Share of services in GDP (%) (X_4)
5. Gross domestic savings (% of GDP) (X_5)
6. Energy use per capita (kg. of oil equivalent) (X_6)
7. Life expectancy at birth (Yrs.) (X_7)
8. Employment in services (% of total employment) (X_8)
9. Urban population (% of total) (X_9)
10. Daily calorie supply per capita (X_{10})
11. Number of Physicians (per 1000 people) (X_{11})
12. Gross private capital flows (% of GDP) (X_{12})
13. Gross capital formation (% of GDP) (X_{13})
14. Share of manufacture exports in merchandise exports (%) (X_{14})
15. Exports of goods and services (% of GDP) (X_{15})
16. Imports of goods and services (% of GDP) (X_{16})
17. Degree of openness (Exports + Imports as % of GDP) (X_{17})
18. Merchandise trade (% of GDP) (X_{18})
19. Trade in services (% of GDP) (X_{19})
20. International migration stock (% of population) (X_{20})
21. Fuel, ores and metal exports (% of merchandise exports) (X_{21})
22. Percentage of population of working age (15-64 years) (X_{22})

Correlation matrices of the 22 selected variables are given in Tables 7.1, 7.2, 7.3 and 7.4 for the years 1980, 1990, 2000 and 2004 respectively.

From the values of correlation coefficients ranging from –0.372 to +0.943 in 1980, and from –0.455 to +0.960 in 1990, it could be generalized that, in each year, the variables could broadly be clubbed into five sub-groups such that correlation between the variables in the same group have maximum values while with those belonging to the other sub-groups were lower.

There are wide variations in the correlation coefficients for the year 2000 ranging from –0.555 to +0.961 and the variables could broadly be clubbed into five sub-groups on the basis of inter-correlations with variables within the sub-group and with those belonging to other sub-groups. Similarly, the correlation coefficients for the year 2004 ranged from –0.533 to +0.941 and the variables could broadly be clubbed into six sub-groups such that correlation between the variables in the same group have maximum values while with those belonging to the other sub-group were lower.

Table 7.1 also shows correlation coefficients of GNI per capita with 22 variables for the year 1980. The correlation coefficient of GNI per capita with GNI per capita (PPP) was highest, i.e. 0.837. Also, the correlation coefficients of GNI per capita were higher and significant at one percent level with share of industry in GDP, gross domestic savings, energy use per capita, life expectancy at birth, employment in services and urban population. On the other hand, coefficients of correlation of GNI per capita were lower with gross capital formation, exports of goods and services, merchandise trade, international migration stock and population of working age.

Table 7.2 shows that for the year 1990, correlation coefficient of GNI per capita was again highest with GNI per capita (PPP), i.e. 0.894. Also, the correlation coefficients of GNI per capita were higher and significant at one percent level with share of industry in GDP, energy use per capita, life expectancy at birth, urban population and daily calorie supply per capita. On the other hand, coefficients of correlation of GNI per capita were lower with share of services in GDP, exports of goods and services, international migration stock and share of fuel, ores and metal exports in merchandise exports.

TABLE 7.1
Correlations Matrix of 22 Variables : 66 Countries Data for 1980

		GNIPPP	GNI	INDUVAL	SERVALU	GROSSAV	ENERGY	LIFEXP	EMPSERV	URBAN	CALORIE	PHYSICI
		X1	X2	X3	X4	X5	X6	X7	X8	X9	X10	X11
GNIPPP	X1	1	.837**	.590**	0.217	.509**	.714**	.656**	.647**	.783**	.540**	.637**
GNI	X2		1	.693**	0.101	.620**	.797**	.539**	.500**	.697**	.469**	.491**
INDUVAL	X3			1	-0.159	.812**	.673**	.478**	.378**	.543**	.430**	.399**
SERVGVALU	X4				1	-0.19	-0.004	.303*	.397**	.433**	0.239	0.193
GROSSAV	X5					1	.612**	.402**	.298*	.369**	.312*	.285*
ENERGY	X6						1	.512**	.429**	.611**	.549**	.477**
LIFEXP	X7							1	.723**	.711**	.588**	.667**
EMPSERV	X8								1	.726**	.418**	.524**
URBAN	X9									1	.582**	.718**
CALORIE	X10										1	.620**
PHYSICI	X11											1
GPCFLOW	X12											
GCAPFOR	X13											
MANUEXPT	X14											
EXPORTGS	X15											
IMPORTGS	X16											
OPENNES	X17											
MRCHTRAD	X18											
TRADSERV	X19											
MIGRA	X20											
FUEL	X21											
WORKING	X22											

(*Contd.*)

TABLE 7.1 (Contd.)

		GPCFLOW	GCAPFOR	MANUEXPT	EXPORTGS	IMPORTGS	OPENNES	MRCHTRAD	TRADSERV	MIGRA	FUEL	WORKING
		X12	X13	X14	X15	X16	X17	X18	X19	X20	X21	X22
GNIPPP	X1	0.104	.354**	0.085	0.149	-0.133	0.012	0.123	-0.144	0.148	0.211	.381**
GNI	X2	0.081	.368**	-0.084	.320**	-0.046	0.15	.282*	-0.014	.317**	.491**	.294*
INDUVAL	X3	-0.067	.576**	0.035	.383**	-0.055	0.18	.397**	0.001	0.093	.628**	.306*
SERVGVALU	X4	.349**	0.113	0.051	0.172	.400**	.301*	-0.003	.312*	0.129	-0.07	-0.083
GROSSAV	X5	0.196	.630**	-0.075	.522**	-0.051	.257*	.373**	0.02	-0.006	.645**	0.234
ENERGY	X6	0.032	.405**	0.028	.275*	-0.069	0.114	.385**	-0.042	0.135	.371**	.406**
LIFEXP	X7	0.216	.444**	.370**	0.149	0.002	0.082	0.141	-0.095	-0.036	0.109	.574**
EMPSERV	X8	0.193	.362**	0.159	0.198	0.108	0.164	0.117	0.109	0.146	0.133	.290*
URBAN	X9	0.12	.302*	0.113	0.118	-0.066	0.03	0.071	-0.016	0.101	.291*	.414**
CALORIE	X10	-0.03	.406**	0.132	0.015	-0.076	-0.032	0.122	-0.084	0.008	0.175	.527**
PHYSICI	X11	0.196	.254*	.261*	-0.013	-0.15	-0.085	-0.059	-0.129	0.002	-0.001	.634**
GPCFLOW	X12	1	0.117	-0.089	.545**	.453**	.532**	0.033	.358**	-0.013	-0.008	0.078
GCAPFOR	X13		1	0.024	.393**	.314*	.376**	.392**	0.207	.242*	.445**	0.135
MANUEXPT	X14			1	-0.172	-0.103	-0.147	-0.156	-0.067	-0.105	-.372**	.397**
EXPORTGS	X15				1	.769**	.943**	.735**	.654**	.278*	.378**	-0.052
IMPORTGS	X16					1	.937**	.621**	.764**	.411**	0.028	-0.2
OPENNES	X17						1	.723**	.753**	.365**	0.22	-0.131
MRCHTRAD	X18							1	.446**	.309*	.338**	-0.027
TRADSERV	X19								1	.499**	0.121	-0.119
MIGRA	X20									1	0.1	-0.203
FUEL	X21										1	-0.094
WORKING	X22											1

* Correlation is significant at 0.05 percent level.
** Correlation is significant at 0.01 percent level..

TABLE 7.2

Correlations Matrix of 22 Variables : 66 Countries Data for 1990

		GNIPPP	GNI	INDUVAL	SERVALU	GROSSAV	ENERGY	LIFEXP	EMPSERV	URBAN	CALORIE	PHYSICI
		X1	X2	X3	X4	X5	X6	X7	X8	X9	X10	X11
GNIPPP	X1	1	.837**	.590**	0.217	.509**	.714**	.656**	.647**	.783**	.540**	.637**
GNI	X2		1	.693**	0.101	.620**	.797**	.539**	.500**	.697**	.469**	.491**
INDUVAL	X3			1	-0.159	.812**	.673**	.478**	.378**	.543**	.430**	.399**
SERVGVALU	X4				1	-0.19	-0.004	.303*	.397**	.433**	0.239	0.193
GROSSAV	X5					1	.612**	.402**	.298*	.369**	.312*	.285*
ENERGY	X6						1	.512**	.429**	.611**	.549**	.477**
LIFEXP	X7							1	.723**	.711**	.588**	.667**
EMPSERV	X8								1	.726**	.418**	.524**
URBAN	X9									1	.582**	.718**
CALORIE	X10										1	.620**
PHYSICI	X11											1
GPCFLOW	X12											
GCAPFOR	X13											
MANUEXPT	X14											
EXPORTGS	X15											
IMPORTGS	X16											
OPENNES	X17											
MRCHTRAD	X18											
TRADSERV	X19											
MIGRA	X20											
FUEL	X21											
WORKING	X22											

(Contd.)

TABLE 7.2 (Contd.)

		GPCFLOW	GCAPFOR	MANUEXPT	EXPORTGS	IMPORTGS	OPENNES	MRCHTRAD	TRADSERV	MIGRA	FUEL	WORKING
		X12	X13	X14	X15	X16	X17	X18	X19	X20	X21	X22
GNIPPP	**X1**	0.104	.354**	0.085	0.149	-0.133	0.012	0.123	-0.144	0.148	0.211	.381**
GNI	**X2**	0.081	.368**	-0.084	.320**	-0.046	0.15	.282*	-0.014	.317**	.491**	.294*
INDUVAL	**X3**	-0.067	.576**	0.035	.383**	-0.055	0.18	.397**	0.001	0.093	.628**	.306*
SERVGVALU	**X4**	.349**	0.113	0.051	0.172	.400**	.301*	-0.003	.312*	0.129	-0.07	-0.083
GROSSAV	**X5**	0.196	.630**	-0.075	.522**	-0.051	.257*	.373**	0.02	-0.006	.645**	0.234
ENERGY	**X6**	0.032	.405**	0.028	.275*	-0.069	0.114	.385**	-0.042	0.135	.371**	.406**
LIFEXP	**X7**	0.216	.444**	.370**	0.149	0.002	0.082	0.141	-0.095	-0.036	0.109	.574**
EMPSERV	**X8**	0.193	.362**	0.159	0.198	0.108	0.164	0.117	0.109	0.146	0.133	.290*
URBAN	**X9**	0.12	.302*	0.113	0.118	-0.066	0.03	0.071	-0.016	0.101	.291*	.414**
CALORIE	**X10**	-0.03	.406**	0.132	0.015	-0.076	-0.032	0.122	-0.084	0.008	0.175	.527**
PHYSICI	**X11**	0.196	.254*	.261*	-0.013	-0.15	-0.085	-0.059	-0.129	0.002	-0.001	.634**
GPCFLOW	**X12**	1	0.117	-0.089	.545**	.453**	.532**	0.033	.358**	-0.013	-0.008	0.078
GCAPFOR	**X13**		1	0.024	.393**	.314*	.376**	.392**	0.207	.242*	.445**	0.135
MANUEXPT	**X14**			1	-0.172	-0.103	-0.147	-0.156	-0.067	-0.105	-.372**	.397**
EXPORTGS	**X15**				1	.769**	.943**	.735**	.654**	.278*	.378**	-0.052
IMPORTGS	**X16**					1	.937**	.621**	.764**	.411**	0.028	-0.2
OPENNES	**X17**						1	.723**	.753**	.365**	0.22	-0.131
MRCHTRAD	**X18**							1	.446**	.309*	.338**	-0.027
TRADSERV	**X19**								1	.499**	0.121	-0.119
MIGRA	**X20**									1	0.1	-0.203
FUEL	**X21**										1	-0.094
WORKING	**X22**											1

* Correlation is significant at 0.05 percent level.
** Correlation is significant at 0.01 percent level.

TABLE 7.3
Correlations Matrix of 22 Variables : 66 Countries Data for 2000

		GNIPPP	GNI	INDUVAL	SERVALU	GROSSAV	ENERGY	LIFEXP	EMPSERV	URBAN	CALORIE	PHYSICI
		X1	X2	X3	X4	X5	X6	X7	X8	X9	X10	X11
GNIPPP	**X1**	1	.929**	.374**	.496**	.391**	.623**	.702**	.654**	.700**	.509**	.590**
GNI	**X2**		1	.341**	.511**	.339**	.640**	.628**	.657**	.744**	.411**	.611**
INDUVAL	**X3**			1	-.279*	.809**	.399**	.363**	.303*	.413**	.269*	0.151
SERVGVALU	**X4**				1	-0.207	0.196	.506**	.611**	.488**	.336**	.544**
GROSSAV	**X5**					1	.389**	.383**	.243*	.341**	.357**	0.077
ENERGY	**X6**						1	.399**	.431**	.511**	.254*	.260*
LIFEXP	**X7**							1	.658**	.603**	.573**	.597**
EMPSERV	**X8**								1	.761**	.398**	.565**
URBAN	**X9**									1	.491**	.625**
CALORIE	**X10**										1	.448**
PHYSICI	**X11**											1
GPCFLOW	**X12**											
GCAPFOR	**X13**											
MANUEXPT	**X14**											
EXPORTGS	**X15**											
IMPORTGS	**X16**											
OPENNES	**X17**											
MRCHTRAD	**X18**											
TRADSERV	**X19**											
MIGRA	**X20**											
FUEL	**X21**											
WORKING	**X22**											

(Contd.)

TABLE 7.3 (Contd.)

		GPCFLOW	GCAPFOR	MANUEXPT	EXPORTGS	IMPORTGS	OPENNES	MRCHTRAD	TRADSERV	MIGRA	FUEL	WORKING
		X12	X13	X14	X15	X16	X17	X18	X19	X20	X21	X22
GNIPPP	**X1**	0.18	0.095	.269*	.291*	0.094	0.211	0.203	-0.006	0.156	0.077	.671**
GNI	**X2**	0.2	0.028	0.141	0.219	0.018	0.133	0.11	-0.03	0.191	0.114	.539**
INDUVAL	**X3**	.316**	.255*	-0.003	.522**	0.106	.348**	.450**	0.052	0.133	.590**	.337**
SERVGVALU	**X4**	0.049	0.033	.295*	-0.124	0.032	-0.056	-0.19	0.031	0.085	-.284*	.450**
GROSSAV	**X5**	.344**	.310*	0.065	.571**	0.069	.358**	.387**	-0.004	-0.011	.521**	.393**
ENERGY	**X6**	0.085	0.006	0.024	.332**	0.106	0.24	.324**	-0.026	0.208	.328**	.436**
LIFEXP	**X7**	0.227	.363**	.392**	.302*	0.21	.272*	0.197	0.092	0.047	0.009	.772**
EMPSERV	**X8**	0.223	-0.037	0.023	0.163	0.035	0.11	0.079	-0.006	0.204	0.241	.465**
URBAN	**X9**	.276*	0.07	0.015	0.148	-0.041	0.065	0.119	-0.042	.244*	.319**	.440**
CALORIE	**X10**	0.041	.337**	.299*	0.187	0.071	0.141	0.126	0.081	0.047	0.08	.604**
PHYSICI	**X11**	0.148	0.072	0.174	-0.04	-0.075	-0.059	-0.12	-0.043	0.023	-0.023	.514**
GPCFLOW	**X12**	1	0.227	-0.102	.504**	.381**	.469**	.358**	.303*	-0.057	0.132	0.133
GCAPFOR	**X13**		1	0.226	.277*	.371**	.335**	.320**	0.219	-0.095	-0.127	.297*
MANUEXPT	**X14**			1	0.096	0.181	0.141	0.129	0.151	-0.081	-.555**	.533**
EXPORTGS	**X15**				1	.816**	.961**	.864**	.634**	0.226	0.199	.290*
IMPORTGS	**X16**					1	.944**	.811**	.789**	0.24	-0.186	0.164
OPENNES	**X17**						1	.881**	.739**	.244*	0.025	.244*
MRCHTRAD	**X18**							1	.520**	0.229	0.096	0.173
TRADSERV	**X19**								1	.342**	-0.157	0.095
MIGRA	**X20**									1	0.151	-0.145
FUEL	**X21**										1	-0.076
WORKING	**X22**											1

* Correlation is significant at 0.05 percent level.
** Correlation is significant at 0.01 percent level.

TABLE 7.4
Correlations Matrix of 22 Variables : 66 Countries Data for 2004

		GNIPPP	GNI	INDUVAL	SERVALU	GROSSAV	ENERGY	LIFEXP	EMPSERV	URBAN	CALORIE	PHYSICI
		X1	X2	X3	X4	X5	X6	X7	X8	X9	X10	X11
GNIPPP	X1	1	.891**	.461**	.377**	.310*	.653**	.679**	.639**	.696**	.477**	.471**
GNI	X2		1	.481**	.337**	.288*	.787**	.583**	.609**	.688**	.340**	.343**
INDUVAL	X3			1	-.298*	.691**	.485**	.353**	.314*	.473**	.300*	0.07
SERVGVALU	X4				1	-0.163	0.094	.484**	.472**	.348**	.299*	.361**
GROSSAV	X5					1	.285*	.373**	0.183	.263*	0.206	-0.037
ENERGY	X6						1	.337**	.401**	.467**	0.171	0.149
LIFEXP	X7							1	.618**	.595**	.563**	.473**
EMPSERV	X8								1	.775**	.373**	.397**
URBAN	X9									1	.507**	.504**
CALORIE	X10										1	.327**
PHYSICI	X11											1
GPCFLOW	X12											
GCAPFOR	X13											
MANUEXPT	X14											
EXPORTGS	X15											
IMPORTGS	X16											
OPENNES	X17											
MRCHTRAD	X18											
TRADSERV	X19											
MIGRA	X20											
FUEL	X21											
WORKING	X22											

(Contd.)

TABLE 7.4 (Contd.)

		GPCFLOW	GCAPFOR	MANUEXPT	EXPORTGS	IMPORTGS	OPENNES	MRCHTRAD	TRADSERV	MIGRA	FUEL	WORKING
		X12	X13	X14	X15	X16	X17	X18	X19	X20	X21	X22
GNIPPP	**X1**	.304*	0.086	.288*	.366**	0.164	.283*	.283*	0.029	0.13	0.071	.767**
GNI	**X2**	.409**	0.023	0.165	.397**	0.185	.317**	.283*	0.028	0.219	0.191	.619**
INDUVAL	**X3**	.248*	.283*	-0.055	.535**	0.137	.368**	.408**	-0.055	0.145	.607**	.424**
SERVGVALU	**X4**	0.154	0.008	.415**	-0.066	0.158	0.058	-0.056	0.103	0.095	-.373**	.385**
GROSSAV	**X5**	0.079	.432**	0.138	.419**	0.01	0.236	.262*	-0.123	-0.193	.397**	.459**
ENERGY	**X6**	.348**	0.049	0.053	.370**	0.181	.302*	.312*	-0.027	0.181	.308*	.503**
LIFEXP	**X7**	.281*	.288*	.369**	.258*	0.213	.251*	0.198	0.07	0.076	-0.07	.793**
EMPSERV	**X8**	.314*	-0.054	0.004	0.21	0.065	0.158	0.105	-0.012	0.192	.267*	.488**
URBAN	**X9**	.329**	0.032	0.024	0.24	0.02	0.145	0.135	-0.121	0.229	.298*	.519**
CALORIE	**X10**	0.122	0.208	.349**	0.222	0.102	0.169	0.148	0.074	0.107	0.011	.556**
PHYSICI	**X11**	.284*	0.049	0.133	0.043	0.019	0.037	0.003	-0.006	0.074	-0.136	.339**
GPCFLOW	**X12**	1	0.003	0.013	.472**	.439**	.493**	.307*	.479**	0.083	0.093	.262*
GCAPFOR	**X13**		1	0.213	0.141	0.2	0.187	0.163	0.109	-0.102	0.034	.338**
MANUEXPT	**X14**			1	0.054	0.196	0.109	0.195	0.145	0.016	-.533**	.506**
EXPORTGS	**X15**				1	.782**	.941**	.860**	.534**	0.231	0.189	.285*
IMPORTGS	**X16**					1	.931**	.831**	.706**	.339**	-0.219	0.15
OPENNES	**X17**						1	.873**	.668**	.309*	0.013	0.242
MRCHTRAD	**X18**							1	.446**	.289*	0.011	0.203
TRADSERV	**X19**								1	.251*	-0.204	0.063
MIGRA	**X20**									1	0.055	-0.052
FUEL	**X21**										1	-0.001
WORKING	**X22**											1

* Correlation is significant at 0.05 percent level.
** Correlation is significant at 0.01 percent level.

In Table 7.3, it was seen that for the year 2000, correlation coefficient of GNI per capita was again highest with GNI per capita (PPP), i.e. 0.929. The correlation coefficients of GNI per capita were higher and significant at one percent level with share of services in GDP, energy use per capita, life expectancy at birth, employment in services, urban population, physicians per 1000 people and population of working age. On the other hand, coefficients of correlation of GNI per capita were lower with share of industry in GDP, gross domestic savings and daily calorie supply per capita.

Table 7.4 shows that for the year 2004, correlation coefficient of GNI per capita was highest with GNI per capita (PPP), i.e. 0.891. Also, the correlation coefficients of GNI per capita were higher and significant at one percent level with energy use per capita, life expectancy at birth, employment in services, urban population and population of working age. On the other hand, coefficients of correlation of GNI per capita were lower with share of services in GDP, gross domestic savings, daily calorie supply per capita, physicians per 1000 people, exports of goods and services, degree of openness, merchandise trade and population of working age.

FACTOR ANALYSIS

The technique of Factor Analysis was used to find out the variables responsible for economic development of developing countries.

The results of the Factor Analysis with Varimax Rotation for the year 1980 are given in Table 7.5. The highest loadings in each row are clubbed together to identify the variables falling in each of the factors. Factor 1 included variables like GNI per capita (X_2), GNI (PPP) (X_1), share of services in GDP (X_4), life expectancy at birth (X_7), employment in services (X_8), urban population (X_9), daily calorie supply (X_{10}) and physicians per 1000 people (X_{11}). This factor could be termed as consisting of socio-economic and structural variables in the set of economic development variables.

Factor 2 included exports of goods and services (X_{15}), imports of goods and services (X_{16}), degree of openness (X_{17}), merchandise trade (X_{18}), trade in services (X_{19}) and international

TABLE 7.5

Economic Development : Results of Factor Analysis (1980)

	Factor 1	*Factor 2*	*Factor 3*	*Factor 4*	*Factor 5*	*Communalities*	*Weights*
(1)	*(2)*	*(3)*	*(4)*	*(5)*	*(6)*	*(7)*	*(8)*
GNI per capita, (current US$) (X2)	**0.689**	0.036	0.553	-0.152	-0.163	0.832	17.077
GNI per capita, PPP (current international $) (X1)	**0.831**	-0.072	0.341	0.000	-0.059	0.815	20.597
Services, value added (% of GDP) (X4)	**0.566**	0.377	-0.479	-0.214	0.113	0.751	14.029
Life expectancy at birth, total (years) (X7)	**0.768**	0.062	0.200	0.383	0.159	0.805	19.036
Employment in services (% of total employment) (X8)	**0.796**	0.165	0.051	0.052	0.015	0.666	19.730
Urban population (% of total) (X9)	**0.913**	-0.017	0.181	-0.012	0.002	0.867	22.630
Daily Calorie Supply (per capita) (X10)	**0.647**	-0.052	0.243	0.284	-0.067	0.565	16.037
Physicians (per 1,000 people) (X11)	**0.757**	-0.108	0.106	0.341	0.136	0.731	18.763
Exports of goods and services (% of GDP) (X15)	0.052	**0.849**	0.415	-0.094	0.203	0.945	17.686
Imports of goods and services (% of GDP) (X16)	-0.037	**0.965**	-0.094	-0.035	-0.002	0.942	20.103
Degree of Openness (Exports+Imports) % to GDP (X17)	0.008	**0.963**	0.170	-0.069	0.108	0.973	20.061
Merchandise trade (% of GDP) (X18)	-0.031	**0.669**	0.491	0.059	-0.231	0.746	13.937
Trade in services (% of GDP) (X19)	-0.025	**0.849**	-0.075	-0.056	-0.116	0.743	17.686
International migration stock (% of population) (X20)	0.180	**0.469**	-0.025	-0.197	-0.677	0.750	9.770

(Contd.)

TABLE 7.5 (Contd.)

(1)	(2)	(3)	(4)	(5)	(6)	(7)	(8)
Industry, value added (% of GDP) (X3)	0.388	0.046	**0.828**	0.087	-0.081	0.852	14.891
Gross domestic savings (% of GDP) (X5)	0.259	0.106	**0.874**	-0.009	0.209	0.886	15.718
Energy Use per capita (kg. of oil equivalent) (X6)	0.574	0.021	**0.607**	0.087	-0.125	0.722	10.916
Gross capital formation (% of GDP) (X13)	0.301	0.358	**0.533**	0.111	-0.072	0.521	9.585
Fuel+ores and metal exports (% of merchandise exports) (X21)	0.118	0.090	**0.723**	-0.430	0.001	0.729	13.002
Manufactures exports (% of merchandise exports) (X14)	0.137	-0.043	-0.183	**0.794**	-0.066	0.689	6.515
Percentage of population of working age (15-64 yrs.) (X22)	0.407	-0.143	0.189	**0.690**	0.189	0.733	5.662
Gross private capital flows (% of GDP) (X12)	0.213	0.500	-0.091	-0.104	**0.713**	0.823	4.176
Percentage of Variance Explained	24.786	20.832	17.984	8.206	5.857		
Percentage of Cumulative Variance Explained	24.786	45.618	63.602	71.809	77.666		

Extraction Method: Principal Component Analysis. *Rotation Method*: Varimax with Kaiser Normalization.

migration stock (X_{20}). This factor included globalization-related variables.

Factor 3 included share of industry in GDP (X_3), gross domestic savings (X_5), energy use per capita (X_6), gross capital formation (X_{13}) and share of fuel, ores & metal exports in merchandise exports (X_{21}). This factor could be termed as consisting of a mix of structural, financial and globalization-related variables. Factor 4 included share of manufacture exports in merchandise exports (X_{14}) and population of working age (X_{22}). This factor could be termed as consisting of globalization and demographic variables. Gross private capital flows (X_{12}) alone formed Factor 5, which is globalization-related variable. Factor 1 explained 24.786 percent of the variations, Factor 2 explained 20.832 percent, Factor 3 explained 17.984 percent, Factor 4 explained 8.206 percent and Factor 5 could explain 5.857 percent of the variations. The five factors together explained 77.666 percent variations in the variable set.

The results of the Factor Analysis with Varimax Rotation for the year 1990 are given in Table 7.6.

Again, the highest loadings in each row are clubbed together to identify the variables falling in each of the factors. Factor 1 included variables like GNI per capita (X_2), GNI (PPP) (X_1), share of services in GDP (X_4), energy use per capita (X_6), life expectancy at birth (X_7), employment in services (X_8), urban population (X_9), daily calorie supply (X_{10}), physicians per 1000 people (X_{11}) and population of working age (X_{22}). This Factor could be termed as consisting of socio-economic and structural variables in the set of economic development variables.

Factor 2 included exports of goods and services (X_{15}), imports of goods and services (X_{16}), degree of openness (X_{17}), merchandise trade (X_{18}), trade in services (X_{19}) and international migration stock (X_{20}). This Factor included globalization-related variables.

Factor 3 included gross domestic savings (X_5), gross capital formation (X_{13}) and share of manufacture exports in merchandise exports (X_{14}). This Factor could be termed as consisting of a mix of financial and globalization related variables. Factor 4 included share of industry in GDP (X_3) and share of fuel, ores and metal exports in merchandise exports (X_{21}), whereas gross private capital flows (X_{12}) alone formed

TABLE 7.6

Economic Development : Results of Factor Analysis (1990)

	Factor 1	*Factor 2*	*Factor 3*	*Factor 4*	*Factor 5*	*Communalities*	*Weights*
(1)	*(2)*	*(3)*	*(4)*	*(5)*	*(6)*	*(7)*	*(8)*
GNI per capita, (current US$) (X2)	**0.783**	0.093	0.057	0.399	-0.152	0.808	20.694
GNI per capita, PPP (current international $) (X1)	**0.871**	0.025	0.223	0.207	-0.117	0.865	23.020
Services, value added (% of GDP) (X4)	**0.525**	0.254	-0.068	-0.580	0.004	0.681	13.875
Energy Use per capita (kg of oil equivalent) (X6)	**0.653**	0.065	0.085	0.461	-0.055	0.653	17.258
Life expectancy at birth, total (years) (X7)	**0.773**	0.163	0.468	0.016	0.096	0.852	20.430
Employment in services (% of total employment) (X8)	**0.778**	0.136	-0.052	-0.101	0.073	0.641	20.562
Urban population (% of total) (X9)	**0.910**	0.059	-0.007	0.142	0.073	0.857	24.050
Daily Calorie Supply (per capita) (X10)	**0.610**	0.052	0.444	0.156	-0.028	0.597	16.122
Physicians (per 1,000 people) (X11)	**0.763**	-0.083	0.143	-0.086	0.279	0.695	20.165
Percentage of population of working age (15-64 yrs.) (X22)	**0.509**	-0.086	0.668	-0.030	0.283	0.793	13.452
Exports of goods and services (% of GDP) (X15)	0.221	**0.898**	0.078	0.206	0.185	0.937	19.446
Imports of goods and services (% of GDP) (X16)	-0.036	**0.968**	0.103	-0.138	0.051	0.970	20.962
Degree of Openness (Exports+Imports) % to GDP (X17)	0.098	**0.972**	0.092	0.034	0.123	0.979	21.049
Merchandise trade (% of GDP) (X18)	0.042	**0.804**	0.246	0.256	-0.069	0.779	17.411
Trade in services (% of GDP) (X19)	0.010	**0.887**	-0.048	-0.251	-0.105	0.864	19.208
International migration stock (% of population) (X20)	0.192	**0.496**	-0.301	0.089	-0.577	0.714	10.741

Gross domestic savings (% of GDP) (X5)	0.292	0.079	**0.643**	0.458	0.106	0.726	8.391
Gross capital formation (% of GDP) (X13)	-0.019	0.346	**0.800**	0.070	-0.106	0.776	10.440
Manufactures exports (% of merchandise exports) (X14)	0.141	0.027	**0.718**	-0.388	-0.072	0.691	9.370
Industry, value added (% of GDP) (X3)	0.463	0.073	0.281	**0.730**	0.090	0.840	8.530
Fuel+ores and metal exports (% of merchandise exports) (X21)	0.191	0.066	-0.273	**0.799**	0.031	0.754	9.336
Gross private capital flows (% of GDP) (X12)	0.209	0.343	-0.139	0.147	**0.781**	0.812	4.492
Percentage of Variance Explained	26.429	21.655	13.050	11.685	5.752		
Percentage of Cumulative Variance Explained	26.429	48.084	61.134	72.819	78.572		

Extraction Method: Principal Component Analysis. *Rotation Method*: Varimax with Kaiser Normalization.

Factor 5. These two Factors could be termed as consisting of a mix of globalization and structural variables. Factor 1 explained 26.429 percent of the variations, Factor 2 explained 21.655 percent, Factor 3 explained 13.050 percent, Factor 4 explained 11.685 percent and Factor 5 could explain 5.752 percent of the variations. The five Factors together explained 78.572 percent variations in the variable set.

The results of the Factor Analysis with Varimax Rotation for the year 2000 are given in Table 7.7.

Factor 1 included variables like GNI per capita (X_2), GNI (PPP) (X_1), share of services in GDP (X_4), energy use per capita (X_6), life expectancy at birth (X_7), employment in services (X_8), urban population (X_9), daily calorie supply (X_{10}), physicians per 1000 people (X_{11}) and population of working age (X_{22}). This Factor could be termed as consisting of socio-economic and structural variables in the set of economic development variables.

Factor 2 included exports of goods and services (X_{15}), imports of goods and services (X_{16}), degree of openness (X_{17}), merchandise trade (X_{18}), trade in services (X_{19}) and international migration stock (X_{20}). This Factor included globalization-related variables.

Factor 3 included share of industry in GDP (X_3), gross domestic savings (X_5) and share of fuel, ores and metal exports in merchandise exports (X_{21}). Share of manufacture exports in merchandise exports (X_{14}) alone formed Factor 4. These two Factors could be termed as consisting of a mix of structural, financial and globalization related variables. Factor 5 included gross private capital flows (X_{12}) and gross capital formation (X_{13}). This factor could be termed as consisting of globalization and financial variables. Factor 1 explained 26.607 percent of the variations, Factor 2 explained 21.206 percent, Factor 3 explained 14.448 percent, Factor 4 explained 9.157 percent and Factor 5 could explain 6.605 percent of the variations. The five Factors together explained 78.124 percent variations in the variable set.

The results of the Factor Analysis with Varimax Rotation for the year 2004 are presented in Table 7.8.

Six Factors were derived from the set of 22 variables. Factor 1 included variables like exports of goods and services (X_{15}), imports of goods and services (X_{16}), degree of openness

TABLE 7.7

Economic Development : Results of Factor Analysis (2000)

	Factor 1	Factor 2	Factor 3	Factor 4	Factor 5	Communalities	Weights
(1)	(2)	(3)	(4)	(5)	(6)	(7)	(8)
GNI per capita, (current US$) (X2)	**0.848**	0.039	0.204	0.078	-0.195	0.807	22.563
GNI per capita, PPP (current international $) (X1)	**0.834**	0.095	0.240	0.233	-0.153	0.839	22.190
Services, value added (% of GDP) (X4)	**0.752**	-0.028	-0.490	0.112	-0.005	0.819	20.008
Energy Use per capita (kg of oil equivalent) (X6)	**0.502**	0.119	0.452	0.108	-0.411	0.650	13.357
Life expectancy at birth, total (years) (X7)	**0.768**	0.178	0.164	0.333	0.191	0.797	20.434
Employment in services (% of total employment) (X8)	**0.853**	0.052	0.090	-0.164	-0.083	0.773	22.696
Urban population (% of total) (X9)	**0.853**	0.006	0.244	-0.152	-0.071	0.816	22.696
Daily Calorie Supply (per capita) (X10)	**0.543**	0.045	0.222	0.395	0.145	0.523	14.448
Physicians (per 1,000 people) (X11)	**0.797**	-0.104	-0.088	0.036	0.144	0.676	21.206
Percentage of population of working age (15-64 yrs.) (X22)	**0.636**	0.119	0.199	0.560	0.205	0.813	16.922
Exports of goods and services (% of GDP) (X15)	0.100	**0.876**	0.404	0.031	0.008	0.941	18.576
Imports of goods and services (% of GDP) (X16)	0.003	**0.968**	-0.093	0.102	0.021	0.956	20.527
Degree of Openness (Exports+Imports) % to GDP (X17)	0.061	**0.963**	0.186	0.072	0.009	0.970	20.421
Merchandise trade (% of GDP) (X18)	-0.008	**0.836**	0.346	0.106	-0.081	0.837	17.728
Trade in services (% of GDP) (X19)	-0.015	**0.840**	-0.195	0.020	-0.051	0.747	17.813
International migration stock (% of population) (X20)	0.152	**0.327**	-0.008	-0.148	-0.691	0.629	6.934

(Contd.)

TABLE 7.7 (Contd.)

(1)	(2)	(3)	(4)	(5)	(6)	(7)	(8)
Industry, value added (% of GDP) (X3)	0.223	0.211	**0.858**	-0.007	0.063	0.834	12.396
Gross domestic savings (% of GDP) (X5)	0.204	0.187	**0.858**	0.100	0.192	0.860	12.396
Fuel+ores and metal exports (% of merchandise exports) (X21)	0.083	-0.095	**0.732**	-0.501	-0.134	0.820	10.576
Manufactures exports (% of merchandise exports) (X14)	0.166	0.129	-0.164	**0.832**	0.087	0.770	7.618
Gross private capital flows (% of GDP) (X12)	0.271	0.493	0.138	-0.423	**0.510**	0.774	3.368
Gross capital formation (% of GDP) (X13)	0.061	0.332	0.165	0.340	**0.527**	0.535	3.480
Percentage of Variance Explained	26.607	21.206	14.448	9.157	6.605		
Percentage of Cumulative Variance Explained	26.607	47.914	62.362	71.519	78.124		

Extraction Method: Principal Component Analysis. *Rotation Method*: Varimax with Kaiser Normalization.

TABLE 7.8
Economic Development : Results of Factor Analysis (2004)

	Factor 1	*Factor 2*	*Factor 3*	*Factor 4*	*Factor 5*	*Factor 6*	*Communalities*	*Weights*
(1)	*(2)*	*(3)*	*(4)*	*(5)*	*(6)*	*(7)*	*(8)*	*(9)*
Exports of goods and services (% of GDP) (X15)	**0.851**	0.042	0.288	0.258	-0.172	0.079	0.912	17.134
Imports of goods and services (% of GDP) (X16)	**0.941**	0.023	0.032	0.029	0.189	0.121	0.937	18.946
Degree of Openness (Exports+Imports) % to GDP (X17)	**0.948**	0.044	0.170	0.148	-0.014	0.092	0.961	19.087
Merchandise trade (% of GDP) (X18)	**0.816**	-0.091	0.251	0.218	0.023	0.231	0.839	16.429
Trade in services (% of GDP) (X19)	**0.810**	0.080	-0.197	-0.104	0.144	-0.083	0.740	16.309
Gross private capital flows (% of GDP) (X12)	**0.582**	0.396	0.197	-0.146	-0.178	-0.425	0.767	11.718
Services, value added (% of GDP) (X4)	0.012	**0.601**	0.103	-0.187	0.545	-0.003	0.704	10.557
Life expectancy at birth, total (years) (X7)	0.112	**0.692**	0.304	0.395	0.241	-0.006	0.798	12.155
Employment in services (% of total employment) (X8)	0.035	**0.751**	0.380	-0.018	-0.174	0.094	0.749	13.191
Urban population (% of total) (X9)	-0.001	**0.758**	0.416	0.114	-0.230	0.177	0.845	13.314
Daily Calorie Supply (per capita) (X10)	0.053	**0.591**	0.046	0.432	0.160	0.265	0.636	10.381
Physicians (per 1,000 people) (X11)	0.014	**0.747**	0.015	-0.039	0.078	-0.092	0.575	13.121

(*Contd.*)

TABLE 7.8 (Contd.)

(1)	(2)	(3)	(4)	(5)	(6)	(7)	(8)	(9)
GNI per capita, (current US$) (X2)	0.161	0.447	**0.820**	0.040	-0.004	0.035	0.901	12.315
GNI per capita, PPP (current international $) (X1)	0.116	0.547	**0.718**	0.173	0.125	0.035	0.875	10.783
Energy Use per capita (kg of oil equivalent) (X6)	0.160	0.124	**0.870**	0.032	-0.109	0.010	0.811	13.066
Fuel+ores and metal exports (% of merchandise exports) (X21)	-0.084	0.016	**0.229**	0.215	-0.852	0.071	0.837	3.439
Percentage of population of working age (15-64 yrs.) (X22)	0.080	0.487	**0.511**	0.496	0.307	-0.106	0.856	7.674
Industry, value added (% of GDP) (X3)	0.206	0.118	0.452	**0.586**	-0.495	0.148	0.871	6.772
Gross domestic savings (% of GDP) (X5)	0.063	-0.006	0.329	**0.789**	-0.226	-0.134	0.804	9.118
Gross capital formation (% of GDP) (X13)	0.138	0.070	-0.156	**0.736**	0.103	-0.096	0.609	8.505
Manufactures exports (% of merchandise exports) (X14)	0.077	0.087	0.164	0.308	**0.809**	0.070	0.795	8.831
International migration stock (% of population) (X20)	0.306	0.157	0.069	-0.230	-0.064	**0.795**	0.812	3.950
Percentage of Variance Explained	20.134	17.565	15.018	11.556	10.917	4.969		
Percentage of Cumulative Variance Explained	20.134	37.699	52.717	64.273	75.190	80.159		

Extraction Method: Principal Component Analysis. *Rotation Method*: Varimax with Kaiser Normalization.

(X_{17}), merchandise trade (X_{18}), trade in services (X_{19}) and gross private capital flows (X_{12}). This Factor consisted of globalization-related variables.

Factor 2 included share of services in GDP (X_4), life expectancy at birth (X_7), employment in services (X_8), urban population (X_9), daily calorie supply (X_{10}) and physicians per 1000 people (X_{11}). Factor 3 included GNI per capita (X_2), GNI (PPP) (X_1), energy use per capita (X_6), share of fuel, ores and metal exports in merchandise exports (X_{21}) and population of working age (X_{22}). These two Factors consisted of mix of socio-economic and structural variables.

Factor 4 included share of industry in GDP (X_3), gross domestic savings (X_5) and gross capital formation (X_{13}). This factor could be termed as consisting of structural and financial variables. Factor 5 included share of manufacture exports in merchandise exports (X_{14}) whereas international migration stock (X_{20}) formed Factor 6. This Factor consisted of globalization related variables.

Factor 1 explained 20.134 percent of the variations, Factor 2 explained 17.565 percent, Factor 3 explained 15.018 percent, Factor 4 explained 11.556 percent, Factor 5 and Factor 6 explained 10.917 and 4.969 percent of the variations in the variable set respectively. Thus, the 22 variables together explained 80.159 percent of the variations in economic development of the developing countries.

Thus, the results of Factor Analysis showed that globalization has positive impact on economic development of developing countries. Globalization-related variables like exports of goods and services, imports of goods and services, degree of openness, merchandise trade, trade in services, international migration stock and gross private capital flows explained sizeable share of the variations. In 1980 and 1990, globalization-related variables collectively explained 26.689 percent and 27.407 percent of the variations. But in 2000 and 2004, globalization-related variables explained 30.363 percent and 36.020 percent of the variations. This indicated increased role of globalization in economic development of developing countries.

MEASURING ECONOMIC DEVELOPMENT : COMPOSITE INDEX, GNI PER CAPITA, GNI PER CAPITA PPP AND PQLI

Economic development is a relative term and its precise measurement is a difficult proposition. GNI per capita has been commonly used for measuring the economic development of countries. But this measure has been widely criticized and estimates of per capita income, based on purchasing power parity (PPP) have been developed for international comparisons. But, as these measures fail to reflect the other aspects of development and welfare of the masses, another important measure of economic development, Physical Quality of Life Index (PQLI), was developed which is based on three indicators; infant mortality rate, life expectancy at age one and literacy rate. Using methodology developed by Morris (1979), PQLI index was constructed for 66 countries. As economic development is a multi-dimensional phenomenon, therefore, there is need of a composite index to measure it, which should reflect all factors regarding structure, human aspects, social and institutional aspects, etc. These countries were ranked on the basis of 4 measures, i.e. composite index, GNI per capita, GNI per capita PPP and PQLI. Then, their relative positions were compared when ranked with these measures.

Table 7.9 shows the composite indices and corresponding ranks of 66 countries, as derived from Factor Analysis for the years 1980, 1990, 2000 and 2004 respectively. In 1980, Trinidad and Tobago was ranked at No. 1, followed by Panama, Jordan and Bulgaria; while Nepal, Burkina Faso, Uganda, Burundi and Chad were ranked at the bottom. India ranked at No. 58 and Pakistan at No. 52. In the year 1990, there was improvement in the ranks of 31 countries, deterioration in the ranks of another 31 countries and ranks remained same for the remaining 4 countries (Brazil, Benin, Burkina Faso and Burundi) in comparison to the ranking based on composite index for the year 1980.

Out of 31 countries with improved position, ranks for 5 countries (Mauritius, Dominican Republic, Thailand, The Gambia and Turkey) improved by 10 or more positions. For 7 countries (Malaysia, China, Morocco, Ecuador, India, Ghana

TABLE 7.9
Composite Index of Economic Development

Sl. No.	Country	1980		1990		2000		2004	
		Composite Index	Rank	Composite Index	Rank	Composite Index	Rank	Composite Index	Rank
	(1)	(2)	(3)	(4)	(5)	(6)	(7)	(8)	(9)
1.	Trinidad and Tobago	0.6191	1	0.5302	5	0.5646	2	0.5591	4
2.	Panama	0.5864	2	0.5508	3	0.5268	7	0.4989	8
3.	Jordan	0.5539	3	0.6203	1	0.5281	6	0.5619	3
4.	Bulgaria	0.5342	4	0.5217	6	0.5298	4	0.5662	2
5.	Venezuela, RB	0.5005	5	0.4665	11	0.4516	16	0.3875	21
6.	Gabon	0.4938	6	0.4511	14	0.4049	21	0.4116	19
7.	Argentina	0.4895	7	0.4458	15	0.5154	8	0.4176	17
8.	Uruguay	0.4731	8	0.4788	9	0.5096	9	0.4361	14
9.	Oman	0.4706	9	0.5057	7	0.5283	5	0.5276	5
10.	Jamaica	0.4617	10	0.4814	8	0.4713	13	0.5126	6
11.	Malaysia	0.4507	11	0.5553	2	0.6457	1	0.6774	1
12.	Chile	0.4505	12	0.4666	10	0.4885	10	0.4498	12
13.	South Africa	0.4433	13	0.4209	18	0.3971	24	0.3516	30

(Contd.)

TABLE 7.9 (Contd.)

	(1)	(2)	(3)	(4)	(5)	(6)	(7)	(8)	(9)
14.	Mauritius	0.4409	14	0.5461	4	0.5417	3	0.5108	7
15.	Congo, Rep.	0.4251	15	0.3458	28	0.3851	26	0.4187	16
16.	Tunisia	0.4221	16	0.4585	12	0.4570	15	0.4480	13
17.	Costa Rica	0.4169	17	0.4518	13	0.4772	12	0.4660	10
18.	Algeria	0.4140	18	0.3807	23	0.4005	23	0.3801	22
19.	Mexico	0.3974	19	0.4318	16	0.4838	11	0.4339	15
20.	Egypt, Arab Rep.	0.3652	20	0.3523	27	0.3534	31	0.3319	36
21.	Peru	0.3634	21	0.3399	29	0.3813	27	0.3212	37
22.	Syrian Arab Republic	0.3580	22	0.3376	30	0.3663	29	0.3340	35
23.	Colombia	0.3565	23	0.3809	22	0.3930	25	0.3415	32
24.	Brazil	0.3556	24	0.3742	24	0.4048	22	0.3408	33
25.	Paraguay	0.3525	25	0.3818	20	0.3483	34	0.3375	34
26.	Ecuador	0.3493	26	0.3865	19	0.4057	20	0.3647	28
27.	Togo	0.3346	27	0.2719	42	0.2488	47	0.2745	43
28.	Sri Lanka	0.3339	28	0.3084	37	0.3505	32	0.3445	31
29.	Iran, Islamic Rep.	0.3276	29	0.3735	25	0.3751	28	0.3801	23
30.	Dominican Republic	0.3230	30	0.4272	17	0.4618	14	0.4561	11
31.	Cote d'Ivoire	0.3189	31	0.2447	46	0.2574	45	0.2728	45

32. Indonesia	0.3085	32	0.3037	38	0.3293	36	0.3179	39
33. Honduras	0.3078	33	0.3110	36	0.3378	35	0.3619	29
34. Philippines	0.3041	34	0.3212	32	0.4065	19	0.4031	20
35. Nicaragua	0.3023	35	0.3190	34	0.3055	41	0.3085	40
36. Bolivia	0.2989	36	0.2892	40	0.3244	37	0.2865	42
37. Zambia	0.2971	37	0.2485	45	0.1828	58	0.1935	58
38. El Salvador	0.2929	38	0.3169	35	0.3649	30	0.3692	26
39. Morocco	0.2920	39	0.3368	31	0.3502	33	0.3731	25
40. Papua New Guinea	0.2867	40	0.2787	41	0.3225	38	0.3680	27
41. Thailand	0.2838	41	0.3815	21	0.4328	17	0.4844	9
42. Kenya	0.2754	42	0.2554	44	0.2220	50	0.2294	50
43. Nigeria	0.2701	43	0.2424	47	0.2691	44	0.2739	44
44. Gambia, The	0.2695	44	0.3210	33	0.2723	43	0.3063	41
45. Turkey	0.2685	45	0.3700	26	0.4309	18	0.4143	18
46. Guatemala	0.2644	46	0.2599	43	0.2816	42	0.2726	46
47. Senegal	0.2632	47	0.2311	49	0.2494	46	0.2713	47
48. China	0.2614	48	0.2997	39	0.3219	39	0.3771	24
49. Cameroon	0.2569	49	0.2170	50	0.2050	52	0.2033	56
50. Haiti	0.2364	50	0.2007	51	0.2041	53	0.2428	49
51. Niger	0.2167	51	0.1461	60	0.1652	59	0.1483	63

(Contd.)

TABLE 7.9 (Contd.)

(1)	(2)	(3)	(4)	(5)	(6)	(7)	(8)	(9)
52. Pakistan	0.2138	52	0.2402	48	0.2240	49	0.2290	51
53. Central African Republic	0.1941	53	0.1639	56	0.1342	62	0.1297	64
54. Benin	0.1883	54	0.1837	54	0.1926	57	0.1925	59
55. Malawi	0.1813	55	0.1610	58	0.1128	63	0.1503	62
56. Madagascar	0.1735	56	0.1678	55	0.2024	54	0.2237	54
57. Sudan	0.1698	57	0.1443	62	0.1982	55	0.1950	57
58. India	0.1630	58	0.1958	52	0.2298	48	0.2429	48
59. Ghana	0.1519	59	0.1923	53	0.3065	40	0.3202	38
60. Bangladesh	0.1298	60	0.1582	59	0.2068	51	0.2210	55
61. Mali	0.1255	61	0.1611	57	0.1533	61	0.1802	60
62. Nepal	0.1171	62	0.1447	61	0.1940	56	0.2248	53
63. Burkina Faso	0.1133	63	0.1335	63	0.1114	64	0.1181	65
64. Uganda	0.1071	64	0.0740	66	0.0875	65	0.1638	61
65. Burundi	0.0988	65	0.0827	65	0.0436	66	0.0692	66
66. Chad	0.0970	66	0.1327	64	0.1644	60	0.2264	52

and Paraguay) ranks improved by 5 to 9 positions and for 19 countries (Tunisia, Costa Rica, Iran Islamic Republic, Pakistan, Mali, Mexico, El Salvador, Guatemala, Jordan, Oman, Jamaica, Chile, Philippines, Chad, Colombia, Nicaragua, Madagascar, Bangladesh and Nepal) ranks improved by less than 5 positions.

Of the 31 countries with deteriorated positions, ranks for 3 countries (Congo Republic, Togo and Cote d'Ivoire) deteriorated by 10 or more positions and for 13 countries (South Africa, Algeria, Sudan, Venezuela RB, Indonesia, Egypt Arab Rep., Gabon, Argentina, Peru, Syrian Arab Rep., Zambia, Sri Lanka and Niger) ranks deteriorated by 5 to 9 positions. For 15 countries (Panama, Uruguay, Papua New Guinea, Cameroon, Haiti, Bulgaria, Kenya, Senegal, Uganda, Honduras, Central African Rep., Malawi, Trinidad and Tobago, Bolivia and Nigeria) ranks deteriorated by less than 5 positions.

While comparing the ranks for the year 2000 with ranks of 1990, it was found that, in the year 2000, there was improvement in the ranks of 35 countries, deterioration in the ranks of 27 countries and for 4 countries (China, Chile, Uruguay and Algeria) the ranks remained same.

There were 2 countries (Ghana and Philippines) whose ranks improved by 10 or more positions and 8 countries (Turkey, Bangladesh, Sudan, Argentina, Mexico, El Salvador, Nepal and Sri Lanka) whose ranks improved by 5 to 9 positions. In case of remaining 25 countries (Thailand, India, Chad, Dominican Republic, Papua New Guinea, Senegal, Trinidad and Tobago, Bolivia, Nigeria, Oman, Brazil, Bulgaria, Indonesia, Peru, Congo Rep., Mauritius, Malaysia, Costa Rica, Guatemala, Madagascar, Uganda, Honduras, Syrian Arab Rep., Niger and Cote d'Ivorie) the ranks improved by less than 5 positions.

Of the 31 countries with deteriorated positions, ranks for 3 countries (The Gambia, Zambia and Paraguay) deteriorated by 10 or more positions and for 10 countries (Jordan, Jamaica, Malawi, Venezuela RB, Togo, Kenya, Central African Rep., South Africa, Nicaragua and Gabon) ranks deteriorated by 5 to 9 positions. For 14 countries (Ecuador, Pakistan, Burkina Faso, Burundi, Morocco, Cameroon, Haiti, Tunisia, Iran Islamic Rep., Colombia, Benin, Mali, Panama and Egypt Arab Rep.) ranks deteriorated by less than 5 positions.

While comparing the ranks for the year 2000 with ranks for 1980, it was found that, in the year 2000, there was improvement in the ranks of 29 countries, deterioration in the ranks of 35 countries and for 2 countries (Bulgaria and Mali) the ranks remained same.

There were 8 countries (Turkey, Thailand, Ghana, Dominican Rep., Philippines, Mauritius, Malaysia and India) whose ranks improved by 10 or more positions and 9 countries (China, Bangladesh, El Salvador, Mexico, Chad, Morocco, Nepal, Ecuador and Costa Rica) whose ranks improved by 5 to 9 positions. In case of remaining 12 countries (Oman, Guatemala, Pakistan, Papua New Guinea, Madagascar, Sudan, Chile, Brazil, Iran Islamic Rep., Tunisia, The Gambia and Senegal) the ranks improved by less than 5 positions.

Of the 35 countries with deteriorated positions, ranks for 8 countries (Congo Rep., Egypt Arab Rep., Venezuela RB, South Africa, Cote d'Ivoire, Gabon, Togo and Zambia) deteriorated by 10 or more positions and for 10 countries (Algeria, Panama, Nicaragua, Peru, Syrian Arab Rep., Malawi, Kenya, Niger, Paraguay and Central African Rep.) ranks deteriorated by 5 to 9 positions. For 17 countries (Uganda, Nigeria, Burundi, Burkina Faso, Trinidad and Tobago, Bolivia, Uruguay, Argentina, Honduras, Colombia, Jamaica, Haiti, Jordan, Benin, Cameroon, Sri Lanka and Indonesia) ranks deteriorated by less than 5 positions.

In the year 2004, there was improvement in the ranks of 27 countries, deterioration in the ranks of another 28 countries and ranks remained same for the remaining 11 countries (Turkey, Nigeria, India, Oman, Malaysia, Madagascar, Cote d'Ivoire, Burundi, Kenya, Zambia and Paraguay) in comparison to the ranking based on composite index for the year 2000.

Out of 27 countries with improved positions, ranks for 3 countries (China, Papua New Guinea and Congo Rep.) improved by 10 or more positions. For 6 countries (Thailand, Chad, Morocco, Jamaica, Honduras and Iran Islamic Rep.) ranks improved by 5 to 9 positions and for 18 countries (El Salvador, Uganda, Togo, Nepal, Dominican Rep., Jordan, Ghana, Bulgaria, Haiti, Costa Rica, Tunisia, Gabon, The Gambia, Sri Lanka, Algeria, Mali, Malawi and Nicaragua) ranks improved by less than 5 positions.

Of the 28 countries with deteriorated positions, ranks for 2 countries (Peru and Brazil) deteriorated by 10 or more positions and for 9 countries (Bolivia, Uruguay, Egypt Arab Rep., Venezuela RB, Syrian Arab Rep., South Africa, Colombia, Ecuador and Argentina) ranks deteriorated by 5 to 9 positions. For 17 countries (Philippines, Senegal, Burkina Faso, Panama, Sudan, Trinidad and Tobago, Chile, Pakistan, Benin, Central African Rep., Indonesia, Bangladesh, Mexico, Mauritius, Guatemala, Niger and Cameroon) ranks deteriorated by less than 5 positions.

While comparing the ranks of the year 2004 with ranks of 1980, it was found that, in the year 2004, there was improvement in the ranks of 29 countries, deterioration in the ranks of 32 countries and for 5 countries (Guatemala, Sudan, Chile, Senegal and Jordan) the ranks remained same.

There were 12 countries (Thailand, Turkey, China, India, Ghana, Dominican Rep., Philippines, Chad, Morocco, Papua New Guinea, El Salvador and Malaysia) whose ranks improved by 10 or more positions and 5 countries (Nepal, Mauritius, Costa Rica, Iran Islamic Republic and Bangladesh) whose ranks improved by 5 to 9 positions. In case of remaining 12 countries (Mexico, Oman, Honduras, Jamaica, Tunisia, The Gambia, Uganda, Madagascar, Bulgaria, Haiti, Pakistan and Mali) the ranks improved by less than 5 positions.

Of the 32 countries with deteriorated positions, ranks for 12 countries (Argentina, Central African Rep., Niger, Syrian Arab Rep., Gabon, Cote d'Ivoire, Peru, Egypt Arab Rep., Venezuela RB, Togo, South Africa and Zambia) deteriorated by 10 or more positions and for 12 countries (Benin, Nicaragua, Bolivia, Uruguay, Panama, Cameroon, Indonesia, Malawi, Kenya, Brazil, Colombia and Paraguay) ranks deteriorated by 5 to 9 positions. For 8 countries (Nigeria, Burundi, Congo Rep., Ecuador, Burkina Faso, Trinidad and Tobago, Sri Lanka and Algeria) ranks deteriorated by less than 5 positions.

While comparing the ranks of the year 2004 with those of 1990, it was found that, in the year 2004, there was improvement in the ranks of 32 countries and deterioration in the ranks of 34 countries.

There were 7 countries (China, Ghana, Papua New Guinea, Congo Republic, Philippines, Thailand and Chad) whose ranks improved by 10 or more positions and 9 countries (El Salvador, Turkey, Nepal, Honduras, Sri Lanka, Dominican Republic, Morocco, Sudan and Uganda) whose ranks improved by 5 to 9 positions. In case of remaining 16 countries (Bulgaria, Bangladesh, Costa Rica, Nigeria, Haiti, India, Oman, Jamaica, Iran Islamic Rep., Senegal, Trinidad and Tobago, Malaysia, Algeria, Mexico, Cote d'Ivoire and Madagascar) the ranks improved by less than 5 positions.

Of the 34 countries with deteriorated positions, ranks for 5 countries (Venezuela RB, Colombia, South Africa, Zambia and Paraguay) deteriorated by 10 or more positions and for 14 countries (Panama, Gabon, Uruguay, Syrian Arab Republic, Benin, Nicaragua, Kenya, Cameroon, Peru, The Gambia, Central African Republic, Egypt Arab Republic, Brazil and Ecuador) ranks deteriorated by 5 to 9 positions. For 15 countries (Tunisia, Togo, Indonesia, Burundi, Jordan, Argentina, Chile, Bolivia, Burkina Faso, Mauritius, Guatemala, Niger, Pakistan, Mali and Malawi) ranks deteriorated by less than 5 positions.

Effort have been made to examine the effect of globalization on economic development through analysis of different globalization related variables in case of countries which improved or deteriorated their positions (5 or more positions) in terms of Composite Index of development during the period 1990-2004. Table 7.10 shows the data of globalization-related variables of 16 countries which showed improvement during 1990-2004. It is seen that in case of all these variables, all the 16 countries showed improvement in the year 2004 over 1990. Only in case of international migration stock and gross private capital flows, a few countries showed some deterioration. Also, the average figures of these countries for all the variables improved sizably in the year 2004 over those of 1990. The average degree of openness increased from 56 to 85 percent, merchandise trade (% of GDP) from 42 to 72 percent, manufacture exports (% of merchandise exports) from 33 to 46 percent, imports (as % of GDP) from 31 to 44 percent and exports (% of GDP) from 25 to 41 percent during the period 1990-2004, showing that these countries gained largely due to globalization.

On the other hand, Table 7.11 shows the data of globalization-related variables of 19 countries which showed

TABLE 7.10

Globalization-Related Variables of 16 Countries which showed Improvement in Ranks During 1990-2004 (In Terms of Composite Index of Development)

Sl. No.	Country Name	Imports of goods and services (% of GDP)		Exports of goods and services (% of GDP)		Degree of Openness (Exports+Imports) % of GDP		Merchandise trade (% of GDP)	
		1990	2004	1990	2004	1990	2004	1990	2004
(1)	(2)	(3)	(4)	(5)	(6)	(7)	(8)	(9)	(10)
1.	Chad	28	36	13	52	41	88	27.2	70.4
2.	China	16	31	19	34	35	65	32.5	59.8
3.	Congo, Rep.	46	57	54	84	99	142	57.2	129.4
4.	Dominican Republic	44	49	34	50	78	98	73.2	72.8
5.	El Salvador	31	44	19	27	50	71	38.4	60.4
6.	Ghana	26	54	17	35	43	89	35.7	77.8
7.	Honduras	40	59	36	37	76	96	57.9	74.0
8.	Morocco	32	39	26	33	59	72	43.4	54.7
9.	Nepal	22	31	11	17	32	49	24.1	39.2
10.	Papua New Guinea	49	60	41	71	90	131	73.6	107.8
11.	Philippines	33	51	28	52	61	102	47.8	97.0
12.	Sri Lanka	33	45	29	36	67	82	57.3	68.5
13.	Sudan	18	21	13	18	32	39	7.5	37.2
14.	Thailand	42	66	34	71	76	136	65.7	119.2
15.	Turkey	18	35	13	29	31	64	23.4	53.1
16.	Uganda	19	28	7	14	27	41	10.2	31.2
	Average	**31**	**44**	**25**	**41**	**56**	**85**	**42**	**72**

(Contd.)

TABLE 7.10 (Contd.)

Sl. No.	Country Name	Trade in services (% of GDP)		International migration stock (% of population)		Gross private capital flows (% of GDP)		Manufactures exports (% of merchandise exports)	
		1990	2004	1990	2004	1990	2004	1990	2004
(1)	(2)	(11)	(12)	(13)	(14)	(15)	(16)	(17)	(18)
1.	Chad	15.5	26.0	1.23	1.31	5.6	7.9	8	10
2.	China	2.9	7.0	0.03	0.05	2.5	10.0	72	91
3.	Congo, Rep.	31.0	17.7	5.22	6.81	6.6	11.7	3	10
4.	Dominican Republic	21.7	25.4	1.45	1.70	5.0	13.5	78	84
5.	El Salvador	13.4	13.0	0.93	29.00	2.0	12.5	38	60
6.	Ghana	6.6	19.9	4.63	8.87	2.9	6.8	8	14
7.	Honduras	11.7	19.1	5.56	0.44	7.2	8.0	9	16
8.	Morocco	13.4	20.3	0.35	0.46	5.5	7.6	47	69
9.	Nepal	10.2	12.4	2.16	3.13	3.5	6.8	57	74
10.	Papua New Guinea	18.9	34.0	0.80	0.40	5.7	34.6	5	6
11.	Philippines	11.3	11.2	0.27	0.49	4.4	13.7	38	55
12.	Sri Lanka	13.4	17.1	2.71	2.00	13.1	5.2	48	74
13.	Sudan	3.0	5.3	4.88	2.00	0.3	10.4	2	2
14.	Thailand	14.9	26.1	0.72	1.60	13.5	7.9	44	75
15.	Turkey	7.4	11.7	2.05	1.60	4.3	12.8	68	85
16.	Uganda	4.5	16.8	3.10	1.90	1.1	4.8	4	13
	Average	**12**	**18**	**2**	**4**	**5**	**11**	**33**	**46**

Source : Tabulated from World Development Indicators; Various Issues.

TABLE 7.11

Globalization-Related Variables of 19 Countries which showed Deterioration in Ranks During 1990-2004 (In Terms of Composite Index of Development)

Sl. No.	Country Name	Imports of goods and services (% of GDP)		Exports of goods and services (% of GDP)		Degree of Openness (Exports+Imports) % of GDP		Merchandise trade (% of GDP)	
		1990	2004	1990	2004	1990	2004	1990	2004
(1)	(2)	(3)	(4)	(5)	(6)	(7)	(8)	(9)	(10)
1.	Benin	26	26	14	15	41	42	30.0	37.7
2.	Brazil	7	13	8	18	15	31	11.7	26.9
3.	Cameroon	17	26	20	26	37	51	30.5	33.4
4.	Central African Republic	28	16	15	11	42	27	18.4	20.7
5.	Colombia	15	22	21	21	35	43	30.7	33.7
6.	Ecuador	32	29	33	27	65	55	44.2	51.2
7.	Egypt, Arab Rep.	33	29	20	29	53	58	36.8	26.0
8.	Gabon	31	40	46	61	77	101	52.5	66.0
9.	Gambia, The	72	52	60	42	131	94	69.1	53.5
10.	Kenya	31	32	26	26	57	58	37.9	45.0
11.	Nicaragua	46	54	25	26	71	80	95.9	65.2
12.	Panama	79	65	87	63	165	128	35.4	32.6
13.	Paraguay	39	37	33	36	73	73	43.9	58.3
14.	Peru	14	18	16	21	30	39	22.3	33.0
15.	South Africa	19	27	24	27	43	54	37.4	48.5
16.	Syrian Arab Republic	28	34	28	35	56	69	53.7	46.7
17.	Uruguay	18	28	24	30	42	58	32.7	45.9
18.	Venezuela, RB	20	20	39	36	60	56	52.8	44.7
19.	Zambia	37	27	36	20	72	47	76.9	68.
	Average	**31**	**31**	**30**	**30**	**61**	**61**	**43**	**44**

(Contd.)

TABLE 7.11 (Contd.)

Sl. No.	Country Name	Trade in services (% of GDP)		International migration stock (% of population)		Gross private capital flows (% of GDP)		Manufactures exports (% of merchandise exports)	
		1990	2004	1990	2004	1990	2004	1990	2004
(1)	(2)	(11)	(12)	(13)	(14)	(15)	(16)	(17)	(18)
1.	Benin	13.9	12.0	1.47	1.98	10.7	5.7	13	9
2.	Brazil	2.4	4.9	0.54	0.28	1.9	8.8	52	54
3.	Cameroon	12.8	16.0	1.47	0.88	15.5	18.2	9	5
4.	Central African Republic	16.0	22.0	2.09	1.80	2.2	3.5	44	37
5.	Colombia	8.3	6.4	0.29	0.26	3.1	10.9	25	38
6.	Ecuador	13.0	9.0	0.76	0.85	11.0	13.1	2	9
7.	Egypt, Arab Rep.	22.6	28.2	0.32	0.21	6.8	13.3	42	31
8.	Gabon	21.0	16.7	13.34	17.33	18.0	18.7	6	7
9.	Gambia, The	34.5	39.0	12.63	15.00	0.9	7.0	36	27
10.	Kenya	21.4	14.1	0.62	1.30	3.5	7.2	30	21
11.	Nicaragua	17.0	15.1	1.03	0.44	9.0	6.1	8	11
12.	Panama	33.5	30.4	2.56	3.04	106.6	39.0	21	10
13.	Paraguay	16.2	12.6	4.35	3.00	5.4	3.4	10	13
14.	Peru	7.5	6.8	0.26	0.14	3.2	6.8	18	20
15.	South Africa	6.4	8.3	3.48	2.00	2.2	8.6	29	58
16.	Syrian Arab Republic	14.3	19.1	5.53	5.30	18.0	1.6	36	11
17.	Uruguay	9.2	12.6	3.16	2.30	12.7	22.0	39	32
18.	Venezuela, RB	7.9	5.3	5.18	3.90	51.6	16.2	10	12
19.	Zambia	15.0	14.0	3.34	3.34	64.7	9.3	6	21
	Average	**15**	**15**	**3**	**3**	**18**	**12**	**23**	**22**

Source : Tabulated from World Development Indicators; Various Issues.

deterioration of 5 or more positions during 1990-2004. The average degree of openness, merchandise trade (% of GDP), manufacture exports (% of merchandise exports), exports (% of GDP), imports (% of GDP) and other related variables largely remained stagnant during this period. In many countries, the globalization related variables showed deterioration, indicating that these countries could not be a part of increased globalization, hence could not reap the benefits and their ranks deteriorated. This confirmed the observation that the globalization has the potential of benefiting the developing countries.

When the positions of countries in 1990 and 2004 are compared on the GNI per capita basis, there was improvement of 5 or more positions of 15 countries and in case of 19 countries there was deterioration of 5 or more positions. The data regarding globalization related variables in case of these countries are given in Appendices 7.1 and 7.2 respectively. Figures show that in 2004 the magnitude of all the globalization related variables were much higher in case of the countries which improved their positions than the countries which lagged behind. Even when there has been improvement in these variables in case of both categories of countries, but the increase is more rapid in case of countries which have improved their positions as compared to those countries whose positions deteriorated. This also confirms that globalization has helped in economic development. The countries which have lagged behind could not reap the benefits due to their limited exposure and other limitations.

Table 7.12 shows the details of composite index, GNI per capita, GNI per capita PPP, PQLI and the corresponding ranks for 66 countries for the year 1980. When composite index was used *vis-à-vis* GNI per capita, there was improvement in the ranks of 28 countries, fall in the ranks of 35 countries and for 3 countries (Central African Rep., Niger and Trinidad and Tobago) there was no change in ranks.

Out of the 28 countries whose ranks improved with composite index, there were 11 countries (Malawi, Mauritius, Indonesia, Jordan, Jamaica, China, Congo Rep., Panama, Togo, Egypt Arab Rep. and Sri Lanka) whose ranks improved by 10 or more positions, for another 7 countries (Bolivia, Tunisia,

Table 7.12
Ranking of Countries on the Basis of Different Measures (1980)

Sl. No.	Country	GNI	Rank	GNIPPP	Rank	PQLI	Rank	Composite Index	Rank
	(1)	(2)	(3)	(4)	(5)	(6)	(7)	(8)	(9)
1.	Trinidad and Tobago	5160.00	1	4876.57	3	72.53	1	0.6191	1
2.	Panama	1620.00	18	2542.15	17	68.58	12	0.5864	2
3.	Jordan	2000.00	14	2353.53	19	65.75	17	0.5539	3
4.	Bulgaria	2010.00	13	2681.80	14	64.34	21	0.5342	4
5.	Venezuela, RB	4200.00	3	3663.67	7	68.49	13	0.5005	5
6.	Gabon	4790.00	2	3434.91	9	51.16	42	0.4938	6
7.	Argentina	2940.00	5	6272.32	1	71.90	3	0.4895	7
8.	Uruguay	2860.00	6	3992.53	5	72.25	2	0.4731	8
9.	Oman	3850.00	4	3667.64	6	59.49	29	0.4706	9
10.	Jamaica	1230.00	23	1572.65	31	70.26	5	0.4617	10
11.	Malaysia	1830.00	17	2077.14	26	60.44	28	0.4507	11
12.	Chile	2240.00	10	2429.04	18	70.34	4	0.4505	12
13.	South Africa	2510.00	8	5565.98	2	67.51	14	0.4433	13
14.	Mauritius	1210.00	24	2163.16	24	64.37	20	0.4409	14
15.	Congo, Rep.	820.00	31	373.65	65	58.73	31	0.4251	15
16.	Tunisia	1360.00	22	2133.58	25	61.21	26	0.4221	16

17.	Costa Rica	1980.00	15	3408.51	10	62.70	23	0.4169	17
18.	Algeria	2060.00	12	2891.14	11	48.21	45	0.4140	18
19.	Mexico	2520.00	7	4101.46	4	68.69	10	0.3974	19
20.	Egypt, Arab Rep.	500.00	42	1135.76	38	47.43	46	0.3652	20
21.	Peru	1050.00	29	2731.83	12	65.66	18	0.3634	21
22.	Syrian Arab Republic	1560.00	19	1566.39	32	61.30	25	0.3580	22
23.	Colombia	1190.00	25	2663.40	15	68.93	9	0.3565	23
24.	Brazil	2190.00	11	3598.12	8	65.55	19	0.3556	24
25.	Paraguay	1470.00	20	2703.46	13	69.71	7	0.3525	25
26.	Ecuador	1420.00	21	1751.77	29	66.77	15	0.3493	26
27.	Togo	410.00	49	1061.85	40	42.88	53	0.3346	27
28.	Sri Lanka	280.00	57	959.46	42	69.37	8	0.3339	28
29.	Iran, Islamic Rep.	2250.00	9	2661.55	16	53.16	38	0.3276	29
30.	Dominican Republic	1160.00	27	2064.98	28	61.92	24	0.3230	30
31.	Cote d'Ivoire	1120.00	28	1176.29	37	47.06	48	0.3189	31
32.	Indonesia	500.00	43	756.88	46	58.72	32	0.3085	32
33.	Honduras	700.00	36	1[illegible]50.54	34	60.64	27	0.3078	33
34.	Philippines	690.00	37	2238.37	21	66.02	16	0.3041	34
35.	Nicaragua	640.00	38	2230.15	22	68.65	11	0.3023	35
36.	Bolivia	590.00	41	1336.33	36	54.36	36	0.2989	36

(Contd.)

Table 7.12 (Contd.)

	(1)	(2)	(3)	(4)	(5)	(6)	(7)	(8)	(9)
37.	Zambia	600.00	40	591.98	52	53.06	39	0.2971	37
38.	El Salvador	760.00	34	2208.01	23	59.46	30	0.2929	38
39.	Morocco	970.00	30	1480.87	33	45.81	51	0.2920	39
40.	Papua New Guinea	780.00	33	1089.89	39	50.93	43	0.2867	40
41.	Thailand	730.00	35	1344.22	35	70.08	6	0.2838	41
42.	Kenya	460.00	45	572.39	54	57.02	34	0.2754	42
43.	Nigeria	810.00	32	507.84	57	47.16	47	0.2701	43
44.	Gambia, The	370.00	52	908.05	44	33.11	64	0.2695	44
45.	Turkey	1920.00	16	2274.18	20	54.49	35	0.2685	45
46.	Guatemala	1190.00	26	2070.40	27	57.81	33	0.2644	46
47.	Senegal	500.00	44	725.88	47	37.35	62	0.2632	47
48.	China	220.00	64	411.54	62	63.84	22	0.2614	48
49.	Cameroon	620.00	39	1012.66	41	52.84	40	0.2569	49
50.	Haiti	270.00	58	1680.10	30	40.19	56	0.2364	50
51.	Niger	390.00	51	605.09	51	34.27	63	0.2167	51
52.	Pakistan	330.00	54	624.16	50	39.75	58	0.2138	52
53.	Central African Republic	340.00	53	761.80	45	46.98	49	0.1941	53
54.	Benin	390.00	50	480.79	58	42.39	54	0.1883	54

55.	Malawi	190.00	65	330.95	66	32.70	65	0.1813	55
56.	Madagascar	440.00	47	624.56	49	49.98	44	0.1735	56
57.	Sudan	450.00	46	568.31	55	44.50	52	0.1698	57
58.	India	270.00	59	637.85	48	45.94	50	0.1630	58
59.	Ghana	410.00	48	924.66	43	54.19	37	0.1519	59
60.	Bangladesh	220.00	62	584.44	53	39.80	57	0.1298	60
61.	Mali	250.00	60	440.17	61	24.92	66	0.1255	61
62.	Nepal	140.00	66	446.55	60	37.49	61	0.1171	62
63.	Burkina Faso	310.00	55	447.82	59	37.65	60	0.1133	63
64.	Uganda	300.00	56	552.00	56	51.30	41	0.1071	64
65.	Burundi	220.00	63	396.37	63	41.36	55	0.0988	65
66.	Chad	230.00	61	380.42	64	38.14	59	0.0970	66

Malaysia, Haiti, The Gambia, Peru and Bulgaria) the ranks improved by 5 to 9 positions. For the remaining 10 countries (India, Bangladesh, Pakistan, Colombia, Kenya, Zambia, Nicaragua, Philippines, Honduras and Nepal) the ranks improved by less than 5 positions.

Of the 35 countries whose ranks deteriorated with composite index, there were 9 countries (Turkey, Guatemala, Iran Islamic Rep., Brazil, Mexico, Ghana, Sudan, Nigeria and Cameroon) whose ranks deteriorated by 10 or more positions in comparison to the ranks with GNI per capita. There were another 12 countries (Madagascar, Morocco, Uganda, Burkina Faso, Papua New Guinea, Thailand, Algeria, Chad, Ecuador, Paraguay, South Africa and Oman) whose ranks deteriorated by 5 to 9 positions and for the remaining 14 countries (Benin, El Salvador, Gabon, Senegal, Cote d'Ivoire, Dominican Rep., Syrian Arab Rep., Burundi, Costa Rica, Chile, Uruguay, Argentina, Venezuela RB and Mali) the ranks deteriorated by less than 5 positions.

When composite index was used *vis-à-vis* GNI per capita PPP, there was improvement in the ranks of 26 countries, fall in the ranks of 35 countries and for 5 countries (Senegal, Mali, Niger, Bolivia and The Gambia) there was no change in ranks.

Out of the 26 countries whose ranks improved with composite index, there were 17 countries (Syrian Arab Rep., Bulgaria, Mauritius, Malawi, Kenya, Togo, Nigeria, Indonesia, China, Sri Lanka, Zambia, Malaysia, Panama, Jordan, Egypt Arab Rep., Jamaica and Congo Rep.) whose ranks improved by 10 or more positions, for another 3 countries (Cote d'Ivoire, Chile and Tunisia) the ranks improved by 5 to 9 positions. For the remaining 6 countries (Honduras, Venezuela RB, Trinidad and Tobago, Ecuador, Gabon and Benin) the ranks improved by less than 5 positions.

Of the 35 countries whose ranks deteriorated with composite index, there were 13 countries (Turkey, Haiti, Guatemala, Brazil, Ghana, Mexico, El Salvador, Iran Islamic Rep., Nicaragua, Philippines, Paraguay, South Africa and India) where the ranks deteriorated by 10 or more positions in comparison to the ranks with GNI per capita PPP. There were another 12 countries (Peru, Cameroon, Uganda, Central African Rep., Colombia, Madagascar, Algeria, Costa Rica, Bangladesh,

Morocco, Thailand and Argentina) whose ranks deteriorated by 5 to 9 positions and for the remaining 10 countries (Burkina Faso, Oman, Uruguay, Sudan, Chad, Dominican Rep., Burundi, Pakistan, Nepal and Papua New Guinea) the ranks deteriorated by less than 5 positions.

When composite index was used *vis-a-vis* PQLI, there was improvement in the ranks of 29 countries, fall in the ranks of 33 countries and for 4 countries (Bolivia, Trinidad and Tobago, Benin and Indonesia) there was no change in ranks.

Out of the 29 countries whose ranks improved with composite index, there were 17 countries (Tunisia, Malawi, Panama, Morocco, Niger, Jordan, Senegal, Congo Rep., Cote d'Ivoire, Bulgaria, Malaysia, Oman, The Gambia, Togo, Egypt Arab Rep., Algeria and Gabon) whose ranks improved by 10 or more positions, for another 7 countries (Mali, Haiti, Costa Rica, Pakistan, Mauritius, Venezuela RB and Iran Islamic Rep.) the ranks improved by 5 to 9 positions. For the remaining 5 countries (South Africa, Zambia, Papua New Guinea, Syrian Arab Rep., and Nigeria) the ranks improved by less than 5 positions.

Of the 33 countries whose ranks deteriorated with composite index, there were 14 countries (Thailand, China, Nicaragua, Uganda, Ghana, Sri Lanka, Philippines, Paraguay, Colombia, Guatemala, Madagascar, Ecuador, Turkey and Burundi) whose ranks deteriorated by 10 or more positions in comparison to the ranks with PQLI. There were another 13 countries (Mexico, Cameroon, El Salvador, India, Chile, Kenya, Chad, Uruguay, Dominican Rep., Honduras, Brazil, Sudan and Jamaica) whose ranks deteriorated by 5 to 9 positions and for the remaining 6 countries (Central African Rep., Argentina, Peru, Bangladesh, Burkina Faso and Nepal) the ranks deteriorated by less than 5 positions.

When GNI per capita PPP was used *vis-à-vis* GNI per capita, there was improvement in the ranks of 28 countries, fall in the ranks of 33 countries and for 5 countries (Thailand, Uganda, Burundi, Mauritius and Niger) there was no change in ranks.

Of the 28 countries whose ranks improved with GNI per capita PPP, there were 8 countries (Haiti, Peru, Nicaragua, Philippines, Sri Lanka, El Salvador, India and Colombia) whose ranks improved by 10 or more positions in comparison to the ranks with GNI per capita. There were another 10 countries (Bangladesh, Togo, Central African Rep., The Gambia, Paraguay, Nepal, South Africa, Ghana, Bolivia, and Costa Rica) whose ranks improved by 5 to 9 positions and for the remaining 10 countries (Argentina, Pakistan, Egypt Arab Rep., Mexico, Brazil, China, Honduras, Uruguay, Panama and Algeria) the ranks improved by less than 5 positions.

Out of the 33 countries whose ranks deteriorated, there were 4 countries (Zambia, Syrian Arab Rep., Nigeria and Congo Rep.) whose ranks deteriorated by 10 or more positions, for another 12 countries (Jordan, Papua New Guinea, Iran Islamic Rep., Gabon, Ecuador, Chile, Jamaica, Benin, Kenya, Sudan, Cote d'Ivoire and Malaysia) the ranks deteriorated by 5 to 9 positions. For the remaining 17 countries (Guatemala, Dominican Rep., Mali, Malawi, Bulgaria, Madagascar, Cameroon, Trinidad and Tobago, Oman, Chad, Indonesia, Tunisia, Morocco, Senegal, Turkey, Burkina Faso and Venezuela RB) the ranks deteriorated by less than 5 positions.

When PQLI was used *vis-à-vis* GNI per capita, there was improvement in the ranks of 32 countries, fall in the ranks of 31 countries and for 3 countries (Malawi, Trinidad & Tobago and Congo Rep.) there was no change in ranks.

Of the 32 countries whose ranks improved with PQLI, there were 13 countries (Sri Lanka, China, Thailand, Nicaragua, Philippines, Jamaica, Colombia, Uganda, Paraguay, Peru, Ghana, Indonesia and Kenya) whose ranks improved by 10 or more positions in comparison to the ranks with GNI per capita. There were another 9 countries (India, Honduras, Burundi, Panama, Ecuador, Chile, Bangladesh, Nepal and Bolivia) whose ranks improved by 5 to 9 positions and for the remaining 10 countries (El Salvador, Central African Rep., Uruguay, Mauritius, Dominican Rep., Madagascar, Haiti, Argentina, Chad and Zambia) the ranks improved by less than 5 positions.

Out of the 31 countries whose ranks deteriorated, there were 14 countries (Venezuela RB, Papua New Guinea, Malaysia, The Gambia, Niger, Nigeria, Senegal, Turkey, Cote d'Ivoire, Morocco, Oman, Iran Islamic Rep., Algeria and Gabon) whose ranks deteriorated by 10 or more positions, for another 9 countries (Burkina Faso, South Africa, Mali, Sudan, Syrian Arab

Rep., Guatemala, Costa Rica, Brazil and Bulgaria) the ranks deteriorated by 5 to 9 positions. For the remaining 8 countries (Cameroon, Mexico, Jordan, Togo, Pakistan, Egypt Arab Rep., Tunisia and Benin) the ranks deteriorated by less than 5 positions.

When PQLI was used *vis-à-vis* GNI per capita PPP, there was improvement in the ranks of 32 countries, fall in the ranks of 33 countries and for Bolivia, there was no change in rank.

Of the 32 countries whose ranks improved with PQLI, there were 13 countries (China, Sri Lanka, Thailand, Jamaica, Kenya, Uganda, Indonesia, Ecuador, Chile, Zambia, Nicaragua and Nigeria) whose ranks improved by 10 or more positions in comparison to the ranks with GNI per capita PPP. There were another 10 countries (Burundi, Honduras, Syrian Arab Rep., Colombia, Paraguay, Ghana, Philippines, Panama, Madagascar and Chad) whose ranks improved by 5 to 9 positions and for the remaining 9 countries (Mauritius, Dominican Rep., Benin, Uruguay, Sudan, Trinidad and Tobago, Jordan, Malawi and Cameroon) the ranks improved by less than 5 positions.

Out of the 33 countries whose ranks deteriorated, there were 15 countries (Brazil, Cote d'Ivoire, South Africa, Niger, Togo, Costa Rica, Senegal, Turkey, Morocco, The Gambia, Iran Islamic Rep., Oman, Haiti, Gabon and Algeria) whose ranks deteriorated by 10 or more positions, for another 9 countries (Mali, Peru, Mexico, Guatemala, Venezuela RB, El Salvador, Bulgaria, Pakistan and Egypt Arab Rep.) the ranks deteriorated by 5 to 9 positions. For the remaining 9 countries (Nepal, Tunisia, Burkina Faso, India, Argentina, Malaysia, Bangladesh, Central African Rep. and Papua New Guinea) the ranks deteriorated by less than 5 positions.

Table 7.13 shows composite index, GNI per capita, GNI per capita PPP, PQLI and the corresponding ranks for 66 countries for the year 1990. When composite index was used *vis-à-vis* GNI per capita, there was improvement in the ranks of 32 countries and deterioration in the ranks of 34 countries.

When composite index was used *vis-à-vis* GNI per capita PPP, there was improvement in the ranks of 26 countries, deterioration in the ranks of 33 countries and for 7 countries (Gabon, Senegal, Papua New Guinea, Indonesia, Honduras, Sri Lanka and Madagascar) there was no change in ranks. When composite index

TABLE 7.13
Ranking of Countries on the Basis of Different Measures (1990)

Sl. No.	*Country*	*GNI*	*Rank*	*GNIPPP*	*Rank*	*PQLI*	*Rank*	*Composite Index*	*Rank*
	(1)	*(2)*	*(3)*	*(4)*	*(5)*	*(6)*	*(7)*	*(8)*	*(9)*
1.	Jordan	1390.00	22	2979.10	26	71.07	13	0.6203	1
2.	Malaysia	2420.00	12	4326.84	16	61.81	37	0.5553	2
3.	Panama	2210.00	16	3558.09	22	71.32	11	0.5508	3
4.	Mauritius	2300.00	13	5271.53	6	65.91	26	0.5461	4
5.	Trinidad and Tobago	3730.00	3	5229.03	8	74.42	2	0.5302	5
6.	Bulgaria	2260.00	15	5234.04	7	65.07	30	0.5217	6
7.	Oman	5610.00	1	8433.31	1	59.88	43	0.5057	7
8.	Jamaica	1790.00	18	2761.08	28	63.12	35	0.4814	8
9.	Uruguay	2870.00	6	5646.49	5	70.66	16	0.4788	9
10.	Chile	2180.00	17	4505.33	15	66.40	24	0.4666	10
11.	Venezuela, RB	2570.00	10	4588.90	12	70.61	17	0.4665	11
12.	Tunisia	1430.00	21	3582.91	21	63.84	33	0.4585	12
13.	Costa Rica	1770.00	19	4988.91	10	64.09	32	0.4518	13
14.	Gabon	4780.00	2	4515.32	14	60.12	42	0.4511	14
15.	Argentina	3190.00	5	7021.01	3	73.29	5	0.4458	15
16.	Mexico	2830.00	7	6019.40	4	72.91	6	0.4318	16

17.	Dominican Republic	880.00	31	3238.85	23	70.85	15	0.4272	17
18.	South Africa	3390.00	4	7748.06	2	72.04	9	0.4209	18
19.	Ecuador	890.00	29	2513.61	31	73.40	4	0.3865	19
20.	Paraguay	1190.00	24	3963.96	18	73.88	3	0.3818	20
21.	Thailand	1540.00	20	3667.83	20	72.78	7	0.3815	21
22.	Colombia	1190.00	23	4656.28	11	72.74	8	0.3809	22
23.	Algeria	2420.00	11	4269.95	17	61.66	40	0.3807	23
24.	Brazil	2770.00	8	5161.06	9	71.61	10	0.3742	24
25.	Iran, Islamic Rep.	2590.00	9	3764.28	19	65.25	29	0.3735	25
26.	Turkey	2270.00	14	4524.41	13	68.75	20	0.3700	26
27.	Egypt, Arab Rep.	760.00	35	2303.03	32	57.68	48	0.3523	27
28.	Congo, Rep.	880.00	30	656.18	63	63.78	34	0.3458	28
29.	Peru	770.00	34	3035.51	25	70.86	14	0.3399	29
30.	Syrian Arab Republic	880.00	32	2054.46	34	65.62	27	0.3376	30
31.	Morocco	1030.00	25	2635.52	30	55.69	49	0.3368	31
32.	Philippines	740.00	37	3146.54	24	75.12	1	0.3212	32
33.	Gambia, The	310.00	57	1365.12	43	47.13	61	0.3210	33
34.	Nicaragua	330.00	54	2276.89	33	65.30	28	0.3190	34
35.	El Salvador	930.00	28	2880.76	27	68.67	21	0.3169	35
36.	Honduras	710.00	39	1902.12	36	67.33	22	0.3110	36

(*Contd.*)

Table 7.13 (Contd.)

	(1)	*(2)*	*(3)*	*(4)*	*(5)*	*(6)*	*(7)*	*(8)*	*(9)*
37.	Sri Lanka	470.00	43	1894.28	37	71.14	12	0.3084	37
38.	Indonesia	620.00	41	1766.19	38	70.37	18	0.3037	38
39.	China	320.00	55	1306.55	45	70.21	19	0.2997	39
40.	Bolivia	740.00	36	1641.12	39	66.23	25	0.2892	40
41.	Papua New Guinea	830.00	33	1470.61	41	61.76	38	0.2787	41
42.	Togo	380.00	51	1252.58	48	55.29	50	0.2719	42
43.	Guatemala	950.00	27	2691.01	29	64.27	31	0.2599	43
44.	Kenya	380.00	50	895.56	52	67.31	23	0.2554	44
45.	Zambia	420.00	46	717.77	58	61.69	39	0.2485	45
46.	Cote d'Ivoire	730.00	38	1258.36	47	51.35	53	0.2447	46
47.	Nigeria	280.00	60	645.14	64	52.03	51	0.2424	47
48.	Pakistan	420.00	45	1329.30	44	50.45	54	0.2402	48
49.	Senegal	660.00	40	1112.67	49	50.00	56	0.2311	49
50.	Cameroon	960.00	26	1594.98	40	60.54	41	0.2170	50
51.	Haiti	390.00	47	1934.30	35	52.01	52	0.2007	51
52.	India	390.00	48	1369.71	42	58.04	46	0.1958	52
53.	Ghana	380.00	49	1262.69	46	61.94	36	0.1923	53
54.	Benin	330.00	53	677.73	60	45.96	62	0.1837	54

55.	Madagascar	230.00	63	748.73	55	57.77	47	0.1678	55
56.	Central African Repub	460.00	44	990.25	51	49.93	57	0.1639	56
57.	Mali	260.00	62	553.66	65	39.11	65	0.1611	57
58.	Malawi	180.00	66	406.45	66	48.59	60	0.1610	58
59.	Bangladesh	300.00	58	1005.56	50	50.26	55	0.1582	59
60.	Niger	280.00	59	662.57	62	27.29	66	0.1461	60
61.	Nepal	200.00	65	847.27	53	49.01	59	0.1447	61
62.	Sudan	550.00	42	841.08	54	58.13	45	0.1443	62
63.	Burkina Faso	350.00	52	724.10	57	44.07	64	0.1335	63
64.	Chad	260.00	61	731.26	56	45.68	63	0.1327	64
65.	Burundi	210.00	64	674.81	61	49.31	58	0.0827	65
66.	Uganda	320.00	56	706.79	59	59.09	44	0.0740	66

was used *vis-à-vis* PQLI, there was improvement in the ranks of 31 countries and deterioration in the ranks of 35 countries. When GNI per capita PPP was used *vis-à-vis* GNI per capita, there was improvement in the ranks of 32 countries, fall in the ranks of 30 countries and for 4 countries (Thailand, Malawi, Tunisia and Oman) there was no change in ranks.

When PQLI was used *vis-à-vis* GNI per capita, there was improvement in the ranks of 31 countries, deterioration in the ranks of 34 countries and for Argentina, there was no change in rank. When PQLI was used *vis-à-vis* GNI per capita PPP, there was improvement in the ranks of 29 countries, deterioration in the ranks of 36 countries and for Mali, there was no change in rank.

Table 7.14 shows composite index, GNI per capita, GNI per capita PPP, PQLI and the corresponding ranks for 66 countries for the year 2000. When composite index was used *vis-à-vis* GNI per capita, there was improvement in the ranks of 29 countries, deterioration in the ranks of 35 countries and for remaining 2 countries (Burundi and Mali) there was no change in the ranks.

When composite index was used *vis-à-vis* GNI per capita PPP, there was improvement in the ranks of 28 countries, deterioration in the ranks of 33 countries and for 5 countries (Gabon, Benin, Mali, Dominican Rep. and Mauritius) there was no change in ranks. When composite index was used *vis-à-vis* PQLI, there was improvement in the ranks of 30 countries, deterioration in the ranks of 35 countries and for Bangladesh, there was no change in the rank.

When GNI per capita PPP was used *vis-à-vis* GNI per capita, there was improvement in the ranks of 33 countries, fall in the ranks of 27 countries and for 6 countries (Brazil, Mexico, Syrian Arab Rep., Haiti, Mali and Chile) there was no change in ranks. When PQLI was used *vis-à-vis* GNI per capita, there was improvement in the ranks of 31 countries, deterioration in the ranks of 34 countries and for Zambia, there was no change in rank. When PQLI was used *vis-à-vis* GNI per capita PPP, there was improvement in the ranks of 31 countries, deterioration in the ranks of 34 countries and for Sudan, there was no change in rank.

Table 7.15 shows composite index, GNI per capita, GNI per capita PPP, PQLI and the corresponding ranks for 66 countries for the year 2004. When composite index was used *vis-à-vis* GNI

Table 7.14
Ranking of Countries on the Basis of Different Measures (2000)

Sl. No.	Country	GNI	Rank	GNIPPP	Rank	PQLI	Rank	Composite Index	Rank
	(1)	(2)	(3)	(4)	(5)	(6)	(7)	(8)	(9)
1.	Malaysia	3430.00	12	8174.58	9	62.04	42	0.6457	1
2.	Trinidad and Tobago	5230.00	4	8278.19	8	77.23	12	0.5646	2
3.	Mauritius	3690.00	10	9546.20	3	73.91	23	0.5417	3
4.	Bulgaria	1600.00	26	5828.27	19	76.39	14	0.5298	4
5.	Oman	6610.00	2	12247.12	1	69.92	32	0.5283	5
6.	Jordan	1760.00	23	3908.07	28	77.57	10	0.5281	6
7.	Panama	740.00	8	5838.90	17	77.42	11	0.5268	7
8.	Argentina	7470.00	1	11850.38	2	78.16	5	0.5154	8
9.	Uruguay	6150.00	3	8659.16	7	76.17	15	0.5096	9
10.	Chile	4860.00	6	8776.73	6	69.32	34	0.4885	10
11.	Mexico	5110.00	5	8815.06	5	78.12	6	0.4838	11
12.	Costa Rica	3700.00	9	7944.19	10	69.09	35	0.4772	12
13.	Jamaica	2940.00	16	3500.68	31	75.44	19	0.4713	13
14.	Dominican Republic	2170.00	17	6072.00	14	74.84	21	0.4618	14
15.	Tunisia	2080.00	18	5947.00	16	71.66	28	0.4570	15

(Contd.)

TABLE 7.14 (Contd.)

	(1)	(2)	(3)	(4)	(5)	(6)	(7)	(8)	(9)
16.	Venezuela, RB	4100.00	7	5617.76	20	77.72	8	0.4516	16
17.	Thailand	1990.00	22	6181.45	13	79.82	1	0.4328	17
18.	Turkey	2980.00	15	6563.27	12	75.98	16	0.4309	18
19.	Philippines	1040.00	32	4198.19	26	79.65	2	0.4065	19
20.	Ecuador	1340.00	30	3074.77	36	78.44	4	0.4057	20
21.	Gabon	3090.00	13	5259.96	21	57.00	50	0.4049	21
22.	Brazil	3590.00	11	7083.35	11	76.45	13	0.4048	22
23.	Algeria	1570.00	27	5143.24	22	69.76	33	0.4005	23
24.	South Africa	3050.00	14	9194.16	4	71.15	29	0.3971	24
25.	Colombia	2060.00	19	6071.06	15	77.92	7	0.3930	25
26.	Congo, Rep.	520.00	43	676.52	64	68.05	36	0.3851	26
27.	Peru	2050.00	20	4597.25	23	77.59	9	0.3813	27
28.	Iran, Islamic Rep.	1670.00	25	5829.47	18	73.17	24	0.3751	28
29.	Syrian Arab Republic	910.00	35	3091.52	35	72.80	25	0.3663	29
30.	El Salvador	2000.00	21	4505.74	25	74.10	22	0.3649	30
31.	Egypt, Arab Rep.	1460.00	28	3631.51	30	65.07	40	0.3534	31
32.	Sri Lanka	810.00	37	3392.61	33	75.11	20	0.3505	32
33.	Morocco	1220.00	31	3421.86	32	61.78	43	0.3502	33
34.	Paraguay	1460.00	29	4553.07	24	78.93	3	0.3483	34

35.	Honduras	860.00	36	2441.13	38	72.55	26	0.3378	35
36.	Indonesia	590.00	41	2827.46	37	75.57	18	0.3293	36
37.	Bolivia	1000.00	33	2334.45	40	71.95	27	0.3244	37
38.	Papua New Guinea	650.00	40	2236.33	41	65.12	39	0.3225	38
39.	China	930.00	34	3880.24	29	75.86	17	0.3219	39
40.	Ghana	330.00	51	1836.98	43	67.40	37	0.3065	40
41.	Nicaragua	750.00	38	3109.61	34	69.93	31	0.3055	41
42.	Guatemala	1740.00	24	3931.27	27	70.03	30	0.2816	42
43.	Gambia, The	320.00	52	1643.95	46	52.47	56	0.2723	43
44.	Nigeria	280.00	55	791.17	60	58.27	47	0.2691	44
45.	Cote d'Ivoire	650.00	39	1469.53	48	45.09	63	0.2574	45
46.	Senegal	450.00	47	1405.35	51	55.89	53	0.2494	46
47.	Togo	270.00	57	1407.25	50	58.32	46	0.2488	47
48.	India	450.00	46	2395.11	39	59.73	45	0.2298	48
49.	Pakistan	480.00	45	1874.67	42	51.39	58	0.2240	49
50.	Kenya	430.00	48	1008.32	55	66.18	38	0.2220	50
51.	Bangladesh	390.00	49	1589.25	47	56.80	51	0.2068	51
52.	Cameroon	580.00	42	1756.40	45	64.32	41	0.2050	52
53.	Haiti	490.00	44	1805.12	44	56.43	52	0.2041	53
54.	Madagascar	240.00	60	810.24	58	57.89	48	0.2024	54

(*Contd.*)

TABLE 7.14 (Contd.)

(1)		(2)	(3)	(4)	(5)	(6)	(7)	(8)	(9)
55.	Sudan	310.00	53	1422.18	49	57.12	49	0.1982	55
56.	Nepal	220.00	62	1327.69	52	53.27	55	0.1940	56
57.	Benin	340.00	50	953.97	57	48.67	60	0.1926	57
58.	Zambia	290.00	54	736.24	62	54.72	54	0.1828	58
59.	Niger	160.00	64	696.72	63	34.01	66	0.1652	59
60.	Chad	180.00	63	809.64	59	46.56	62	0.1644	60
61.	Mali	220.00	61	769.92	61	40.98	64	0.1533	61
62.	Central African Republic	270.00	56	1134.92	54	49.43	59	0.1342	62
63.	Malawi	150.00	65	574.03	66	52.18	57	0.1128	63
64.	Burkina Faso	250.00	59	996.50	56	39.54	65	0.1114	64
65.	Uganda	260.00	58	1213.78	53	60.03	44	0.0875	65
66.	Burundi	110.00	66	607.76	65	48.43	61	0.0436	66

Table 7.15
Ranking of Countries on the Basis of Different Measures (2004)

Sl. No.	Country	GNI	Rank	GNIPPP	Rank	PQLI	Rank	Composite Index	Rank
	(1)	(2)	(3)	(4)	(5)	(6)	(7)	(8)	(9)
1.	Malaysia	4520.00	6	9715.00	7	71.02	36	0.6774	1
2.	Bulgaria	2750.00	17	7936.33	11	77.54	21	0.5662	2
3.	Jordan	2190.00	26	4765.11	28	79.98	9	0.5619	3
4.	Trinidad and Tobago	8730.00	2	11431.24	4	80.63	7	0.5591	4
5.	Oman	9070.00	1	14677.54	1	68.70	38	0.5276	5
6.	Jamaica	3300.00	15	3950.48	33	75.27	27	0.5126	6
7.	Mauritius	4640.00	5	11954.56	3	74.59	28	0.5108	7
8.	Panama	4210.00	8	6725.64	19	79.31	18	0.4989	8
9.	Thailand	2490.00	19	7932.80	13	79.98	10	0.4844	9
10.	Costa Rica	4470.00	7	9216.49	9	73.66	31	0.4660	10
11.	Dominican Republic	2100.00	27	6862.93	18	79.76	14	0.4561	11
12.	Chile	5220.00	4	10608.31	6	64.59	48	0.4498	12
13.	Tunisia	2650.00	18	7426.84	16	74.34	29	0.4480	13
14.	Uruguay	3900.00	11	9025.66	10	79.38	17	0.4361	14
15.	Mexico	6790.00	3	9644.73	8	79.93	12	0.4339	15

(Contd.)

TABLE 7.15 (Contd.)

	(1)	(2)	(3)	(4)	(5)	(6)	(7)	(8)	(9)
16.	Congo, Rep.	765.00	41	738.93	64	71.50	35	0.4187	16
17.	Argentina	3580.00	14	12525.94	2	79.96	11	0.4176	17
18.	Turkey	3750.00	12	7724.21	14	83.10	2	0.4143	18
19.	Gabon	4080.00	9	5698.82	23	64.45	49	0.4116	19
20.	Philippines	1170.00	33	4946.29	25	81.29	4	0.4031	20
21.	Venezuela, RB	4030.00	10	5829.46	22	78.62	19	0.3875	21
22.	Algeria	2270.00	23	6322.33	20	73.53	34	0.3802	22
23.	Iran, Islamic Rep.	2325.00	22	7532.62	15	76.09	25	0.3801	23
24.	China	1500.00	30	5885.35	21	80.66	6	0.3771	24
25.	Morocco	1570.00	29	4253.36	30	67.50	41	0.3731	25
26.	El Salvador	2320.00	21	4894.38	26	77.62	20	0.3692	26
27.	Papua New Guinea	560.00	46	2276.89	41	64.82	46	0.3680	27
28.	Ecuador	2210.00	24	3767.94	34	80.07	8	0.3647	28
29.	Honduras	1040.00	36	2760.29	39	77.32	22	0.3619	29
30.	South Africa	3630.00	13	10964.44	5	76.36	24	0.3516	30
31.	Sri Lanka	1010.00	37	4207.61	31	74.25	30	0.3445	31
32.	Colombia	2020.00	28	6944.88	17	79.46	16	0.3415	32
33.	Brazil	3000.00	16	7935.34	12	79.92	13	0.3408	33

34.	Paraguay	1140.00	35	4816.87	27	81.36	3	0.3375	34
35.	Syrian Arab Republic	1230.00	32	3496.28	35	73.58	33	0.3340	35
36.	Egypt, Arab Rep.	1250.00	31	4199.75	32	70.26	37	0.3319	36
37.	Peru	2360.00	20	5395.42	24	79.56	15	0.3212	37
38.	Ghana	380.00	54	2221.43	42	65.05	45	0.3202	38
39.	Indonesia	1140.00	34	3484.66	36	80.88	5	0.3179	39
40.	Nicaragua	830.00	39	3480.80	37	76.09	26	0.3085	40
41.	Gambia, The	280.00	60	1885.12	46	54.85	59	0.3063	41
42.	Bolivia	960.00	38	2600.27	40	76.88	23	0.2865	42
43.	Togo	310.00	58	1508.03	50	61.44	54	0.2745	43
44.	Nigeria	430.00	52	966.32	59	62.42	52	0.2739	44
45.	Cote d'Ivoire	760.00	42	1473.65	52	51.84	62	0.2728	45
46.	Guatemala	2190 00	25	4262.91	29	73.65	32	0.2726	46
47.	Senegal	630.00	43	1662.21	49	57.00	57	0.2713	47
48.	India	620.00	44	3116.07	38	67.07	43	0.2429	48
49.	Haiti	510.00	48	1805.00	48	62.07	53	0.2428	49
50.	Kenya	480.00	49	1130.43	56	68.39	39	0.2294	50
51.	Pakistan	600.00	45	2174.31	43	59.67	55	0.2290	51
52.	Chad	250.00	61	1336.62	54	44.34	65	0.2264	52
53.	Nepal	250.00	62	1484.90	51	63.56	50	0.2248	53
54.	Madagascar	290.00	59	842.84	62	67.70	40	0.2237	54

(*Contd.*)

TABLE 7.15 (Contd.)

(1)	(2)	(3)	(4)	(5)	(6)	(7)	(8)	(9)
55. Bangladesh	440.00	51	1968.87	45	62.73	51	0.2210	55
56. Cameroon	810.00	40	2117.12	44	64.74	47	0.2033	56
57. Sudan	530.00	47	1811.18	47	67.14	42	0.1950	57
58. Zambia	400.00	53	890.10	61	61.75	1	0.1935	58
59. Benin	450.00	50	1085.18	58	53.02	60	0.1925	59
60. Mali	330.00	56	952.98	60	51.08	63	0.1802	60
61. Uganda	250.00	63	1448.39	53	65.78	44	0.1638	61
62. Malawi	160.00	65	630.91	66	58.71	56	0.1503	62
63. Niger	210.00	64	775.73	63	37.57	66	0.1483	63
64. Central African Republic	310.00	57	1102.91	57	52.46	61	0.1297	64
65. Burkina Faso	350.00	55	1168.17	55	47.41	64	0.1181	65
66. Burundi	90.00	66	662.12	65	56.11	58	0.0692	66

per capita, there was improvement in the ranks of 26 countries, deterioration in the ranks of 37 countries and for remaining 3 countries (Burundi, Haiti and Panama) there was no change in the ranks. When composite index was used *vis-à-vis* GNI per capita PPP, there was improvement in the ranks of 27 countries, deterioration in the ranks of 32 countries and for 7 countries (El Salvador, Mali, Syrian Arab Rep., Haiti, Trinidad and Tobago, Niger and Sri Lanka) there was no change in ranks.

When composite index was used *vis-à-vis* PQLI, there was improvement in the ranks of 33 countries and deterioration in the ranks of other 33 countries.

When GNI per capita PPP was used *vis-à-vis* GNI per capita, there was improvement in the ranks of 29 countries, deterioration in the ranks of 32 countries and for 5 countries (Sudan, Central African Rep., Burkina Faso, Haiti and Oman) there was no change in ranks.

When PQLI was used *vis-à-vis* GNI per capita, there was improvement in the ranks of 31 countries, deterioration in the ranks of 32 countries and for 3 countries (Bangladesh, Papua New Guinea and Nigeria) there was no change in rank. When PQLI was used *vis-à-vis* GNI per capita PPP, there was improvement in the ranks of 30 countries and deterioration in the ranks of other 36 countries.

RANK CORRELATION ANALYSIS

Attempt was made to examine whether the ranks of the countries with different measures changed over time or not. Table 7.16 shows Rank Correlation Matrices between composite index, GNI per capita, GNI per capita PPP and PQLI for the years 1980, 1990, 2000 and 2004 separately. It was seen that in 1980, the rank correlation coefficients ranged between 0.683 to 0.882 within different measures. Similarly, the rank correlation coefficients ranged between 0.633 to 0.906 and 0.734 to 0.950 in the years 1990 and 2000 respectively. In the year 2004, the rank correlation coefficient ranged between 0.611 to 0.926. Thus, in all the years, the rank correlation coefficients were higher and significant at one percent level. This shows that results in

Table 7.16
Rank Correlations Between Different Measures of Economic Development (1980)

	Composite Index 1980	*GNI 1980*	*GNI PPP 1980*	*PQLI 1980*
Composite Index 1980	1	.860**	.795**	.734**
GNI 1980		1	.882**	.683**
GNI PPP 1980			1	.710**
PQLI 1980				1

** Correlation is significant at the .01 level (2-tailed).

Rank Correlations Between Different Measures of Economic Development (1990)

	Composite Index 1990	*GNI 1990*	*GNI PPP 1990*	*PQLI 1990*
Composite Index 1990	1	.861**	.865**	.680**
GNI 1990		1	.906**	.633**
GNI PPP 1990			1	.701**
PQLI 1990				1

** Correlation is significant at the .01 level (2-tailed).

Rank Correlations Between Different Measures of Economic Development (2000)

	Composite Index 2000	*GNI 2000*	*GNI PPP 2000*	*PQLI 2000*
Composite Index 2000	1	.922**	.886**	.763**
GNI 2000		1	.950**	.740**
GNI PPP 2000			1	.734**
PQLI 2000				1

** Correlation is significant at the .01 level (2-tailed).

Rank Correlations Between Different Measures of Economic Development (2004)

	Composite Index 2004	*GNI 2004*	*GNI PPP 2004*	*PQLI 2004*
Composite Index 2004	1	.868**	.835**	.611**
GNI 2004		1	.926**	.624**
GNI PPP 2004			1	.631**
PQLI 2004				1

** Correlation is significant at the .01 level (2-tailed).

different measures were consistent with each other and there was not much change in the ranks.

CORRELATION ANALYSIS OF THE SELECTED VARIABLES WITH COMPOSITE INDEX OF ECONOMIC DEVELOPMENT

An attempt has also been made to study the correlation of globalization, socio-economic and growth related variables with composite index of economic development in order to know the impact of globalization on economic development of developing countries.

Table 7.17 shows the correlation coefficients of composite index with 22 selected variables. It was seen that in the year 1980, variables like GNI per capita, GNI per capita PPP, urban population (% of total) and life expectancy at birth were highly correlated with composite index of economic development. While the correlation of variables like manufacture exports (% of merchandise exports), international migration stock (% of population), gross private flows (% of GDP), trade in services (% of GDP) and services value added (% of GDP), with composite index was weak.

In the year 1990 also, variables like GNI per capita, GNI per capita PPP, urban population (% of total) and life expectancy at birth showed high correlation with composite index of economic development. On the other hand, manufacture exports (% of merchandise exports), international migration stock (% of population), gross private flows (% of GDP) and share of fuel, ores and metal exports (% of merchandise exports) showed weak correlation with composite index.

In 2000, the variables like GNI per capita, GNI per capita PPP, life expectancy at birth, urban population (% of total), employment in services (% of total employment) and percentage of population of working age, were highly correlated with composite index of economic development, while the correlation of variables like manufacture exports (% of merchandise exports), international migration stock (% of population), gross capital formation (% of GDP) and trade in services (% of GDP) was weak.

TABLE 7.17
Correlation Coefficients of Composite Index of Economic Development with 22 Selected Variables at Different Points of Time

Sl. No.	*Variable*	*1980*	*1990*	*2000*	*2004*
1.	GNI per capita, (current US$)	.773**	.736**	.785**	.745**
2.	GNI per capita, PPP (current international $)	.742**	.794**	.838**	.774**
3.	Industry, value added (% of GDP)	.716**	.618**	.527**	.543**
4.	Services, value added (% of GDP)	.365**	.425**	.496**	.395**
5.	Daily Calorie Supply (per capita)	.590**	.664**	.609**	.540**
6.	Energy Use per capita (kg. of oil equivalent)	.712**	.638**	.601**	.572**
7.	Fuel + ores and metal exports (% of merchandise exports)	.465**	.251*	0.170	0.076
8.	Life expectancy at birth, total (years)	.736**	.845**	.828**	.735**
9.	Employment in services (% of total employment)	.714**	.673**	.743**	.625**
10.	Percentage of population of working age (15-64 yrs.)	.371**	.573**	.740**	.722**
11.	Physicians (per 1,000 people)	.586**	.608**	.597**	.422**
12.	Urban population (% of total)	.774**	.786**	.758**	.655**
13.	International migration stock (% of population)	.302*	.283*	0.242	.286*
14.	Gross domestic savings (% of GDP)	.652**	.543**	.514**	.400**
15.	Manufactures exports (% of merchandise exports)	0.072	.278*	.296*	.343**
16.	Exports of goods and services (% of GDP)	.614**	.686**	.591**	.735**
17.	Imports of goods and services (% of GDP)	.364**	.463**	.420**	.624**
18.	Degree of Openness (Exports+Imports) % to GDP	.520**	.599**	.541**	.722**
19.	Gross private capital flows (% of GDP)	.317**	.344**	.383**	.570**
20.	Gross capital formation (% of GDP)	.642**	.407**	.289*	.274*
21.	Merchandise trade (% of GDP)	.521**	.551**	.474**	.638**
22.	Trade in services (% of GDP)	.333**	.391**	.319**	.420**

* Correlation is significant at the 0.05 level (2-tailed).
** Correlation is significant at the 0.01 level (2-tailed).

In the year 2004, GNI per capita, GNI per capita PPP, life expectancy at birth, percentage of population of working age, degree of openness (exports+ imports) % of GDP, exports of goods and services (% of GDP) and merchandise trade (% of GDP) were highly correlated with composite index of economic development. On the other hand, international migration stock, life expectancy at birth and gross capital formation showed weak correlation with composite index.

Thus, in the years 1980 and 1990, generally the correlation of globalization and growth-related variables was weak with composite index of economic development, but these variables showed high correlation in the years 2000 and 2004 which clearly shows the positive impact of globalization on economic development of developing countries.

The table also showed that globalization-related variables like imports of goods and services (% of GDP), exports of goods and services (% of GDP), degree of openness, merchandise trade (% of GDP), gross private capital flows (% of GDP) and trade in services (% of GDP) were weakly correlated with composite index in 1980, but got strengthened throughout the period of study, clearly showing the impact of globalization on economic development.

CONCLUSION

From Factor Analysis, it may be concluded that globalization has positive impact on economic development of developing countries. Indicators of globalization included variables like exports of goods and services, imports of goods and services, degree of openness, merchandise trade, trade in services, international migration stock and gross private capital flows. In 1980 and 1990, globalization-related variables collectively explained 26.689 percent and 27.407 percent of the variations. But in 2000 and 2004, globalization-related variables explained 36.968 percent and 36.020 percent of the variations. This indicated increased role of globalization in economic development of developing countries.

Four measures of economic development, i.e. composite index, GNI per capita, GNI per capita PPP and PQLI were used to measure economic development of developing countries. The countries were ranked on the basis of these measures and their relative positions were compared when ranked with these measures. While comparing the relative positions of developing countries on the basis of composite index, GNI per capita, GNI per capita PPP and PQLI, it was seen that there were not marked differences in ranking of these countries.

Rank correlation analysis showed that in 1980, the rank correlation coefficients ranged between 0.683 to 0.882 in case of different measures. Similarly, the rank correlation coefficients ranged between 0.633 to 0.906 and 0.734 to 0.950 for the years 1990 and 2000 respectively. In the year 2004, the rank correlation coefficients ranged between 0.611 to 0.926. Thus, in all the years, the rank correlation coefficients were high and significant at one percent level. This shows that results of different measures were consistent with each other and there was not marked differences in the ranks.

Composite index can be termed as more scientific measure of economic development as it is representative of broad spectra of indicators. From the results of composite index, it is seen that there were 16 countries (China, Ghana, Papua New Guinea, Congo Republic, Philippines, Thailand, Chad, El Salvador, Turkey, Nepal, Honduras, Sri Lanka, Dominican Republic, Morocco, Sudan and Uganda) whose ranks improved by 5 or more positions in 2004 as compared to 1990. These countries have been developing at a fast speed, in terms of different globalization-related indicators, thereby reaping more gains of globalization as compared to other developing countries.

From correlation coefficients of composite index with 22 selected variables, it was seen that in the years 1980, 1990 and 2000, variables like GNI per capita, GNI per capita PPP, urban population (% of total) and life expectancy at birth were highly correlated with composite index of economic development. While the correlation of globalization-related variables like manufacture exports (% of merchandise exports), international migration stock (% of population), gross private flows (% of GDP) and trade in services (% of GDP), was weak with composite index. But in 2004, degree of openness (exports+ imports % of GDP), exports of goods and services (% of GDP) and merchandise trade (% of GDP) were highly correlated with composite index of economic development. This clearly shows the positive impact of globalization on economic development of developing countries.

Also, the correlation coefficients of the globalization-related variables like imports of goods and services (% of GDP), exports of goods and services (% of GDP), degree of openness, merchandise trade (% of GDP), gross private capital flows (% of GDP) and trade in services (% of GDP) with composite index got strengthened throughout the period of study, clearly showing the impact of globalization on economic development.

Globalization and Economic Development : Convergence and Stability

In this chapter, attempt has been made to find whether developing countries are converging over time or not. Convergence has been examined in the pre and post-globalization period to find the impact of globalization on economic development and convergence in developing countries. Also, attempt was made to find whether developing countries would be able to 'catch-up' the developed countries or not. The chapter has been divided into two sections; first section deals with convergence in the context of globalization while the second section examines the stability of growth parameters in the pre and post-globalization periods.

SECTION I

An attempt has been made here to find whether developing countries would be able to 'catch-up' the developed countries and whether there is possibility of convergence even within the developing countries.

GNI PER CAPITA OF DIFFERENT GROUPS OF COUNTRIES

Table 8.1 shows average GNI per capita of different groups of countries i.e. high income, low income, lower middle income, middle income and upper middle income countries, as classified by the World Bank (2006), in the years 1980, 1990, 2000 and 2004. The figures in the parentheses are the percentages of GNI per capita of the concerned groups of countries to those of high income countries. The table shows that in the year 1980 GNI per capita of low income countries was only 3.03 percent of that of the high income countries which decreased to 1.82 percent in the year 1990, further decreased to 1.45 percent in 2000 and slightly increased to 1.58 percent in the year 2004. Similarly, in case of lower middle income countries, GNI per capita was 5.57 percent of that of high income countries in the year 1980, which decreased to 3.94 percent in the year 1990 and then slightly increased to 4.73 percent and 5.25 percent in the years 2000 and 2004 respectively. The percentage in 2004 was still lower than that in 1980.

In case of middle income countries, GNI per capita was 8.93 percent of that of high income countries in the year 1980 which decreased to 5.98 percent in the year 1990. However, it increased to 6.53 percent in the year 2000 and 7.08 percent in the year 2004. Similarly, in case of upper middle income countries, GNI per capita was 22.62 percent of that of high income countries in the year 1980 which drastically decreased to 14.09 percent in the year 1990 and then slightly increased to 14.12 percent in the year 2000 and 14.85 percent in the year 2004. The percentage figures of all categories of developing countries were invariably lower in 2004 as compared to those in 1980.

This shows no trend towards convergence between developed and developing countries. The gap between the developed and developing countries is in fact increasing rather than decreasing, thus the developing countries have not been able to 'catch-up' the developed countries. However, if we consider the period of globalization, i.e. the period after 1990, then the GNI per capita of all categories of developing countries (except low income category) as percentage of those of high income countries has increased. There appears some tendency

TABLE 8.1
GNI Per Capita (Current US $) in Different Groups of Countries

Countries	*1980*	*1990*	*2000*	*2004*
High Income	10573.88	19619.60	26528.92	32111.74
Low Income	320.55	357.59	383.87	506.91
	(3.03)	(1.82)	(1.45)	(1.58)
Lower Middle Income	589.49	773.59	1254.42	1685.79
	(5.57)	(3.94)	(4.73)	(5.25)
Middle Income	944.15	1174.17	1733.47	2274.08
	(8.93)	(5.98)	(6.53)	(7.08)
Upper Middle Income	2391.29	2763.8	3746.17	4769.46
	(22.62)	(14.09)	(14.12)	(14.85)

Note : Figures in parentheses represent percentages to high income countries.
Source : World Development Indicators; Various Issues.

towards convergence in case of these categories of countries after 1990. But the low income countries have lagged behind even after globalization. Thus, globalization has not proved helpful to low income countries in 'catching-up' the developed countries and they have lagged behind.

GNI PER CAPITA OF DEVELOPING COUNTRIES

Table 8.2 shows GNI per capita of 66 developing countries as percentage of GNI per capita of U.S.A. This was done to see whether there occurred convergence between developed and developing countries or not. The table showed that no trend towards convergence between developed and developing countries except in case of two countries, i.e. China and Mauritius as the percentage of GNI per capita to that USA of these countries only showed an increasing trend.

Attempt has also been made to find whether there has been convergence within the developing countries or not. Table 8.3 shows the GNI per capita of 66 developing countries as percentage of a developing country with highest GNI per capita in 2004, i.e. Oman. It was seen that only one country, i.e. China experienced increase in the percentage of GNI per capita

TABLE 8.2
GNI Per Capita of 66 Developing Countries as Percentage of that of USA

Country	*1980*	*1990*	*2000*	*2004*
(1)	*(2)*	*(3)*	*(4)*	*(5)*
USA (US $)	12980	23330	34400	41440
Algeria (Percentages)	15.87	10.37	4.56	5.48
Argentina	22.65	13.67	21.72	8.64
Bangladesh	1.69	1.29	1.13	1.06
Benin	3.00	1.41	0.99	1.09
Bolivia	4.55	3.17	2.91	2.32
Brazil	16.87	11.87	10.44	7.24
Bulgaria	15.49	9.69	4.65	6.64
Burkina Faso	2.39	1.50	0.73	0.84
Burundi	1.69	0.90	0.32	0.22
Cameroon	4.78	4.11	1.69	1.95
Central African Republic	2.62	1.97	0.78	0.75
Chad	1.77	1.11	0.52	0.60
Chile	17.26	9.34	14.13	12.60
China	1.69	1.37	2.70	3.62
Colombia	9.17	5.10	5.99	4.87
Congo, Rep.	6.32	3.77	1.51	1.83
Costa Rica	15.25	7.59	10.76	10.79
Cote d'Ivoire	8.63	3.13	1.89	1.83
Dominican Republic	8.94	3.77	6.31	5.07
Ecuador	10.94	3.81	3.90	5.33
Egypt, Arab Rep.	3.85	3.26	4.24	3.02
El Salvador	5.86	3.99	5.81	5.60
Gabon	36.90	20.49	8.98	9.85
Gambia, The	2.85	1.33	0.93	0.68
Ghana	3.16	1.63	0.96	0.92
Guatemala	9.17	4.07	5.06	5.28
Haiti	2.08	1.67	1.42	1.23
Honduras	5.39	3.04	2.50	2.51
India	2.08	1.67	1.31	1.50
Indonesia	3.85	2.66	1.72	2.75
Iran, Islamic Rep.	17.33	11.10	4.85	5.60

(Contd.)

TABLE 8.2 (*Contd.*)

(1)	*(2)*	*(3)*	*(4)*	*(5)*
Jamaica	9.48	7.67	8.55	7.96
Jordan	15.41	5.96	5.12	5.28
Kenya	3.54	1.63	1.25	1.16
Madagascar	3.39	0.99	0.70	0.70
Malawi	1.46	0.77	0.44	0.39
Malaysia	14.10	10.37	9.97	10.91
Mali	1.93	1.11	0.64	0.80
Mauritius	9.32	9.86	10.73	11.20
Mexico	19.41	12.13	14.85	16.39
Morocco	7.47	4.41	3.55	3.79
Nepal	1.08	0.86	0.64	0.60
Nicaragua	4.93	1.41	2.18	2.00
Niger	3.00	1.20	0.47	0.51
Nigeria	6.24	1.20	0.81	1.04
Oman	29.66	24.05	19.22	21.89
Pakistan	2.54	1.80	1.40	1.45
Panama	12.48	9.47	10.87	10.16
Papua New Guinea	6.01	3.56	1.89	1.35
Paraguay	11.33	5.10	4.24	2.75
Peru	8.09	3.30	5.96	5.69
Philippines	5.32	3.17	3.02	2.82
Senegal	3.85	2.83	1.31	1.52
South Africa	19.34	14.53	8.87	8.76
Sri Lanka	2.16	2.01	2.35	2.44
Sudan	3.47	2.36	0.90	1.28
Syrian Arab Republic	12.02	3.77	2.65	2.97
Thailand	5.62	6.60	5.78	6.01
Togo	3.16	1.63	0.78	0.75
Trinidad and Tobago	39.75	15.99	15.20	21.07
Tunisia	10.48	6.13	6.05	6.39
Turkey	14.79	9.73	8.66	9.05
Uganda	2.31	1.37	0.76	0.60
Uruguay	22.03	12.30	17.88	9.41
Venezuela, RB	32.36	11.02	11.92	9.72
Zambia	4.62	1.80	0.84	0.97

Source : Calculated from data given in World Development Indicators; Various Issues.

TABLE 8.3

GNI Per Capita of 66 Developing Countries as Percentage of that of Top Country of the Group (Oman)

Country	*1980*	*1990*	*2000*	*2004*
(1)	*(2)*	*(3)*	*(4)*	*(5)*
Oman (US $)	3850	5610	6610	9070
Algeria (Percentages)	53.51	43.14	23.75	25.03
Argentina	76.36	56.86	113.01	39.47
Bangladesh	5.71	5.35	5.90	4.85
Benin	10.13	5.88	5.14	4.96
Bolivia	15.32	13.19	15.13	10.58
Brazil	56.88	49.38	54.31	33.08
Bulgaria	52.21	40.29	24.21	30.32
Burkina Faso	8.05	6.24	3.78	3.86
Burundi	5.71	3.74	1.66	0.99
Cameroon	16.10	17.11	8.77	8.93
Central African Republic	8.83	8.20	4.08	3.42
Chad	5.97	4.63	2.72	2.76
Chile	58.18	38.86	73.52	57.55
China	5.71	5.70	14.07	16.54
Colombia	30.91	21.21	31.16	22.27
Congo, Rep.	21.30	15.69	7.87	8.38
Costa Rica	51.43	31.55	55.98	49.28
Cote d'Ivoire	29.09	13.01	9.83	8.38
Dominican Republic	30.13	15.69	32.83	23.15
Ecuador	36.88	15.86	20.27	24.37
Egypt, Arab Rep.	12.99	13.55	22.09	13.78
El Salvador	19.74	16.58	30.26	25.58
Gabon	124.42	85.20	46.75	44.98
Gambia, The	9.61	5.53	4.84	3.09
Ghana	10.65	6.77	4.99	4.19
Guatemala	30.91	16.93	26.32	24.15
Haiti	7.01	6.95	7.41	5.62
Honduras	18.18	12.66	13.01	11.47
India	7.01	6.95	6.81	6.84
Indonesia	12.99	11.05	8.93	12.57
Iran, Islamic Rep.	58.44	46.17	25.26	25.58

(Contd.)

TABLE 8.3 (*Contd.*)

(1)	(2)	(3)	(4)	(5)
Jamaica	31.95	31.91	44.48	36.38
Jordan	51.95	24.78	26.63	24.15
Kenya	11.95	6.77	6.51	5.29
Madagascar	11.43	4.10	3.63	3.20
Malawi	4.94	3.21	2.27	1.76
Malaysia	47.53	43.14	51.89	49.83
Mali	6.49	4.63	3.33	3.64
Mauritius	31.43	41.00	55.82	51.16
Mexico	65.45	50.45	77.31	74.86
Morocco	25.19	18.36	18.46	17.31
Nepal	3.64	3.57	3.33	2.76
Nicaragua	16.62	5.88	11.35	9.15
Niger	10.13	4.99	2.42	2.32
Nigeria	21.04	4.99	4.24	4.74
Pakistan	8.57	7.49	7.26	6.62
Panama	42.08	39.39	56.58	46.42
Papua New Guinea	20.26	14.80	9.83	6.17
Paraguay	38.18	21.21	22.09	12.57
Peru	27.27	13.73	31.01	26.02
Philippines	17.92	13.19	15.73	12.90
Senegal	12.99	11.76	6.81	6.95
South Africa	65.19	60.43	46.14	40.02
Sri Lanka	7.27	8.38	12.25	11.14
Sudan	11.69	9.80	4.69	5.84
Syrian Arab Republic	40.52	15.69	13.77	13.56
Thailand	18.96	27.45	30.11	27.45
Togo	10.65	6.77	4.08	3.42
Trinidad and Tobago	134.03	66.49	79.12	96.25
Tunisia	35.32	25.49	31.47	29.22
Turkey	49.87	40.46	45.08	41.35
Uganda	7.79	5.70	3.93	2.76
Uruguay	74.29	51.16	93.04	43.00
Venezuela, RB	109.09	45.81	62.03	44.43
Zambia	15.58	7.49	4.39	4.41

Source : Calculated from data taken from World Development Indicators; Various Issues.

throughout the period of study. For the remaining countries, the percentage of GNI per capita either decreased or there were fluctuations in the percentage. This indicates that convergence has not taken place even within the developing countries. However, if we examine the period of globalization, i.e. after 1990, then the GNI per capita of Chile, Costa Rica, Ecuador, El Salvador, Guatemala, Indonesia, Jamaica, Malaysia, Mauritius, Mexico, Panama, Peru, Trinidad and Tobago and Tunisia constituted increasing percentage of GNI per capita of Oman in 2004 as compared to in 1990. This may indicate some gain of globalization to these countries. The remaining developing countries do not indicate trend towards convergence even within the group.

HOGENDORN'S CONCEPT OF BRIDGING THE DEVELOPMENT GAP

Efforts were also made to study the phenomenon of development gap, i.e. whether this gap has narrowed or widened over time. An exercise was made following Hogendorn (1987) to examine whether the gap is widening or narrowing down. The absolute gap in income will increase whenever the ratio of per capita GNI of the target country to the country in question, is greater than inverse ratio of their growth rates, i.e.

$$\frac{Y_1}{Y_2} > \frac{r_2}{r_1}$$

where Y_1 is per capita GNI of the target country being followed and Y_2 is per capita GNI of the follower country and r_1 is rate of growth of GDP of the target country and r_2 is rate of growth of GDP of the follower country. The results of analysis are given in Appendices 8.1, 8.2 and 8.3 for the year 1990, Appendices 8.4, 8.5 and 8.6 for the year 2000 and Appendices 8.7, 8.8 and 8.9 for the year 2004.

Bridging of development gap has been examined for three groups of developing countries; low income, lower middle income and upper middle income countries separately by taking the highest income country of the same group as the target country. Appendix 8.1 shows that in 1990, out of the 36 low income countries taken up for analysis with Cameroon as target country, there was not even a single country in which case the development gap was bridging. Appendix 8.2 shows that in the year 1990, out of 26 lower middle income countries with Brazil taken as target country, there were 2 countries only in whose case the development gap was bridging, i.e. Bulgaria and Thailand. In case of upper middle income countries with Oman as target country in 1990, there was not even a single country for which the gap was bridging (Appendix 8.3).

Similarly in the year 2000, out of 38 low income countries there were only 3 countries (Lesotho, India and Papua New Guinea) for which development gap was bridging with Cote d'Ivoire as target country (Appendix 8.4). In case of lower middle income countries, out of 26 countries with Brazil as target country, development gap was bridging only in case of one country, i.e. Dominican Republic (Appendix 8.5). While Appendix 8.6 shows that development gap was bridging in none of the 18 upper middle income countries with Argentina as target country.

Development gap in the year 2004 was also examined for low income countries with Cameron as target country (Appendix 8.7). Of the 38 countries considered for analysis, development gap was bridging only in case of one country (India). It was only in case of lower middle income countries that the development gap was bridging for 12 countries (46 percent) with Brazil taken as target country (Appendix 8.8). These countries were Romania, Bulgaria, Tunisia, Thailand, Peru, Iran Islamic Republic, Algeria, Ecuador, Jordon, Morocco, China and Angola. For rest of 14 countries, the development gap was not bridging. Appendix 8.9 shows that out of 18 upper middle income countries with Oman taken as target country, there were 2 countries for which the development gap was bridging, i.e. Hungary and Trinidad and Tobago.

Hence, it was seen that in case of low income countries, there was no bridging of development gap during the period 1980-90, but the development gap was bridging in case of 3 countries during the period 1990-2000 and in case of only one country during the period 2000-04. The upper middle income countries presented a gloomy picture in respect of bridging of development gap as there was not even a single country during the period 1980-90 and 1990-2000 for which the gap was bridging. There were only 2 countries (Hungary and Trinidad and Tobago) in which case the development gap was bridging during the period 2000-04. On the other hand, in case of lower middle income countries, development gap was bridging in case of 2 countries during the period 1980-90, in case of only one country in the year 2000, but the number increased to 12 during the period 2000-04. Thus, in the overall period of study, the gap was not bridging in case of low income countries and upper middle income countries, but gap was seen to be bridging to some extent in case of lower middle income countries in the later period only.

COEFFICIENTS OF VARIATION OF DEVELOPMENT INDICATORS

Table 8.4 shows coefficients of variation of 22 development indicators for the year 1980, 1990, 2000 and 2004 worked out for 66 countries. It is seen that in the year 1980 and 1990, coefficient of variation was maximum in case of gross private capital flows (as % of GDP), followed international migration stock (as % of total population), physicians per thousand of population, fuel ore and metal exports (as % of merchandise exports) and energy use per capita (kg of oil equivalent). On the other hand, coefficients of variation were minimum in case of percentage of population of working age (15-64 years), life expectancy at birth, daily calorie supply (per capita), services value-added (as % of GDP) and gross capital formation (as % of GDP).

In the year 2000 and 2004, the coefficient of variation was maximum in case of international migration stock (as % of total population) followed by energy use per capita (kg. of oil equivalent), fuel ore and metal exports (as % of merchandise exports), GNI per capita (current US$) and physicians per thousand of population. On the contrary, coefficient of variation was minimum is case of percentage of population of working age (15-64 years) preceded by daily calorie supply (per capita), life expectancy at birth, services value-added (as % of GDP) and gross capital formation (as % of GDP).

Table 8.4
Coefficients of Variation of 22 Development Indicators for 66 Developing Countries

(*Percent*)

	1980	*1990*	*2000*	*2004*
Industry, value added (% of GDP)	44.34	37.62	40.67	39.17
Services, value added (% of GDP)	23.00	20.93	23.45	22.95
GNI per capita, (current US$)	93.13	93.38	103.27	101.01
GNI per capita, PPP (current international $)	75.39	71.97	75.77	76.24
Gross domestic savings (% of GDP)	84.44	59.03	75.89	53.69
Energy Use per capita (kg. of oil equivalent)	102.02	110.03	124.19	132.51
Fuel+ores and metal exports (% of merchandise exports)	106.09	113.94	114.05	109.44
Manufactures exports (% of merchandise exports)	98.88	83.04	80.71	77.90
Life expectancy at birth, total (years)	15.73	15.51	18.25	18.55
Percentage of population of working age (15-64 yrs.)	7.74	8.94	9.81	10.33
Employment in services (% of total employment)	52.49	52.60	46.42	44.22
Urban population (% of total)	51.39	46.71	43.11	42.09
Daily Calorie Supply (per capita)	16.41	15.94	16.10	17.08
Physicians (per 1,000 population)	127.20	114.46	93.12	89.01
International migration stock (% of population)	154.43	151.25	179.76	183.14
Gross private capital flows (% of GDP)	328.95	170.85	80.96	80.82
Gross capital formation (% of GDP)	33.49	35.37	28.84	25.10
Exports of goods and services (% of GDP)	62.62	58.67	61.67	55.33
Imports of goods and services (% of GDP)	49.57	52.60	47.63	43.02
Degree of Openness (Exports+Imports) % to GDP	52.20	53.17	51.81	43.37
Merchandise trade (% of GDP)	49.55	54.20	52.21	49.24
Trade in services (% of GDP)	68.48	73.51	60.38	58.49

Source : Worked out from data given in World Development Indicators; various issues.

It was also seen that coefficient of variation in case of gross private capital flows (as % of GDP), gross capital formation (as % of GDP), degree of openness, manufacture exports (as % of merchandise exports), physicians per thousand of population and urban population (as % of total population) decreased continuously throughout the period of study. Thus economic development in terms of these four variables indicated convergence within developing countries. On the other hand, coefficients of variation in case of energy use per capita (kg of oil equivalent) and percentage of population of working age (15-64 years) consistently increased throughout the period of study, indicating divergence among the developing countries in terms of these two indicators. On the whole, it appears that convergence has not taken place in the developing countries as the coefficients of variation in case of two most accepted indicators of development, i.e. GNI per capita and GNI per capita (PPP) indicated increasing trend.

Table 8.5 shows the results of simple regression analysis of 22 selected economic development indicators for the year 1980 with GDP growth rate (1980-2004) as dependent variable. The graphic presentation is shown in Appendix 8.10.

Table shows that regression coefficient of GNI per capita (current US $) was negative and non-significant showing some indication of convergence in terms of GNI per capita. However, in case of GNI per capita PPP, the coefficient was negative and significant showing clear-cut contribution of this indicator to convergence. It was also seen that the regression coefficients of indicators like services value added (% of GDP), daily calorie supply per capita, energy use per capita (kg. of oil equivalent), fuel, ore and metal exports (% of merchandise exports), employment in services (% of total), physicians (per 1000 people), exports of goods and services, imports of goods and services, degree of openness, gross private capital flows, merchandise trade and trade in services were negative and non-significant, showing some contribution of these indicators to convergence in growth. On the other hand, regression coefficients of indicators like industry value added, life expectancy at birth, population of working age, international migration stock, gross domestic savings, manufacture exports and gross capital formation were positive and non-significant

Table 8.5
Simple Regression Analysis with Growth Rate (1980-2004) as Dependent Variable

Variable (1980 Values)	*Constant*	*Regression Coefficient*	r^2	*F-Value*
(1)	(2)	(3)	(4)	(5)
GNI per capita	3.5637 (11.617)	-0.0002 (-1.263)	0.024	1.6
GNI per capita PPP	3.844 (11.284)	-0.0003* (-2.071)	0.063	4.29
Industry Value Added	3.2743 (6.256)	0.0002 (0.010)	0	0.0001
Services Value Added	4.7025 (5.059)	-0.0316 (-1.571)	0.037	2.47
Daily Calorie Supply	3.7073 (2.830)	-0.0002 (-0.331)	0.002	0.11
Energy use per capita	3.6761 (12.775)	-0.0006 (-1.953)	0.057	3.85
Fuel, ore and metal exports	3.3053 (11.370)	-0.0008 (-0.131)	0	0.02
Life Expectancy at Birth	2.0771 (1.529)	0.0211 (0.896)	0.012	0.8
Employment in Services	3.8534 (8.581)	-0.0186 (-1.442)	0.031	2.08
Population of Working Age	-0.5085 (-0.188)	0.0703 (1.402)	0.03	1.97
Physicians per 1000 people	3.4098 (12.740)	-0.256 (-0.787)	0.01	0.62
Urban Population	4.0873 (9.084)	-0.0212* (-2.016)	0.06	4.07
International Migration Stock	3.2283 (12.839)	0.0142 (0.369)	0.002	0.14
Gross Domestic Savings	3.2192 (9.812)	0.0035 (0.238)	0.001	0.06
Manufacture Exports	2.8948 (9.868)	0.0206 (1.835)	0.05	3.37
Exports of Goods and Services	3.3718 (8.448)	-0.0034 (-0.273)	0.001	0.07

(*Contd.*)

TABLE 8.5 (*Contd.*)

(1)	(2)	(3)	(4)	(5)
Imports of Goods and Services	3.2932 (6.896)	-0.0004 (-0.033)	0	0.0011
Degree of Openness	3.3463 (7.303)	-0.0011 (-0.165)	0	0.03
Gross Private Capital Flows	3.291 (14.931)	-0.0012 (-0.184)	0.001	0.03
Gross Capital Formation	2.6691 (4.023)	0.0267 (0.969)	0.014	0.94
Merchandise Trade	3.5027 (7.348)	-0.0046 (-0.523)	0.004	0.27
Trade in Services	3.4023 (9.083)	-0.0089 (-0.398)	0.002	0.16

Note : Figures in parentheses are t-values.
* Regression coefficient significant at 5 percent level.

showing some contribution of these indicators to divergence in growth. Out of 22 indicators, there were only two indicators, i.e. GNI per capita PPP and urban population in which case the regression coefficients were negative and significant showing that improvement in these indicators could lead to convergence in growth. On the whole, in the simple regression analysis, there was no clear indication of convergence or divergence in economic development of developing countries as the improvement in the indicators did not significantly contribute to convergence.

STEP-WISE (STEP-UP) REGRESSION ANALYSIS

Table 8.6 shows step-up regression analysis with 5 independent variables selected on the basis of correlation analysis with the dependent variable (GDP growth rate), i.e. gross capital formation (% of GDP), urban population (% of total population), GNI per capita PPP, services value added (% of GDP) and manufacture exports (% of merchandise exports). In the step-wise analysis, GDP growth rates for the years 1980-90, 1990-2000 and 2000-04 were taken as dependent variables. The independent variables were taken at initial year values.

Table shows that in the year 1980, when gross capital formation (% of GDP) alone was taken as independent variable, the regression coefficient was positive and non-significant showing that there was some indication of divergence in terms of gross capital formation. When the variable urban population (% of total population) was added as independent variable in the second step, coefficient of gross capital formation (% of GDP) was still positive and non-significant but that of urban population (% of total) was negative and significant showing clear-cut convergence in the economic development as a result of urbanization. Similarly, in the third step, GNI per capita PPP was included as independent variable in the regression. Coefficient of gross capital formation was still positive and non-significant showing some contribution of this variable in divergence in growth, but coefficients of both GNI per capita PPP and urban population were negative and non-significant showing some indication of convergence as a result of improvement in these two variables. In the fourth step of step-wise regression, coefficient of services value added (% of GDP) was negative and non-significant which shows some contribution of this variable in convergence. In the fifth step, manufacture exports (% of merchandise exports) was included as fifth variable. In this step, coefficients of gross capital formation, urban population, GNI per capita PPP and services value added continued showing similar results as in the previous steps. However, the coefficient of manufacture exports was positive and significant showing its contribution to divergence in growth. This also indicates that structure of exports is important for rapid growth. The countries with higher share of manufacture exports could experience rapid growth rate of GDP.

Similarly, in the year 1990, GDP growth rate was taken as dependent variable alongwith gross capital formation as independent variable in the first step of step-wise regression analysis. Coefficient of gross capital formation was positive and significant showing clear-cut divergence in terms of gross capital formation. In the second step, urban population was included as independent variable, coefficient of which was negative and non-significant showing some indication of convergence as a result of urbanization, but coefficient of gross

TABLE 8.6
Step-up Regression Analysis with Growth Rate as Dependent Variable

(A) Step-up Regression Analysis 1980 (Growth Rate for 1980-90)

	Constant	*Gross Capital Formation*	*Urban Population*	*GNI Per capita PPP*	*Services Value Added*	*Manufacture Exports*	R^2	*Adjusted* R^2	*F-Value*
(1)	*(2)*	*(3)*	*(4)*	*(5)*	*(6)*	*(7)*	*(8)*	*(9)*	*(10)*
Step 1	2.315 (2.538)	0.018 (0.480)					0.004	-0.012	0.232
Step 2	3.248 (3.586)	0.053 (1.434)	-0.046* (-3.130)				0.138	0.11	5.032
Step 3	2.993 (3.212)	0.062 (1.632)	-0.026 (-1.188)	0.0003 (-1.128)			0.155	0.114	3.793
Step 4	4.845 (3.522)	0.064 (1.703)	-0.008 (-0.310)	-0.001 (-1.514)	-0.053 (-1.804)		0.198	0.145	3.761
Step 5	4.194 (3.234)	0.065 (1.858)	-0.013 (-0.551)	-0.001 (-1.612)	-0.053 (-1.938)	0.044* (3.210)	0.315	0.258	5.529

(Contd.)

TABLE 8.6 (Contd.)

(B) Step-up Regression Analysis 1990 (Growth Rate for 1990-2000)

	Constant	*Gross Capital Formation*	*Urban Population*	*GNI Per capita PPP*	*Services Value Added*	*Manufacture Exports*	R^2	*Adjusted* R^2	*F-Value*
(1)	*(2)*	*(3)*	*(4)*	*(5)*	*(6)*	*(7)*	*(8)*	*(9)*	*(10)*
Step 1	1.772 (2.416)	0.088* (2.570)					0.094	0.079	6.605
Step 2	1.891 (2.112)	0.088* (2.557)	-0.003 (-0.235)				0.094	0.066	3.282
Step 3	1.857 (1.981)	0.089* (2.504)	-0.001 (-0.044)	-0.0002 (-0.137)			0.095	0.051	2.16
Step 4	0.626 (0.445)	0.088* (2.490)	-0.006 (-0.325)	-0.0001 (-0.179)	0.032 (1.169)		0.114	0.056	1.971
Step 5	0.862 (0.606)	0.072 (1.868)	-0.005 (-0.248)	-0.0001 (-0.274)	0.026 (0.936)	0.013 (1.065)	0.131	0.058	1.808

(C) Step-up Regression Analysis 2000 (Growth Rate for 2000-04)

	Constant	*Gross Capital Formation*	*Urban Population*	*GNI Per capita PPP*	*Services Value Added*	*Manufacture Exports*	R^2	*Adjusted* R^2	*F-Value*
(1)	*(2)*	*(3)*	*(4)*	*(5)*	*(6)*	*(7)*	*(8)*	*(9)*	*(10)*
Step 1	1.083 (1.024)	0.123* (2.457)					0.086	0.072	6.036
Step 2	2.216 (2.238)	0.131* (2.745)	-0.035* (-2.622)				0.176	0.15	6.734
Step 3	2.674 (2.245)	0.130* (2.699)	-0.039* (-2.089)	0.0004 (0.324)			0.178	0.138	4.46
Step 4	2.858 (1.753)	0.130* (2.674)	-0.038* (-1.991)	0.0001 (0.353)	-0.005 (-0.167)		0.178	0.124	3.3
Step 5	2.759 (1.690)	0.142* (2.843)	-0.045* (-2.210)	0.0001 (0.649)	0.004 (0.127)	-0.011 (-1.037)	0.192	0.125	2.858

Note : Figures in the parentheses are t-values.
* Regression coefficient significant at 5 percent level.

capital formation was still positive and significant showing divergence as a result of improvement in this variable. GNI per capita PPP was included as independent variable in the third step. Coefficient of gross capital formation was positive and significant indicating divergence in terms of gross capital formation but coefficients of urban population and GNI per capita PPP were negative and non-significant showing some indication of convergence as a result of improvement in these two variables. In the fourth step, services value added (% of GDP) was added as independent variable. Coefficient of gross capital formation was positive and significant, the coefficient of services value added was positive but non-significant showing some contribution of this variable in divergence. On the other hand, coefficient of GNI per capita PPP was negative and non-significant showing some indication of convergence as a result of improvement in this variable but coefficient of urban population was negative and significant showing clear-cut convergence in terms of increase in urban population. In the fifth step, manufacture exports (% of merchandise exports) was added as independent variable. Coefficients of gross capital formation, services value added and manufacture exports were positive and non-significant showing some contribution of these variables in divergence. On the other hand, coefficients of urban population and GNI per capita PPP were negative and non-significant showing some indication of convergence as a result of improvement in these two variables.

In the year 2000, gross capital formation was again taken as independent variable in the first step alongwith GDP growth rate. Coefficient of gross capital formation was positive and significant indicating clear-cut divergence in terms of gross capital formation. In the second step, urban population was included as independent variable. Coefficient of gross capital formation was still positive and significant showing clear-cut divergence, but coefficient of urban population was negative and significant showing clear-cut convergence as a result of urbanization. GNI per capita PPP was included as independent variable in the third step. Coefficient of gross capital formation was positive and significant showing clear-cut divergence in terms of gross capital formation and coefficient of GNI per capita PPP was positive and non-significant showing some contribution in divergence. But coefficient of urban population was negative and significant showing convergence as a result of urbanization. In the fourth step, services value added was added as independent variable. Gross capital formation showed same result as in previous step, but coefficient of GNI per capita PPP was positive and non-significant showing some indication of divergence as a result of improvement in this variable. Coefficient of services value added was negative and non-significant showing some contribution of this variable in convergence. But coefficient of urban population was negative and significant showing clear-cut convergence as a result of urbanization. In the fifth step, manufacture exports (% of merchandise exports) was added as independent variable. Again, coefficient of gross capital formation was positive and significant showing clear-cut divergence in terms of gross capital formation. Also, coefficients of GNI per capita PPP and services value added were positive and non-significant showing some contribution of these variables in divergence. But coefficient of urban population was negative and significant showing clear-cut convergence as a result of urbanization. On the other hand, coefficient of manufacture exports was negative and non-significant showing some indication of convergence as a result of improvement in manufacture exports.

Thus, throughout the period of study, there was no clear-cut indication of convergence or divergence in economic development of developing countries in the step-wise regression analysis. Some variables led to convergence but others led to divergence in growth.

On the whole, this indicates that globalization has not helped the developing countries to 'catch-up' the developed countries. Not to speak of convergence between developed and developing countries, convergence has not taken place even among the developing countries. No clear cut trend towards convergence was seen within the developing countries. The gap was not bridging in case of the low income and upper middle income countries. The gap was bridging to some extent only in case of lower middle income countries in the later period only.

SECTION II

In developing countries, economic growth is the principal objective in policy-making and designing investment projects. However, growth may be fluctuating and may not be stable over a longer period. A relatively lower but stable growth is better than highly fluctuating one which may indicate poor foundations of growth. Hence, stability in growth is an important aspect which needs examination in the context of globalization, i.e. whether globalization has promoted stability in growth or not.

CORRELATION ANALYSIS

Coefficients of correlation were worked out between the GDP growth rates during the different sub-periods of study i.e. 1980-90, 1990-2000, 1980-2000, 2000-04, 1990-04 and 1980-2004 to examine the stability in the growth rates. GDP growth rates of 66 developing countries for different time periods and overall period are given in Appendix 8.11. Table 8.7 shows correlation coefficients between GDP growth rates of different time periods.

It was seen that the correlation coefficient of GDP growth rates of the periods 1980-90 and 1990-2000 was 0.317 and that for the periods 1980-90 and 2000-04 was 0.423. Also, the correlation coefficients of GDP growth rates for the periods 1980-90 and 1990-2004 was 0.458. The correlation coefficient of the growth rates for the periods 1980-90 and the overall period of study (1980-2004) was 0.824, which shows improvement in the stability of growth rate. The correlation of the growth rates for the periods 1990-2000 and the overall period of study was 0.711, indicating that globalization has led to stability in growth.

RANK CORRELATION ANALYSIS

Countries were ranked in different time periods, i.e. 1980, 1990, 2000 and 2004; on the basis of different measures of economic development like Composite Index (CINDEX), GNI per capita, GNI PPP and PQLI and the results have been shown in Chapter 7 (Tables 7.10, 7.11, 7.12 and 7.13).

Table 8.7
Correlation Matrix of GDP Growth Rates

	GDP Growth 1980-2004	*GDP Growth 1980-90*	*GDP Growth 1990-2000*	*GDP Growth 2000-04*	*GDP Growth 1980-2000*	*GDP Growth 1990-2004*
(1)	*(2)*	*(3)*	*(4)*	*(5)*	*(6)*	*(7)*
GDP Growth 1980-2004	1	.824**	.711**	.609**	.971**	.845**
GDP Growth 1980-90		1	.317**	.423**	.834**	.458**
GDP Growth 1990-2000			1	.277**	.754**	.904**
GDP Growth 2000-04				1	.453**	.631**
GDP Growth 1980-2000					1	.818**
GDP Growth 1990-2004						1

** Correlation is significant at the 0.01 level.

Table 8.8
Rank Correlations Between Ranks in Terms of Different Measures of Growth

	CINDX 1980	GNI 1980	GNIPPP 1980	PQLI 1980	CINDX 1990	GNI 1990	GNIPPP 1990	PQLI 1990	CINDX 2000	GNI 2000	GNIPPP 2000	PQLI 2000	CINDX 2004	GNI 2004	GNIPPP 2004	PQLI 2004
(1)	(2)	(3)	(4)	(5)	(6)	(7)	(8)	(9)	(10)	(11)	(12)	(13)	(14)	(15)	(16)	(17)
CINDX 1980	1	.860**	.795**	.734**	.936**	.827**	.779**	.628**	.888**	.838**	.739**	.644**	.835**	.829**	.729**	.554**
GNI 1980		1	.882**	.683**	.861**	.926**	.841**	.620**	.845**	.872**	.794**	.625**	.772**	.867**	.776**	.546**
GNIPPP 1980			1	.710**	.817**	.875**	.947**	.680**	.810**	.890**	.889**	.691**	.716**	.849**	.861**	.584**
PQLI 1980				1	.773**	.677**	.737**	.910**	.782**	.788**	.752**	.885**	.732**	.756**	.739**	.793**
CINDX 1990					1	.861**	.865**	.680**	.965**	.907**	.853**	.722**	.933**	.903**	.846**	.632**
GNI 1990						1	.906**	.633**	.861**	.922**	.872**	.647**	.801**	.923**	.861**	.557**
GNIPPP 1990							1	.701**	.878**	.938**	.972**	.731**	.805**	.916**	.960**	.623**
PQLI 1990								1	.713**	.723**	.713**	.946**	.654**	.687**	.704**	.900**
CINDX 2000									1	.922**	.886**	.763**	.967**	.923**	.887**	.647**
GNI 2000										1	.950**	.740**	.858**	.976**	.932**	.641**
GNIPPP 2000											1	.734**	.825**	.930**	.992**	.630**
PQLI 2000												1	.716**	.710**	.732**	.896**
CINDX 2004													1	.868**	.835**	.611**
GNI 2004														1	.926**	.624**
GNIPPP 2004															1	.631**
PQLI 2004																1

**Correlation is significant at the .01 level.

Attempt was made to examine stability of growth through Rank Correlation Analysis. Table 8.8 shows rank correlation coefficients of composite index, GNI per capita, GNI per capita PPP and Physical Quality of Life Index (PQLI) in different time periods. The rank correlations between all sets of measures were significant at one percent level of significance showing that there was not much difference in rankings of the countries in the different time periods, which indicates stability. The Table shows that rank correlation of composite index of 1980 with composite index of 1990 was 0.936. The rank correlation coefficient between composite indices for the years 1990 and 2000 was 0.965. Also, the rank correlation of composite index of 2000 with composite index of 2004 was 0.967. The increase in rank correlations indicates stability.

It was also seen that rank correlation of GNI per capita 1980 with GNI per capita of 1990 was 0.926. The rank correlation of GNI per capita in 1990 with that of 2000 slightly decreased to 0.922. But the rank correlation of GNI per capita during the periods 2000 and 2004 increased to 0.976, again showing stability in growth in terms of GNI per capita.

In case of GNI per capita PPP, the rank correlation of the variable between the periods 1980 and 1990 was 0.947, between the periods 1990 and 2000 was 0.972. The rank correlation of GNI per capita PPP for the periods 2000 and 2004 was 0.992. Thus, increase in the rank correlation in the subsequent time periods indicated stability in growth in terms of GNI per capita PPP.

In case of PQLI, the rank correlation of the Index between the periods 1980 and 1990 was 0.910, which increased to 0.946 for the periods 1990 and 2000. The rank correlation coefficient of PQLI for the periods 2000 and 2004 was 0.896.

Thus, the rank correlation analysis also indicated stability of growth in terms of different measures of growth. The stability largely improved during the globalization

FASTEST AND SLOWEST GROWING COUNTRIES

Table 8.9 shows fastest and slowest growing countries, selected on the basis of growth rate of GDP 1980-2004. Table shows GDP growth rate of different time periods, i.e. 1980-2004,

TABLE 8.9
Countries with Fastest and Slowest Growth Rates During 1980-2004

(a) Fastest Growing Countries, GDP (Average Annual % Growth)

Sl. No.	Country Name	1980-2004	1980-90	1990-2000	2000-04
1.	China	9.73	10.30	10.60	9.40
2.	Oman	6.33	8.40	4.50	3.00
3.	Malaysia	6.29	5.30	7.00	4.40
4.	Thailand	6.05	7.60	4.20	5.40
5.	India	5.78	5.70	6.00	6.20
6.	Uganda	5.43	2.90	7.10	5.80
7.	Indonesia	5.41	6.10	4.20	4.60
8.	Mauritius	5.35	6.00	5.20	4.40
9.	Chad	5.35	6.10	1.90	14.10
10.	Pakistan	5.16	6.30	3.80	4.10
11.	Chile	5.10	4.20	6.60	3.70
12.	Egypt, Arab Rep.	4.97	5.40	4.70	3.40
13.	Jordan	4.63	2.50	5.00	5.50
14.	Sri Lanka	4.55	4.00	5.30	3.70

(b) Slowest Growing Countries, GDP (Average Annual % Growth)

Sl. No.	Country Name	1980-2004	1980-90	1990-2000	2000-04
(1)	(2)	(3)	(4)	(5)	(6)
1.	Haiti	-0.33	-0.20	-1.50	-0.40
2.	Central African Republic	0.76	1.40	2.00	-2.00
3.	Cote d'Ivoire	0.76	0.70	3.30	-0.70
4.	Venezuela, RB	1.25	1.10	1.60	-1.20
5.	Madagascar	1.32	1.10	2.00	0.90
6.	Bulgaria	1.35	3.40	-1.80	4.80
7.	Niger	1.36	-0.10	2.40	4.10
8.	Nicaragua	1.50	-1.90	3.70	2.50
9.	Uruguay	1.53	0.50	3.40	-1.20

(Contd.)

TABLE 8.9 (Contd.)

(1)	(2)	(3)	(4)	(5)	(6)
10.	El Salvador	1.55	0.20	4.80	1.90
11.	Jamaica	1.56	2.00	0.90	1.50
12.	Zambia	1.58	1.00	0.50	4.40
13.	Argentina	1.59	-0.70	4.30	-0.10
14.	Burundi	1.69	4.40	-2.60	2.70
15.	Trinidad and Tobago	1.89	-3.30	3.20	7.20
16.	Bolivia	1.94	-0.20	4.00	2.60
17.	Peru	2.10	-0.10	4.60	3.70
18.	South Africa	2.13	1.00	2.10	3.20
19.	Gabon	2.20	0.90	2.80	1.60
20.	Togo	2.45	1.70	3.50	2.60
21.	Brazil	2.45	2.70	2.90	2.00
22.	Ecuador	2.48	2.10	1.90	4.20

Source : World Development Indicators; Various Issues.

1980-90, 1990-2000 and 2000-04. Countries were divided into three categories; fastest, medium and slowest growing countries using Cumulative Frequency Cube-Root method. Accordingly, the countries with growth rate higher than 4.50 percent were categorized as fastest growing, between 4.50 and 2.50 percent as medium and below 2.50 percent as slowest growing countries. The results showed that out of 66 countries, 14 were fastest growing and 22 were slowest growing countries. Out of 14 countries, it was seen that China was the fastest growing country followed by Oman, Malaysia, Thailand and India. It was seen that almost all the fastest growing countries in the overall period were also in the same category in other time periods, which shows stability in the growth rates. In the period 1980-90, two countries, i.e. Uganda and Jordan experienced low growth rates, but their growth rates were higher in 1990-2000 and 2000-04, so they fell in the category of fastest growing country on the basis of growth rate of overall period. Similarly, in the period 1990-2000, Chad and Pakistan were not fastest growing countries but their growth rates were high enough in 1980-90 and 2000-04, so on the basis of overall period growth rate, these were included in the category of fastest growing countries. Also, in the period 2000-04, countries like Oman, Chile, Egypt Arab Republic and Sri Lanka experienced lower growth rates as compared to other countries but their growth in other periods were high. Thus, even when there were exceptions, broadly some stability is indicated.

The Table also shows 22 slowest growing countries during 1980-2004 out of which Haiti had the negative growth rate preceded by Central African Republic, Cote d'Ivoire, Venezuela RB and Madagascar. It was seen that most of the slowest growing countries in the overall period were in the same category in the other time periods, showing stability in the growth rates. Although, growth rate of Burundi was high during the period 1980-90, but it was included in the slowest growing countries as its growth rate in other periods was very low. Similarly, in the period 1990-2000, El Salvador, Argentina, Bolivia and Peru experienced higher growth rates, but their growth rates in other periods were low enough to make them fall in the category of slowest growing countries. Also, it was seen that in the period 2000-04, countries like Bulgaria, Niger, Zambia, Trinidad and Tobago and Ecuador experienced high growth rates, but were included in slowest growing countries on the basis of growth rates during other periods.

Correlation coefficients of growth rate of periods 1980-90, 1990-2000 and 2000-04 with that of 1980-2004 (overall period), were 0.788, 0.694 and 0.388. Thus, the correlation coefficients of growth rate of all periods, except 2000-04, were high and significant with growth rate of overall period. This indicates that there was some indication of stability in the growth of fastest growing countries.

On the other hand, in case of slowest growing countries, correlation coefficients of growth rates of periods 1980-90, 1990-2000 and 2000-04 with that of 1980-2004 (overall period), were 0.141, 0.389 and 0.516. Thus, the correlation coefficients of growth rate of all periods, except 2000-04, were low and non-significant with growth rate of overall period. This indicates that there was not much stability in growth rate of slowest growing countries. However, there was some improvement in stability of growth over time.

STABILITY OF REGRESSION PARAMETERS (CHOW TEST)

Chow Test was applied to examine the stability in regression parameters of different time periods. Those variables were selected for this analysis whose correlation coefficients were high and significant with GDP growth rate. GDP growth rate was taken as dependent variable (Y) alongwith gross capital formation (% of GDP) (X_1), urban population (% of total) (X_2), GNI per capita PPP (X_3), services value added (% of GDP) (X_4) and manufacture exports (% of merchandise exports) (X_5) as independent variables.

For checking stability of regression parameters of the period 1980-1990, following regression equations were obtained:

For 1980;

$Y_1 = 4.19 + 0.06X_1 - 0.01X_2 - 0.001X_3 - 0.05X_4 + 0.04X_5 + u_1$ ($n_1 = 66$) (Eq. 1)

For 1990;

$Y_2 = 0.86 + 0.07X_1 - 0.04X_2 - 0.001X_3 + 0.03X_4 + 0.01X_5 + u_2$ ($n_2 = 66$) (Eq. 2)

Pooled for 1980-90;

$Y_3 = 3.11 + 0.03X_1 - 0.02X_2 + 0.002X_3 - 0.01X_4 + 0.03X_5 + u_3$ ($n_1+n_2=132$) (Eq. 3)

Chow F-Statistics for the period 1980-90 was 3.1858, which was greater than tabulated value of F-Statistic and null hypothesis was rejected. Thus, the regression parameters in the period 1980-90 were instable.

For checking stability of regression parameters of the period 1980-2000, following regression equations were obtained:

For 1980;

$Y_1 = 4.19 + 0.06X_1 - 0.01X_2 - 0.001X_3 - 0.05X_4 + 0.04X_5 + u_1$ ($n_1 = 66$) (Eq. 1)

For 2000;

$Y_2 = 2.75 + 0.14X_1 - 0.04X_2 + 0.001X_3 + 0.003X_4 - 0.01X_5 + u_2$ ($n_2 = 66$) (Eq. 2)

Pooled for 1980-2000;

$Y_3 = 3.95 + 0.05X_1 - 0.03X_2 + 0.0008X_3 - 0.02X_4 + 0.01X_5 + u_3$ ($n_1+n_2=132$) (Eq. 3)

Chow F-Statistics for the period 1980-2000 was 4.0697, which was greater than tabulated value of F-Statistic and null hypothesis was rejected. Thus, the regression parameters in the period 1980-2000 were instable.

For checking stability of regression parameters of the period 1990-2000, following regression equations were obtained:

For 1990;

$Y_1 = 0.86 + 0.07X_1 - 0.04X_2 - 0.001X_3 + 0.03X_4 + 0.01X_5 + u_2$ $(n_2 = 66)$ (Eq. 1)

For 2000;

$Y_2 = 2.75 + 0.14X_1 - 0.04X_2 + 0.001X_3 + 0.003X_4 - 0.01X_5 + u_2$ $(n_2 = 66)$ (Eq. 1)

Pooled for 1990-2000;

$Y_3 = 1.90 + 0.10X_1 - 0.02X_2 - 0.0005X_3 + 0.01X_4 - 0.007X_5 + u_3$ $(n_1+n_2=132)$ (Eq. 3)

Chow F-Statistiçs for the period 1990-2000 was 1.1450, which was smaller than tabulated value of F-Statistic and null hypothesis was not rejected. Thus, the regression parameters in the period 1990-2000 were stable.

Table 8.10 shows that in the period 1980-90 and 1980-2000, the regression coefficients were instable. On the other hand, the regression coefficients for the period 1990-2000 were stable. This shows that in the era of globalization, i.e. 1990-2000, the coefficients were stable.

TABLE 8.10
Testing Stability of Regression Parameters: Chow Test

Sl. No.	*Comparison Years*	*Chow F-Statistics*	*Decision about Null-Hypothesis*	*Stability/Instability of Regression Coff.*
1.	1980-90	3.1858	Rejected	Instable
2.	1980-2000	4.0697	Rejected	Instable
3.	1990-2000	1.1450	Not Rejected	Stable

Note : All values are compared with the tabulated value of F obtained for $V_1 = 6$ and $V_2 = 120$ degrees of freedom and at 5 percent level of significance.

Thus, broadly, the analysis showed stability in growth variables. The correlation analysis showed stability in growth rates. In rank correlation analysis, stability was seen in ranks although there were some fluctuations. It was also seen that most of the fastest and slowest growing countries in the overall period were in the same category in the other time periods, which shows stability in the growth rates. It also showed that stability was more in fastest growing countries as compared to slowest growing countries. Results of Chow test showed that there was stability in regression parameters during the period of globalization.

Summary and Conclusions

Globalization—the integration of the world economy—has been a widely debated theme in the past two decades or so. It is associated with increasing economic openness, growing economic interdependence and deepening governance at global level. The process has brought about profound changes in the international context which have far reaching implications. The growth of cross-border economic activity has changed the structure of economies and the political and social organization of countries. However, not all effects of globalization can be measured directly.

Many factors have accelerated the pace of globalization. Barriers to international trade and investment are coming down. Technological progress has dramatically cut transportation and communication costs, enabling production processes and distribution networks to move from local to global. Some previously non-tradable services can now be traded easily around the world. Efficiency gains due to resource allocation at global scale have made globalization an increasingly powerful source of growth. Under globalization, the changes in one country have effects on others immediately. Globalization has important bearing on growth, structural and demographic changes and the effect appears to have strengthened since early nineties.

In the above-mentioned context, the present study was undertaken to examine the relationship of Globalization and Economic Development and their correlates at four points of time, i.e. in early eighties, early nineties, early 2K and as at present and also to construct and compare alternative measures of economic development in this context. As the pace of globalization sharply increased during early nineties, the analysis of later periods' data could help in examining the impact of globalization on economic development of developing countries.

OBJECTIVES OF THE STUDY

The specific objectives of the study were:

1. To examine the relationship of structural and demographic variables with level of per capita income, particularly since early nineties.
2. To construct alternative measures of economic development on the basis of economic, structural and demographic variables.
3. To examine whether development levels are converging, especially since early nineties.
4. To establish relationship between rate of growth and level of growth and examine stability of rate of growth.
5. To bring out policy implications in the context of emerging pattern of development.

HYPOTHESES OF THE STUDY

In the light of the above mentioned objectives, the study attempts to test the following hypotheses:

1. Structural and demographic changes have taken place with economic growth in the developing countries.
2. Different measures of economic development are consistent with each other.
3. There is a positive impact of globalization on the

economic development of developing countries.

4. Globalization has led to convergence between the developing and developed countries, and also within the developing countries.
5. Globalization has led to stability in the growth rate of the developing countries.

PLAN OF THE STUDY

To meet the objectives, the study was organized in nine chapters. The first chapter introduces the topic. The second chapter deals with the theoretical issues of globalization and economic development. The third chapter reviews the literature pertaining to various aspects of globalization and economic development. Data base and methodology used in the study have been described in the fourth chapter. The relationship between economic growth and structural changes has been established in fifth chapter, while that of economic growth and demographic changes has been taken up in the sixth chapter. The seventh chapter deals with the empirical investigation of the factors in economic development and presents a comparative study of different measures of economic development. The eighth chapter examines the issues of convergence and stability of rate of growth. The present chapter 9 presents the summary and brings out implications of the study.

DATA BASE AND METHODOLOGY

The nature of the study was such that it required secondary data regarding a number of variables concerning developing countries. The data were collected mainly from various World Bank publications such as World Tables, World Development Indicators, World Development Indicators (CD version), World Development Report, World Development Report (CD version), UNCTAD's Handbook of Statistics and UNDP's Human Development Report, etc. Attempts were made to collect data for maximum number of developing countries and for maximum number of variables since 1980. The number of countries varied between 66 and 113 in case of each variable, depending upon the availability of data and the number of countries for which data were available for different indicators increased since 1980. The technique of Interpolation and Extrapolation was used in case of a few of countries for some variables where data for some relevant years were not available.

The study covered the period of 1980 to 2004 (the latest year for which data were available). Keeping in view the long time-period and number of countries, the data was collected at four points of time viz. 1980, 1990, 2000 and 2004. Countries were categorized as developing countries on the basis of World Bank's grouping of countries.

The statistical techniques which were used to analyze the data included Tabular Analysis, Ratios, Percentages, Chi-Square Test, Correlation Analysis, Rank Correlation Analysis, Simple and Multiple Regression Analysis, Factor Analysis and Chow Test, etc.

MAIN FINDINGS

Globalization has many aspects such as economic, political, social, cultural etc., but this study focused mainly on economic globalization. The process of globalization accelerated during the last quarter of twentieth century. Essentially, there are four channels of globalization process through which there is interaction with the development process—trade in goods and services, movement of persons, financial flows and technological diffusion.

Trade dimension of globalization is the most prominent. In the past two decades or so growth in trade has outpaced the growth in production by at least a factor of two and this phenomenon is likely to sustain in the next two decades. Opening up to the international trade has helped many countries grow far more quickly than they would otherwise have done.

Migration is another widespread channel of globalization having bearing on countries of in-migration and out-migration alike. International migration of persons has increased rapidly in the past 20 years or so. The greatest beneficiaries of this migration are the migrants themselves and the sending countries. The migrants are not only the source of funds but also potential for change and innovation. Even when the issue of 'brain-drain' persists, but due to inability of the developing countries to absorb the technically trained, on the whole, international migration has benefited such countries.

Financial globalization, which refers to increasing global linkages created through cross-border financial flows, helped the developing countries in raising their growth rate. Opening to foreign direct investment has also brought important benefits, including knowledge about technologies and markets and an upgrading of the skills of domestic workers.

Technological innovations in the financial markets and their integration have changed the financial system of the world dramatically. Communication revolution, increased training and skills have increased the pace of diffusion, which have played significant role in productivity growth. The current effects of new technology have also given a distinctive character to the process of globalization. The natural barriers of time and space have been vastly reduced. The cost of moving information, people, goods and capital across the globe has fallen dramatically, while global communications is becoming cheap and instantaneous. This has vastly expanded the feasibility of economic transactions across the world. Markets are becoming global in scope with expanding range of goods and services.

As every coin has two sides, similarly, there are both positive and negative aspects of globalization. While globalization is a catalyst for and a consequence of economic development, it is also a messy process that creates significant challenges and problems. Concerns have emerged over equality of opportunity and the unequal distribution of benefits of globalization. Many poor countries and poor people in many countries have not been able to take full advantage of the opportunities brought by globalization and failed to reap adequate benefits from the process.

It is now increasingly recognized that the process of globalization entails significant risks and potentially large economic and social costs. Openness to global capital markets has brought greater volatility in domestic financial markets, particularly in countries whose financial systems were weak to begin with and economic policies lacked credibility. Large reversals in short-term capital flows (induced by the volatility of world capital markets) have led to severe financial crises and sharp increases in unemployment and poverty in the short run. Similarly, trade liberalization has led in some countries to reduce demand for unskilled labour (also for certain categories of skilled labours) and lower real wages in the short run; combined with a low degree of inter-sectoral labour mobility, job losses and income declines have often translated into higher poverty rates.

Thus, having pluses and minuses, globalization is an emerging and powerful global reality which has a momentum of its own. Some countries gained, some lost partly because of the prevailing political circumstances. Developing countries have to manage the process of globalization with a view to drive maximum benefits while minimizing the risks. It can potentially benefit developing countries directly and indirectly through cultural, social, scientific and technological changes as well as through trade and finance. A comprehensive approach towards globalization managed by good policies at country and global level can magnify the effects of growth promoting measures.

In the chapter on economic growth and structural changes, attempt was made to establish the relationship between level of growth and 30 selected structural indicators of developing countries. The developing countries were divided into 3 categories; low income countries, lower-middle income countries and upper-middle income countries, as classified by World Bank on the basis of gross national income per capita.

The majority of structural indicators included in the analysis showed significant association with level of growth of developing countries. As the trade dimension of globalization is most prominent, therefore, to examine the effect of globalization trends, the trade-related variables were examined. It was seen that the share of manufacture exports in merchandise exports increased over time especially during 1990-2004 period. On the other hand, the share of food and agriculture raw material in merchandise exports decreased. Thus, with globalization, the developing countries started exporting larger share of manufactured goods, though earlier these countries exported mainly the primary goods.

The exposure of developing countries to international trade picked up in 1990s, coinciding with their movement towards trade liberalization. It was also seen that the average annual growth rate of export volume and import volume were positively associated with level of economic growth during the period 1990-2000, which clearly showed the positive impact of globalization on developing countries. The export-GDP ratio and degree of openness were positively associated with level of economic growth. This showed that due to increased openness and major reductions in barriers to international trade, globalization has opened the door for export-led growth.

With globalization, the MNCs became more active and increased their area of work, and due to this there was a boost in services sector. Thus, services sector of developing countries developed more due to globalization. The trade in services increased at higher level of economic growth especially during the period of 1990s. At lower level of economic growth, the developing countries lagged behind in trade in services sector and there was predominance of agricultural sector in the trade. The study also brought out that the gross private capital flows and total debt service also showed positive association with level of economic growth, indicating that developing countries might have gained from private capital flows and external debt.

Net resource flows to developing countries, consisting official flows, direct investment, equity investment, bonds and others increased to $230.8 billion in 2001. While some components experienced cyclical fluctuations, foreign direct investment has remained largely independent of the cycles. During the nineties, private flows largely concentrated in middle-income countries while low-income countries have got a smaller share. However, still FDI creates positive impact through competition and linkage effects. It helps in raising level of technology, improves access to international markets and raises trade flows.

Technological innovations in the financial markets and their integration have changed the financial system of the world dramatically. With increasing share of developing countries in trade, the importance of their currencies has increased and some such currencies have been strengthened. Saving and investment rates in these countries have picked up. There is North-South and South-South flow of capital.

These changes in trade, FDI and financial flows are increasingly becoming part of a new systemic whole. An important factor is that all these elements necessarily evolved in the context of increasing economic openness and the growing influence of global market forces.

The analysis of various indicators confirmed that structural changes go along with economic development. Share of agriculture and level of growth were negatively associated showing that at higher levels of economic growth, the share of agriculture in GDP of developing countries declined. On the other hand, share of industry and services were positively associated with level of development. Thus, structural changes took place in developing countries and share of agricultural sector in GDP declined whereas that of industry and service sectors increased.

The study also showed that the sectoral shifts in labour force took place with time in the developing countries. Employment in agriculture and level of growth were negatively and significantly associated. On the other hand, employment in industry and services both were positively associated with level of growth. This shows that with economic growth, the labour force shifted from agricultural sector to industrial and services sectors showing that structural changes took place in developing countries.

GNI per capita (PPP), energy use per capita and daily calorie supply per capita were also positively associated with level of economic growth.

It can be concluded that there was positive impact of globalization on the relationship of economic growth and structural indicators and the relationship between economic growth and share of industry in GDP, share of services in GDP, gross domestic savings, energy use per capita, employment in industry, employment in services, etc. in the developing countries got strengthened after 1990s.

Economic development involves not only change in structure of output and employment, etc. but also an improvement in the quality of life of people. Economic development essentially affects living standards which have strong bearing on demographic aspects. For decades, economists and social thinkers have debated the influence of population change on economic growth and *vice-versa*. It is believed that economic growth affects, and is in turn, affected by demographic indicators. Thus, it was pertinent to examine the relationship of economic growth and demographic indicators.

The sixth chapter examined the relationship between economic growth and 11 selected demographic indicators of developing countries. The majority of these indicators showed significant association with level of growth of developing countries.

Number of physicians and life expectancy at birth showed positive and significant association with level of economic growth, showing that these increased with higher levels of economic growth in the developing countries. On the whole, the medical facilities improved at higher levels of economic growth.

A low death and infant mortality rates are signs of economic development. The birth rate, death rate and infant mortality rate were negatively associated with level of economic growth. Thus, birth rate, death rate and infant mortality rate declined with economic growth due to increased medical and other facilities in the developing countries. The relationship between population change and economic growth has assumed added importance in recent years because of demographic trends in the developing world. Developing countries have been undergoing demographic transition at varying rates, from high to low rates of mortality and fertility. This transition is producing a "boom" generation (working generation)—a generation that is larger in proportion than those immediately before and after it—that is gradually working its way through nations' age structures.

Also, working age population and level of growth were positively associated showing that population of working age increased at higher levels of economic growth and in turn might affect economic growth as well. People's economic behavior and needs vary at different stages of life, so changes in a country's age structure can have significant effect on its economic performance. Nations with a high proportion of children are likely to devote a high proportion of resources to their care, which tends to depress the pace of economic growth. By contrast, if larger proportion of a nation's population falls within the working age, the added productivity of this group can produce a "demographic dividend" of economic growth, assuming that policies to take the advantage of this are in place. In fact, the combined effect of this large working-age population and health, family, labor and human capital policies can effect virtuous cycles of wealth creation. And if a large proportion of a nation's population consists of the elderly, the effects can be similar to those of a very young population. A large share of resources is needed by a relatively less productive segment of the population, which likewise can inhibit economic growth.

The study showed that urban population and international migration stock were positively associated with level of growth. The industries and services sectors develop generally in urban areas, thus workers shift from rural areas to the urban areas and settle there. Similarly, skilled workers prefer to shift to developed countries as they find more employment opportunities and higher wages there. Due to globalization, this trend is increasing in developing countries and it got strengthened mainly after 1990.

The cross-border movement of people is a substantial and widespread phenomenon involving more than 10 million people a year over the past decade, as well as increasing number of countries. In some cases this movement has been temporary, while in other cases it has involved migration leading to permanent settlement. What was once a predominantly only South to North flow, now has a significant intra-developing country dimension also. These cross-border movements have occurred despite a tightening of immigration controls in the industrialized countries and (in contrast to the cross-border movement of goods, services and capital) without any concerted effort to promote it.

This pattern of migration is clearly linked to increasing globalization. Declining costs of transportation and the advent of cheap mass travel have greatly reduced one important barrier to movement. The ICT (Information and Communications Technology) revolution and the universal reach of the media have created fast diffusion of awareness about differences in living standards between rich and poor countries that has added to the allurement of migration. New market institutions have emerged which facilitate the process, in the shape of intermediaries and agents. Managers in the transnational enterprises move around the world for "shopping" overseas for specialized skills ("body-shopping"), and labour markets for some highly skilled professionals are effectively already global. The globalization of higher education systems has reinforced this trend.

The study showed that adult literacy rate, primary school enrolment ratio and secondary school enrollment ratio were also positively associated with level of economic growth throughout the period of study. This shows that with economic growth, the literacy rate increased in the developing world due to increased educational facilities. Under the impact of globalization the youth prefer to go in for higher studies in order to get jobs in MNCs as these require educated and skilled persons. Also, due to the sectoral changes with economic growth, demand of educated persons has increases in services sector.

There are other far-reaching ways in which globalization has touched the lives of people. The massive increase in global interconnectivity is affecting people's lives in different ways, some predictable and others unforeseen. One important change is an increase in global awareness. People anywhere are now much more aware of events and issues everywhere.

Thus, it can be concluded that globalization and economic development involved positive effects on education, health-related and other demographic indicators.

The seventh chapter involved empirical study of the factors in economic development. Also, economic development of developing countries was measured using different measures. Composite Index of economic development was developed using structural, demographic and social indicators.

The results of Factor Analysis showed that globalization has positive impact on economic development of developing countries. Indicators of globalization included variables like exports of goods and services, imports of goods and services, degree of openness, merchandise trade, trade in services, international migration stock and gross private capital flows. In 1980 and 1990, globalization-related variables collectively explained 26.689 percent and 27.407 percent of the variations.

But in 2000 and 2004, globalization-related variables explained 30.363 percent and 36.020 percent of the variations. This indicated increased role of globalization in economic development of developing countries.

Four measures of economic development, i.e. composite index, GNI per capita, GNI per capita PPP and PQLI were used to measure economic development of developing countries. The countries were ranked on the basis of these measures and their relative positions were compared when ranked with different measures. While comparing the relative positions of developing countries on the basis of composite index, GNI per capita, GNI per capita PPP and PQLI, it was seen that there was not marked differences in ranking of these countries.

Attempt was made to examine whether the ranks of the countries with different measures changed over time or not. It was seen that in 1980, the rank correlation coefficients ranged between 0.683 to 0.882 among the different measures. Similarly, the rank correlation coefficients ranged between 0.633 to 0.906 and 0.734 to 0.950 for the years 1990 and 2000 respectively. In the year 2004, the rank correlation coefficients ranged between 0.611 to 0.926. Thus, in all the years, the rank correlation coefficients were positive and significant at one percent level. This shows that results of different measures were consistent with each other and there was not marked differences in the ranks.

From the results of composite index, it can be seen that there were 16 countries (China, Ghana, Papua New Guinea, Congo Republic, Philippines, Thailand, Chad, El Salvador, Turkey, Nepal, Honduras, Sri Lanka, Dominican Republic, Morocco, Sudan and Uganda) whose ranks improved by 5 or more positions in 2004 as compared to 1990. Thus, these countries have been developing at a fast speed as compared to others. When examined in respect of globalization-related variables, it was found that all these variables improved sizably in these countries, which indicated that these countries gained from globalization.

An attempt was made to study the correlation of globalization, socio-economic and growth related variables with composite index of economic development in order to know the impact of globalization on economic development of developing countries. From correlation coefficients of composite index with 22 selected variables, it was seen that in the years 1980, 1990 and 2000, variables like GNI per capita, GNI per capita PPP, urban population (% of total) and life expectancy at birth were highly correlated with composite index of economic development. However, the correlation of globalization-related variables like manufacture exports (% of merchandise exports), international migration stock (% of population), gross private flows (% of GDP) and trade in services (% of GDP) with composite index was weak in the earlier years of study. But in 2004, GNI per capita, GNI per capita PPP, life expectancy at birth, percentage of population of working age, degree of openness (exports + imports % of GDP), exports of goods and services (% of GDP) and merchandise trade (% of GDP) were highly correlated with composite index of economic development. This clearly shows the positive impact of globalization on economic development of developing countries.

Also, the correlations of globalization related variables like imports of goods and services (% of GDP), exports of goods and services (% of GDP), degree of openness, merchandise trade (% of GDP), gross private capital flows (% of GDP) and trade in services (% of GDP) with composite index got strengthened throughout the period of study, clearly showing the increasing impact of globalization on economic development.

In eighth chapter, an attempt was made to find whether developing countries would be able to 'catch-up' with the developed countries and whether there is possibility of convergence even within the developing countries.

The study showed no trend towards convergence between developed and developing countries. The gap between the developed and developing countries is in fact increasing rather than decreasing, thus the developing countries have not been able to 'catch-up' with the developed countries. However, if we consider the period of globalization, i.e. the period after 1990, then the GNI per capita of all categories of developing countries (except low income category) as percentage of those of high income countries has increased. There appears some tendency towards convergence in case of these categories of countries after 1990. But the low income countries have lagged behind even during globalization.

Attempt was also made to find whether there has been convergence within the developing countries or not. The GNI per capita of 66 developing countries as percentage of a developing country with highest GNI per capita (in 2004), i.e. Oman was calculated. It was seen that only one country, i.e. China experienced increase in the percentage of GNI per capita throughout the period of study. For the remaining countries, the percentage of GNI per capita either decreased or there were fluctuations in the percentage. This indicates that convergence has not taken place even within the developing countries. However, if we examine the period of globalization, i.e. after 1990, then the GNI per capita of Chile, Costa Rica, Ecuador, El Salvador, Guatemala, Indonesia, Jamaica, Malaysia, Mauritius, Mexico, Panama, Peru, Trinidad and Tobago and Tunisia constituted increasing percentage of GNI per capita of Oman in 2004 as compared to in 1990. This may indicate some gain of globalization to these countries. The remaining developing countries do not indicate trend towards convergence even within the group.

Step-wise regression analysis was also applied to examine convergence in the developing countries. The results showed no clear-cut indication of convergence or divergence in economic development of developing countries. Some variables contributed towards convergence while others caused divergence in growth.

Efforts were also made to study the phenomenon of development gap, i.e. whether this gap has narrowed or widened over time. Bridging of development gap has been examined for three groups of developing countries; low income, lower middle income and upper middle income countries separately by taking the highest income country of the same group as the target country. It was seen that in case of low income countries, there was no bridging of development gap during the period 1980-90, but the development gap was bridging in case of 3 countries during the period 1990-2000 and in case of only one country during the period 2000-04. The upper middle income countries presented a gloomy picture in respect of bridging of development gap as there was not even a single country during the period 1980-90 and 1990-2000 for which the gap was bridging. There were only 2 countries (Hungary and Trinidad and Tobago) in which case the development gap was bridging during the period 2000-04. On the other hand, in case of lower middle income countries, development gap was bridging in case of 2 countries during the period 1980-90, in case of only one country during the period 1990-2000, but this number increased to 12 during the period 2000-04. Thus, in the overall period of study, the gap was not bridging in case of low income countries and upper middle income countries, but gap was seen to be bridging to some extent in case of lower middle income countries in the later period only.

In developing countries, economic growth is the principal objective in policy-making and designing investment projects. However, growth may be fluctuating and may not be stable over a longer period. A relatively lower but stable growth is better than highly fluctuating one which may indicate poor foundations of growth. Hence, stability in growth is an important aspect which needs examination in the context of globalization, i.e. whether globalization has promoted stability in growth or not.

Coefficients of correlation were worked out between the GDP growth rates of different countries during the different sub-periods of study, i.e. 1980-90, 1990-2000, 1980-2000, 2000-04, 1990-2004 and 1980-2004 to examine the stability in the growth rates. All the correlation coefficients were significant at one percent level. It was seen that the correlation coefficient of GDP growth rates of the periods 1980-90 and 1990-2000 was 0.317 and that for the periods 1980-90 and 2000-04 was 0.423. Also, the correlation coefficients of GDP growth rates for the periods 1980-90 and 1990-2004 was 0.458. The correlation coefficient of the growth rates for the periods 1980-90 and the overall period of study (1980-2004) was 0.824, which shows improvement in the stability of growth rate. The correlation of the growth rates for the periods 1990-2000 and the overall period of study was 0.711, indicating that globalization has led to stability in growth.

Attempt was made to examine stability of growth from different measures of growth through Rank Correlation Analysis. Rank correlation coefficients for the countries in case of composite index, GNI per capita, GNI per capita PPP and Physical Quality of Life Index (PQLI), for different time periods were worked out. The rank correlations between all sets of measures were significant at one percent level of significance showing that there was not marked difference in rankings of the countries in the different time periods, which indicates stability. Rank correlation of countries in case of composite index of 1980 with that of 1990 was 0.936. The rank correlation coefficient of composite index of countries for the years 1990 and 2000 was 0.965. Also, the rank correlation of countries between composite index of 2000 and 2004 was 0.967. The improvement in rank correlations indicates stability. Thus, the rank correlation analysis also indicated stability of growth in terms of different measures of growth. The stability largely improved during the globalization period.

Cumulative Frequency Cube-Root method was used to divide countries into three categories; fastest, medium and slowest growing countries. Accordingly, the countries with growth rate of 4.50 percent or higher were categorized as fastest growing, between 2.50 and 4.50 percent as medium and below 2.50 percent as slowest growing countries. The results showed that out of 66 countries, 14 were fastest growing and 22 were slowest growing countries.

Correlation coefficients of growth rate of the fastest growing countries for the periods 1980-90, 1990-2000 and 2000-04 with that of 1980-2004 (overall period), were 0.788, 0.694 and 0.388. Thus, the correlation coefficients of growth rate of all periods, except 2000-04, were high and significant with growth rate of overall period. This indicates that there was some indication of stability in the growth of fastest growing countries. However, this stability came down during 2000-04. On the other hand, in case of slowest growing countries, correlation coefficients of growth rates of periods 1980-90, 1990-2000 and 2000-04 with that of 1980-2004 (overall period), were 0.141, 0.389 and 0.516 respectively. Thus, the correlation coefficients of growth rate of all periods, except 2000-04, were low and non-significant with growth rate of overall period. This indicates that there was not much stability in growth rate of slowest growing countries. However, there was some improvement in stability of growth over time.

Chow Test was applied to examine the stability in regression parameters of different time periods. Those variables were selected whose correlation coefficients were high and significant with GDP growth rate. GDP growth rate was taken as dependent variable (Y) alongwith gross capital formation (% of GDP) (X_1), urban population (% of total) (X_2), GNI per capita PPP (X_3), services value added (% of GDP) (X_4) and manufacture exports (% of merchandise exports) (X_5) as independent variables.

Chow F-Statistics for the period 1980-90 and 1980-2000 were 3.1858 and 4.0697 respectively which were greater than tabulated value of F-Statistic and null hypothesis was rejected. Thus, the regression parameters for the periods 1980-90 and 1980-2000 were instable. Chow F-Statistics for the period 1990-2000 was 1.1450, which was smaller than tabulated value of F-Statistic and null hypothesis was accepted. Thus, the regression parameters in the period 1990-2000 were stable.

Thus, the study showed that in the period 1980-90 and 1980-2000, the regression coefficients were instable. On the other hand, the regression coefficients for the period 1990-2000 were stable. This shows that in the era of globalization, i.e. 1990-2000, the coefficients were stable.

It can be concluded that, broadly, there was improvement in stability in growth variables. The correlation analysis showed stability in growth rates. In rank correlation analysis, stability was seen in ranks although there were some fluctuations. It was also seen that most of the fastest and slowest growing countries in the overall period were in the same category in the other time periods, which shows stability in the growth rates. It also showed that stability was more in fastest growing countries as compared to slowest growing countries. Results of Chow test also showed that there was stability in regression parameters during the period of globalization.

Thus, on the whole, the study showed that, as globalization progressed, the structural and demographic changes took place at a relatively faster pace, which were favourable with economic development in developing countries. The study of demographic variables such as birth rate, death rate, infant mortality rate, life expectancy at birth, number of physicians, adult literacy rate, etc. proved that the living conditions have improved significantly in all the developing countries. But there is no clear-cut indication of convergence or divergence between developed and developing countries and also within developing countries. Also, the income gap is not bridging. However, the study showed that there is relative stability in growth rates of developing countries. The developing countries across the board have not been able to gain much in the process of globalization, some countries have gained while others have not. This may be partly due to their chosen policies and partly due to factors outside their control.

On the basis of the analysis carried out in the study, following hypotheses are accepted:

- Structural and demographic changes have taken place with economic growth in the developing countries.
- Different measures of economic development are consistent with each other.
- Globalization has led to stability in the growth rate of the developing countries.

The hypothesis of positive impact of globalization on economic development is not conclusively accepted or rejected as there are gainers and losers. The gains of globalization can be reaped if it is properly managed, which requires good governance. However, the hypothesis that 'globalization has led to convergence between developed and developing countries, and also within the developing countries' could not be accepted as the development gap in most of the cases widened.

POLICY IMPLICATIONS

Economic development is the primary objective of the majority of the world's nations. Economic development is necessary for underdeveloped countries because it helps them in solving the problems of general poverty, unemployment, backwardness and low standard of living. Development strategy may vary from one country to another, depending on the nature, structure and degree of interdependence among its primary, secondary and tertiary sectors. The nature and structure of developing countries are so diverse that it is not possible to provide a prescription that suites all the countries. It is essential to identify the political, social and institutional framework that imparts the necessary impetus to the overall development in general, especially in the context of globalization. On the basis of the review of theoretical and empirical studies, some broad observations are made in the succeeding paragraphs.

The recent trends in globalization have entailed expansion in the flow of goods, services, capital and technology. The globalization process driven by several forces is posing challenges to developing countries. With due attention to their problems, developing countries should manage the process of globalization with a view to drive maximum benefits while minimizing the risks. Globalization itself is neither good nor bad. It is like a two-edge sword, which can cut for you and also which can cut you, if not properly managed. Thus, governance is critical in the process of economic development.

In this era of increased role of markets under globalization, the role of the state is more critical and extends beyond correcting the market failures or regulating domestic markets. It should create the initial conditions to capture the benefits from globalization, manage the process of integration into the world economy in terms of pace and sequence, provide social protection and safeguard the vulnerable in the process of change and ensure that economic growth creates employment and livelihood for the people.

Thus, good governance, where government is accountable to citizens and people and is at the centre-stage in the process of development, is essential for creating capabilities, providing opportunities and ensuring rights for ordinary people. Indeed, the quality of governance is an important determinant of success or failure in the process of development.

In terms of global governance, there are hardly any international rules and international institutions governing cross-border movements of the people. Such cross-border movements are governed entirely by national immigration laws and consular practices. There should be exchange of information on surpluses and shortages between labour-exporting and labour-importing countries, which might ultimately provide the basis for the creation of an international labour exchange. Thus, it is essential to work towards a new institutional framework that could govern cross-border movements of people.

There is a need of World Financial Authority that would manage the systemic risks associated with international financial liberalization, coordinate national action against market failure and act as a regulator in international financial markets. Such an authority should have powers of regulation and surveillance. It should also have the ability to coordinate with central banks and the IMF when interventions may be needed from an international lender of the last resort. The activities of transnational corporations have expanded very rapidly, necessitating the creation of an international financial system of governance for transnational corporations.

Based on the present study, following specific policy recommendations are made:

1. Developing countries across the board have not gained from increasing integrated world; some of them might have been left behind due to their own structural weaknesses. Governments in these countries should steer the economy through proper regulatory policies, management of resources, institutional framework and overall good governance.
2. International organizations, such as the World Bank, WTO, IMF, bilateral aid agencies and NGOs should work with developing countries to lay foundation in these countries for global integration and to enable them to reap the benefits of globalization. In this regard, policies should be designed to strengthen international financial system and trade to help the developing countries so that there is bridging of development gap between developing and developed countries and also within developing countries.
3. As the development gap is not bridging, there is need of some drastic measures in view of exploitative and dominating attitude of the developed countries. One of reasons why developing countries could not gain much

from globalization is that the western countries have made poor countries eliminate trade barriers, but kept up their own barriers denying developing countries the access to their markets and depriving them of desperately needed export income. The developed countries should be made to reduce trade barriers and subsidies and make their markets accessible.

4. Realizing that poverty anywhere is threat to prosperity everywhere, the focus of developed countries should be on development in poor countries as partners in development so that they can 'catch-up' with the developed countries and get a fair share of the benefits of integrated world, thereby leading to more inclusive globalization.
5. To take advantage of the opportunities of globalization, developing countries should create necessary infrastructure by creating strong economic and technological capabilities, setting up effective political and legal institutions and policies which integrate economic and social goals.
6. Economic development is a multi-dimensional phenomenon. Composite index is a better measure of economic development as it is constructed on the basis of economic, structural and demographic variables. Therefore, international institutions should categorize countries on the basis of composite index and frame their policies regarding loans, aid and grants, etc. accordingly.

Globalization is inevitable and in this modern world, no nation can survive in isolation. Today, nations have no option but integrate their economies with the world economy. Globalization cannot be washed-off despite its many negative implications. Under the circumstances, it is better to understand the pitfalls, frame the policies accordingly and cope up with the challenges of globalization.

APPENDIX 5.1
Data of Selected Variables For Developing Countries (Averages)

Sl. No.	*Variable*	*1980*	*1990*	*2000*	*2004*
(1)	*(2)*	*(3)*	*(4)*	*(5)*	*(6)*
1.	Agriculture, value added (% of GDP)	20.78	17.95	12.26	11.82
2.	Agriculture, value added (annual % growth)	4.30	4.10	2.01	4.13
3.	Industry, value added (% of GDP)	38.57	36.89	34.96	36.04
4.	Industry, value added (annual % growth)	2.53	2.76	6.31	8.41
5.	Services, value added (% of GDP)	40.68	45.20	52.78	52.15
6.	Services, value added (annual % growth)	5.94	2.81	5.67	5.79
7.	GDP growth (annual %)	5.23	1.84	5.31	7.12
8.	GNI per capita (current US$)	705.70	846.68	1156.33	1501.66
9.	GNI per capita, PPP (current international $)	1309.45	2378.42	3662.64	4725.84
10.	Gross domestic savings (% of GDP)	24.93	25.41	24.83	26.99
11.	Gross capital formation (% of GDP)	26.56	25.23	23.73	25.40
12.	Energy use (kg of oil equivalent per capita)	938.97	1008.02	947.20	1013.82
13.	Fuel, Ore and Metal exports (% of merchandise exports)	21.23	20.48	19.04	17.04
14.	Food & Agricultural raw-materials exports (% of merchandise exports)	13.23	10.71	5.92	5.85
15.	Manufactures exports (% of merchandise exports)	47.54	50.60	62.88	63.94
16.	Exports of goods and services (% of GDP)	16.02	20.46	28.75	33.32
17.	Imports of goods and services (% of GDP)	17.67	20.15	27.68	31.76
18.	Degree of Openness (Exports+Imports) % of GDP	8.29	7.49	31.84	33.96

(Contd.)

APPENDIX 5.1 (Contd.)

(1)	(2)	(3)	(4)	(5)	(6)
19.	Export volume (Average annual % growth)	-1.49	3.60	16.39	15.94
20.	Import volume (Average annual % growth)	9.78	3.88	15.44	18.02
21.	Merchandise trade (% of GDP)	35.75	32.50	48.51	58.07
22.	Trade in services (% of GDP)	7.28	6.99	9.49	10.29
23.	Gross private capital flows (% of GDP)	5.75	5.88	11.38	11.86
24.	Foreign direct investment, net inflows (% of GDP)	0.50	0.73	2.84	2.55
25.	Foreign direct investment, net outflows (% of GDP)	0.03	0.07	0.29	0.50
26.	Total debt service (% of GNI)	4.80	4.52	6.50	5.55
27.	Birth rate, crude (per 1,000 people)	30.05	28.10	23.13	21.99
28.	Death rate, crude (per 1,000 people)	10.73	9.40	9.00	8.93
29.	Life expectancy at birth, total (years)	60.07	63.04	64.46	65.18
30.	Mortality rate, infant (per 1,000 live births)	87.12	69.34	62.64	58.84
31.	Physicians (per 1,000 people)	0.84	1.34	1.96	2.13
32.	Adult Literacy rate (% of people ages 15 and above)	60.23	68.88	76.23	80.06
33.	Population of working age 15-64 (% of total)	57.46	60.24	62.31	63.69
34.	Urban population (% of total)	31.76	36.80	41.35	43.33
35.	International migration stock (% of population)	1.34	1.91	1.55	1.98

Note : The above figures are averages for each year of all the developing countries, as reported in the pulbications of the World Bank.

Source : World Bank, World Development Indicators, Various Issues.

Appendix 7.1

Globalization-Related Variables of 15 Countries which showed Improvement in Ranks During 1990-2004 (In Terms of GNI per capita)

Sl. No.	Country.	Imports of goods and services (% of GDP)		Exports of goods and services (% of GDP)		Degree of Openness (Exports+Imports) % of GDP		Merchandise trade (% of GDP)	
		1990	2004	1990	2004	1990	2004	1990	2004
	(1)	(2)	(3)	(4)	(5)	(6)	(7)	(8)	(9)
1.	Bangladesh	14	21	6	15	20	36	17.6	35.7
2.	Chile	31	30	35	36	66	66	53.1	60.5
3.	China	16	31	19	34	35	65	32.5	59.8
4.	Costa Rica	41	49	35	46	76	96	60.2	78.7
5.	Ecuador	32	29	33	27	65	55	44.2	51.2
6.	El Salvador	31	44	19	27	50	71	38.4	60.4
7.	Indonesia	24	27	25	31	49	58	41.5	49.4
8.	Malaysia	72	100	75	121	147	181	133.4	195.9
9.	Mali	34	36	17	28	51	64	39.7	50.2
10.	Mauritius	71	56	64	56	136	112	118.0	79.2
11.	Nicaragua	46	54	25	26	71	80	95.9	65.2
12.	Nigeria	29	37	43	55	72	92	67.5	48.2
13.	Panama	79	65	87	63	165	128	35.4	32.6
14.	Peru	14	18	16	21	30	39	22.3	33.0
15.	Sri Lanka	38	45	29	36	67	82	57.3	68.5
	Average	38	43	35	42	73	82	57	65

(Contd.)

APPENDIX 7.1 (Contd.)

Sl. No.	Country	Trade in services (% of GDP)		International migration stock (% of population)		Gross private capital flows (% of GDP)		Manufactures exports (% of merchandise exports)	
		1990	2004	1990	2004	1990	2004	1990	2004
	(1)	(10)	(11)	(12)	(13)	(14)	(15)	(16)	(17)
1.	Bangladesh	3.6	5.3	0.85	0.70	0.9	1.9	77	90
2.	Chile	12.9	13.3	0.82	1.25	15.0	21.5	11	13
3.	China	2.9	7.0	0.03	0.05	2.5	10.0	72	91
4.	Costa Rica	20.3	19.2	13.58	5.70	7.0	12.3	27	63
5.	Ecuador	13.0	9.0	0.76	0.85	11.0	13.1	2	9
6.	El Salvador	13.4	13.0	0.93	29.00	2.0	12.5	38	60
7.	Indonesia	7.5	17.9	0.26	0.12	4.1	4.6	35	56
8.	Malaysia	21.2	29.9	5.68	7.00	10.3	22.6	54	76
9.	Mali	19.0	16.3	0.67	0.35	2.0	8.4	2	11
10.	Mauritius	38.0	41.1	0.83	1.53	8.0	7.5	66	71
11.	Nicaragua	17.0	15.1	1.03	0.44	9.0	8.1	8	11
12.	Nigeria	10.3	11.5	0.49	0.75	5.9	11.0	1	2
13.	Panama	33.5	30.4	2.56	3.04	86.0	39.0	21	10
14.	Peru	7.5	6.8	0.26	0.14	3.2	6.8	18	20
15.	Sri Lanka	13.4	17.1	2.71	2.00	13.1	8.0	48	74
	Average	16	17	2	4	12	12	32	44

Source : Tabulated from World Development Indicators; Various Issues.

APPENDIX 7.2
Globalization-Related Variables of 19 Countries which showed Deterioration in Ranks During 1990-2004 (In Terms of GNI per capita)

Sl. No.	Country	Imports of goods and services (% of GDP)		Exports of goods and services (% of GDP)		Degree of Openness (Exports+Imports) (% of GDP)		Merchandise trade (% of GDP)	
		1990	2004	1990	2004	1990	2004	1990	2004
	(1)	(2)	(3)	(4)	(5)	(6)	(7)	(8)	(9)
1.	Algeria	25	26	23	40	48	66	36.6	59.7
2.	Argentina	5	18	10	25	15	43	11.6	37.1
3.	Brazil	7	13	8	18	15	31	11.7	26.9
4.	Cameroon	17	26	20	26	37	51	30.5	33.4
5.	Central African Republic	28	16	15	11	42	27	18.4	20.7
6.	Colombia	15	22	21	21	35	43	30.7	33.7
7.	Congo, Rep.	46	57	54	84	99	142	57.2	129.4
8.	Gabon	31	40	46	61	77	101	52.5	66.0
9.	Ghana	26	54	17	35	43	89	35.7	77.8
10.	Iran, Islamic Rep.	24	30	22	32	46	62	32.9	48.4
11.	Niger	22	26	15	16	37	42	27.0	30.2
12.	Papua New Guinea	49	60	41	71	90	131	73.6	107.8
13.	Paraguay	39	37	33	36	73	73	43.9	58.3
14.	South Africa	19	27	24	27	43	54	37.4	48.5
15.	Sudan	18	21	13	18	32	39	7.5	37.2
16.	Togo	45	47	33	34	79	81	52.1	88.4
17.	Uganda	19	28	7	14	27	41	10.2	31.2
18.	Uruguay	13	28	24	30	42	58	32.7	45.9
19.	Zambia	37	27	36	20	72	47	76.9	68.8
	Average	25	32	24	33	50	64	36	55

(Contd.)

Appendix 7.2 (Contd.)

Sl. No.	Country	Trade in services (% of GDP)		International migration stock (% of population)		Gross private capital flows (% of GDP)		Manufactures exports (% of merchandise exports)	
		1990	2004	1990	2004	1990	2004	1990	2004
	(1)	(10)	(11)	(12)	(13)	(14)	(15)	(16)	(17)
1.	Algeria	2.9	9.0	1.08	0.70	2.6	4.0	3	2
2.	Argentina	3.9	7.8	5.06	3.80	8.2	15.6	29	29
3.	Brazil	2.4	4.9	0.54	0.28	1.9	8.8	52	54
4.	Cameroon	12.8	16.0	1.47	0.88	15.5	18.2	9	5
5.	Central African Republic	16.0	22.0	2.09	1.80	2.2	3.5	44	37
6.	Colombia	8.3	6.4	0.29	0.26	3.1	10.9	25	38
7.	Congo, Rep.	31.0	17.7	5.22	6.81	6.6	11.7	3	10
8.	Gabon	21.0	16.7	13.34	17.33	18.0	18.7	6	7
9.	Ghana	6.6	19.9	4.63	8.87	2.9	6.8	8	14
10.	Iran, Islamic Rep.	3.7	3.6	7.00	2.00	2.6	2.4	1	9
11.	Niger	10.9	9.4	1.36	1.00	2.8	2.3	2	8
12.	Papua New Guinea	18.9	34.0	0.80	0.40	5.7	34.6	5	6
13.	Paraguay	16.2	12.6	4.35	3.00	5.4	3.4	10	13
14.	South Africa	6.4	8.3	3.48	2.00	2.2	8.6	29	58
15.	Sudan	3.0	5.3	4.88	2.00	0.3	10.4	2	2
16.	Togo	24.1	17.0	4.10	3.00	9.6	14.8	9	47
17.	Uganda	4.5	16.8	3.10	1.90	1.1	4.8	4	13
18.	Uruguay	9.2	12.6	3.16	2.30	12.7	22.0	39	32
19.	Zambia	15.0	14.0	3.34	3.34	64.7	9.3	6	21
	Average	11	13	4	3	9	11	15	21

Source : Tabulated from World Development Indicators; Various Issues.

Appendix 8.1
Development Gap Between Low Income Countries with Cameroon as Target GNI per capita (Y_1 = 960 US$) Growth Rate = 3.40

Gap Bridging (Decreasing) Name of Countries	*Gap Not Bridging (Increasing) Name of Countries*	
(1)	*(2)*	
NIL	Congo Rep.	$\frac{960}{880} > \frac{3.30}{3.40}$
	Cote d'Ivoire	$\frac{960}{730} > \frac{0.70}{3.40}$
	Lesotho	$\frac{960}{640} > \frac{4.50}{3.40}$
	Senegal	$\frac{960}{660} > \frac{3.10}{3.40}$
	India	$\frac{960}{390} > \frac{5.80}{3.40}$
	Zimbabwe	$\frac{960}{850} > \frac{3.50}{3.40}$
	Pakistan	$\frac{960}{420} > \frac{6.30}{3.40}$
	Papua New Guinea	$\frac{960}{420} > \frac{6.30}{3.40}$
	Mauritania	$\frac{960}{540} > \frac{1.70}{3.40}$
	Sudan	$\frac{960}{550} > \frac{0.40}{3.40}$
	Haiti	$\frac{960}{390} > \frac{-0.20}{3.40}$

(Contd.)

APPENDIX 8.1 (Contd.)

(1)	(2)	
NIL	Kenya	$\frac{960}{380} > \frac{4.20}{3.40}$
	Benin	$\frac{960}{330} > \frac{2.50}{3.40}$
	Bangladesh	$\frac{960}{300} > \frac{4.30}{3.40}$
	Nigeria	$\frac{960}{280} > \frac{1.60}{3.40}$
	Guinea	$\frac{960}{430} > \frac{4.10}{3.40}$
	Zambia	$\frac{960}{420} > \frac{1.00}{3.40}$
	Ghana	$\frac{960}{380} > \frac{3.00}{3.40}$
	Burkinafaso	$\frac{960}{350} > \frac{3.70}{3.40}$
	Mali	$\frac{960}{260} > \frac{0.80}{3.40}$
	Tanzania	$\frac{960}{200} > \frac{3.80}{3.40}$
	Central African R.	$\frac{960}{460} > \frac{1.40}{3.40}$
	Togo	$\frac{960}{380} > \frac{1.80}{3.40}$
	Somalia	$\frac{960}{140} > \frac{2.10}{3.40}$

(Contd.)

Appendix 8.1 (*Contd.*)

(1)	*(2)*	
NIL	Madagascar	$\frac{960}{230} > \frac{1.10}{3.40}$
	Gambia, The	$\frac{960}{310} > \frac{3.40}{3.40}$
	Mozambique	$\frac{960}{170} > \frac{-0.20}{3.40}$
	Chad	$\frac{960}{260} > \frac{6.10}{3.40}$
	Nepal	$\frac{960}{200} > \frac{4.60}{3.40}$
	Uganda	$\frac{960}{320} > \frac{2.90}{3.40}$
	Niger	$\frac{960}{280} > \frac{-0.10}{3.40}$
	Rwanda	$\frac{960}{360} > \frac{2.30}{3.40}$
	Sierraleone	$\frac{960}{200} > \frac{1.20}{3.40}$
	Guineabissau	$\frac{960}{220} > \frac{4.00}{3.40}$
	Malawi	$\frac{960}{180} > \frac{2.50}{3.40}$
	Ethiopia	$\frac{960}{170} > \frac{1.10}{3.40}$
	Burundi	$\frac{960}{210} > \frac{4.40}{3.40}$
No. of Countries = Nil	No. of Countries = 37	

APPENDIX 8.2
Development Gap Between Lower Middle Income Countries
With Brazil as Target GNI per capita (Y_1 = 2770 US$)
Growth Rate = 2.70

Gap Bridging (Decreasing) Name of Countries		*Gap Not Bridging (Increasing) Name of Countries*	
(1)		(2)	
Bulgaria	$\frac{2770}{2260} < \frac{3.40}{2.70}$	Romania	$\frac{2770}{1730} > \frac{0.50}{2.70}$
Thailand	$\frac{2770}{1540} < \frac{7.60}{2.70}$	Tunisia	$\frac{2770}{1430} > \frac{3.30}{2.70}$
		Peru	$\frac{2770}{770} > \frac{-0.20}{2.70}$
		El Salvador	$\frac{2770}{930} > \frac{0.20}{2.70}$
		Iran Islamic	$\frac{2770}{2590} > \frac{1.50}{2.70}$
		Algeria	$\frac{2770}{2420} > \frac{2.80}{2.70}$
		Ecuador	$\frac{2770}{890} > \frac{2.00}{2.70}$
		Guatemala	$\frac{2770}{950} > \frac{0.80}{2.70}$
		Jordan	$\frac{2770}{1390} > \frac{2.50}{2.70}$
		Dominican	$\frac{2770}{880} > \frac{3.10}{2.70}$
		Colombia	$\frac{2770}{1190} > \frac{3.70}{2.70}$

(Contd.)

APPENDIX 8.2 (*Contd.*)

(1)	(2)	
	Morocco	$\frac{2770}{1030} > \frac{4.20}{2.70}$
	China	$\frac{2770}{320} > \frac{10.20}{2.70}$
	Egypt Arab Rep.	$\frac{2770}{760} > \frac{5.40}{2.70}$
	Syrian Arab Rep.	$\frac{2770}{880} > \frac{1.50}{2.70}$
	Phillippine	$\frac{2770}{740} > \frac{1.00}{2.70}$
	Indonesia	$\frac{2770}{620} > \frac{6.10}{2.70}$
	Paraguay	$\frac{2770}{1190} > \frac{2.50}{2.70}$
	Honduras	$\frac{2770}{710} > \frac{2.70}{2.70}$
	Sri Lanka	$\frac{2770}{470} > \frac{4.00}{2.70}$
	Bolivia	$\frac{2770}{740} > \frac{-0.20}{2.70}$
	Angola	$\frac{2770}{730} > \frac{3.40}{2.70}$
	Nicaragua	$\frac{2770}{330} > \frac{-1.90}{2.70}$
No. of Countries = 2	No. of Countries = 23	

Appendix 8.3
Development Gap Between Upper Middle Income Countries With Oman as Target GNI per capita (Y_1 = 5610 US$) Growth Rate = 8.30

Gap Bridging (Decreasing) Name of Countries	*Gap Not Bridging (Increasing) Name of Countries*	
(1)	*(2)*	
NIL		
	Trinidad & Tobago	$\frac{5610}{3730} > \frac{-0.80}{8.30}$
	Hungary	$\frac{5610}{2880} > \frac{1.30}{8.30}$
	Mexico	$\frac{5610}{2830} > \frac{1.00}{8.30}$
	Poland	$\frac{5610}{1910} > \frac{1.90}{8.30}$
	Chile	$\frac{5610}{2180} > \frac{4.10}{8.30}$
	Mauritius	$\frac{5610}{2300} > \frac{6.20}{8.30}$
	Malaysia	$\frac{5610}{2420} > \frac{5.20}{8.30}$
	Costa Rica	$\frac{5610}{1770} > \frac{3.00}{8.30}$
	Botswana	$\frac{5610}{2450} > \frac{10.30}{8.30}$
	Panama	$\frac{5610}{2210} > \frac{0.50}{8.30}$
	Gabon	$\frac{5610}{4780} > \frac{0.90}{8.30}$

(Contd.)

APPENDIX 8.3 (*Contd.*)

(1)	(2)	
	Venezuela RB	$\frac{5610}{2570} > \frac{1.10}{8.30}$
	Uruguay	$\frac{5610}{2870} > \frac{0.40}{8.30}$
	Turkey	$\frac{5610}{2270} > \frac{5.30}{8.30}$
	South Africa	$\frac{5610}{3390} > \frac{1.00}{8.30}$
	Argentina	$\frac{5610}{3190} > \frac{-0.70}{8.30}$
	Jamaica	$\frac{5610}{1790} > \frac{2.00}{8.30}$
No. of Countries = Nil	No. of Countries = 17	

APPENDIX 8.4

Development Gap Between Low Income Countries With Cote d'Ivoire as Target GNI per capita (Y_1 = 650 US$) Growth Rate = 3.30

Gap Bridging (Decreasing) Name of Countries		*Gap Not Bridging (Increasing) Name of Countries*	
(1)		*(2)*	
Lesotho	$\frac{650}{630} < \frac{3.90}{3.30}$	Cameroon	$\frac{650}{580} > \frac{1.70}{3.30}$
India	$\frac{650}{450} < \frac{6.00}{3.30}$	Congo Rep.	$\frac{650}{520} > \frac{1.20}{3.30}$
Papua New G.	$\frac{650}{650} < \frac{4.30}{3.30}$	Senegal	$\frac{650}{450} > \frac{3.20}{3.30}$
		Zimbabwe	$\frac{650}{460} > \frac{2.10}{3.30}$
		Pakistan	$\frac{650}{480} > \frac{3.80}{3.30}$
		Mauritania	$\frac{650}{460} > \frac{4.60}{3.30}$
		Sudan	$\frac{650}{310} > \frac{5.40}{3.30}$
		Haiti	$\frac{650}{490} > \frac{-1.50}{3.30}$
		Kenya	$\frac{650}{430} > \frac{2.20}{3.30}$
		Benin	$\frac{650}{340} > \frac{4.80}{3.30}$
		Bangaldesh	$\frac{650}{390} > \frac{4.80}{3.30}$
		Nigeria	$\frac{650}{280} > \frac{2.50}{3.30}$

(Contd.)

APPENDIX 8.4 (*Contd.*)

(1)	(2)	
	Guinea	$\frac{650}{400} > \frac{4.40}{3.30}$
	Zambia	$\frac{650}{290} > \frac{0.50}{3.30}$
	Ghana	$\frac{650}{330} > \frac{4.30}{3.30}$
	Burkina Faso	$\frac{650}{250} > \frac{4.00}{3.30}$
	Mali	$\frac{650}{220} > \frac{4.10}{3.30}$
	Tanzania	$\frac{650}{280} > \frac{2.90}{3.30}$
	Central African	$\frac{650}{270} > \frac{2.00}{3.30}$
	Togo	$\frac{650}{270} > \frac{3.50}{3.30}$
	Somalia	$\frac{650}{230} > \frac{2.10}{3.30}$
	Madagascar	$\frac{650}{240} > \frac{2.00}{3.30}$
	Gambia, The	$\frac{650}{320} > \frac{3.00}{3.30}$
	Mozambique	$\frac{650}{210} > \frac{6.40}{3.30}$
	Chad	$\frac{650}{180} > \frac{1.90}{3.30}$
	Nepal	$\frac{650}{220} > \frac{4.90}{3.30}$

(*Contd.*)

APPENDIX 8.4 (Contd.)

(1)	(2)	
	Uganda	$\frac{650}{260} > \frac{7.10}{3.30}$
	Niger	$\frac{650}{160} > \frac{2.40}{3.30}$
	Rwanda	$\frac{650}{250} > \frac{-0.30}{3.30}$
	Sierra Leone	$\frac{650}{140} > \frac{-6.10}{3.30}$
	Guinea Bissau	$\frac{650}{160} > \frac{1.20}{3.30}$
	Malawi	$\frac{650}{150} > \frac{3.70}{3.30}$
	Ethiopia	$\frac{650}{110} > \frac{4.20}{3.30}$
	Burundi	$\frac{650}{110} > \frac{-2.60}{3.30}$
No. of Countries = 3	No. of Countries = 34	

APPENDIX 8.5

Development Gap Between Lower Middle Income Countries With Brazil as Target GNI per capita (Y_1 = 3590 US$) Growth Rate = 2.90

Gap Bridging (Decreasing) Name of Countries		*Gap Not Bridging (Increasing) Name of Countries*	
(1)		(2)	
Dominican Rep.	$\frac{3590}{2170} < \frac{6.10}{2.90}$	Romania	$\frac{3590}{1690} > \frac{-0.60}{2.90}$
		Bulgaria	$\frac{3590}{1600} > \frac{-1.80}{2.90}$
		Tunisia	$\frac{3590}{2080} > \frac{4.70}{2.90}$
		Thailand	$\frac{3590}{1990} > \frac{4.20}{2.90}$
		Peru	$\frac{3590}{2050} > \frac{4.60}{2.90}$
		El Salvador	$\frac{3590}{2000} > \frac{4.80}{2.90}$
		Iran Islamic	$\frac{3590}{1670} > \frac{3.50}{2.90}$
		Algeria	$\frac{3590}{1570} > \frac{1.90}{2.90}$
		Ecuador	$\frac{3590}{1340} > \frac{1.90}{2.90}$
		Guatemala	$\frac{3590}{1740} > \frac{4.20}{2.90}$
		Jordan	$\frac{3590}{1760} > \frac{5.00}{2.90}$
		Colombia	$\frac{3590}{2060} > \frac{2.80}{2.90}$
		Morocco	$\frac{3590}{1220} > \frac{2.30}{2.90}$

(Contd.)

APPENDIX 8.5 (Contd.)

(1)	(2)	
	China	$\frac{3590}{930} > \frac{10.60}{2.90}$
	Egypt Arab Rep.	$\frac{3590}{1460} > \frac{4.70}{2.90}$
	Syrian Arab Rep.	$\frac{3590}{910} > \frac{5.00}{2.90}$
	Phillippine	$\frac{3590}{1040} > \frac{3.40}{2.90}$
	Indonesia	$\frac{3590}{590} > \frac{4.20}{2.90}$
	Paraguay	$\frac{3590}{1460} > \frac{2.20}{2.90}$
	Honduras	$\frac{3590}{860} > \frac{3.20}{2.90}$
	Sri Lanka	$\frac{3590}{810} > \frac{5.30}{2.90}$
	Bolivia	$\frac{3590}{1000} > \frac{4.00}{2.90}$
	Angola	$\frac{3590}{430} > \frac{1.60}{2.90}$
	Nicaragua	$\frac{3590}{750} > \frac{3.70}{2.90}$
No. of Countries = 1	No. of Countries = 24	

Appendix 8.6
Development Gap Between Upper Middle Income Countries With Argentina as Target GNI per capita (Y_1 = 7470 US$) Growth Rate = 4.30

Gap Bridging (Decreasing) *Name of Countries*	*Gap Not Bridging (Increasing)* *Name of Countries*	
(1)	*(2)*	
NIL	Oman	$\frac{7470}{6610} > \frac{4.50}{4.30}$
	Trinidas & Tobago	$\frac{7470}{5230} > \frac{3.20}{4.30}$
	Hungary	$\frac{7470}{4670} > \frac{1.60}{4.30}$
	Mexico	$\frac{7470}{5110} > \frac{3.10}{4.30}$
	Poland	$\frac{7470}{4430} > \frac{4.60}{4.30}$
	Chile	$\frac{7470}{4860} > \frac{6.60}{4.30}$
	Mauritius	$\frac{7470}{3690} > \frac{5.20}{4.30}$
	Malaysia	$\frac{7470}{3430} > \frac{7.00}{4.30}$
	Costa Rica	$\frac{7470}{3700} > \frac{5.30}{4.30}$
	Botswana	$\frac{7470}{2870} > \frac{4.90}{4.30}$
	Panama	$\frac{7470}{3740} > \frac{4.70}{4.30}$
	Gabon	$\frac{7470}{3090} > \frac{2.80}{4.30}$
	Venezuela RB	$\frac{7470}{4100} > \frac{1.60}{4.30}$
	Uruguay	$\frac{7470}{6150} > \frac{3.40}{4.30}$
	Turkey	$\frac{7470}{6150} > \frac{3.40}{4.30}$
	South Africa	$\frac{7470}{3050} > \frac{2.10}{4.30}$
	Jamaica	$\frac{7470}{2940} > \frac{0.90}{4.30}$
No. of Countries = Nil	No. of Countries = 17	

Appendix 8.7
Development Gap Between Low Income Countries With Cameroon as Target GNI per capita (Y_1 = 810 US$) Growth Rate = 4.50

Gap Bridging (Decreasing) *Name of Countries*		*Gap Not Bridging (Increasing)* *Name of Countries*	
(1)		*(2)*	
India	$\frac{810}{620} < \frac{6.20}{4.50}$	Congo Rep.	$\frac{810}{760} > \frac{3.10}{4.50}$
		Cote D'Ivoire	$\frac{810}{760} > \frac{-0.70}{4.50}$
		Lesotho	$\frac{810}{730} > \frac{3.10}{4.50}$
		Senegal	$\frac{810}{630} > \frac{4.40}{4.50}$
		Zimbabwe	$\frac{810}{620} > \frac{-5.90}{4.50}$
		Pakistan	$\frac{810}{600} > \frac{4.10}{4.50}$
		Papua New G.	$\frac{810}{560} > \frac{0.60}{4.50}$
		Mauritania	$\frac{810}{530} > \frac{4.70}{4.50}$
		Sudan	$\frac{810}{530} > \frac{6.00}{4.50}$
		Haiti	$\frac{810}{510} > \frac{-0.40}{4.50}$
		Kenya	$\frac{810}{480} > \frac{2.70}{4.50}$
		Benin	$\frac{810}{450} > \frac{4.50}{4.50}$
		Bangladesh	$\frac{810}{440} > \frac{5.20}{4.50}$
		Nigeria	$\frac{810}{430} > \frac{5.40}{4.50}$
		Guinea	$\frac{810}{410} > \frac{2.90}{4.50}$
		Zambia	$\frac{810}{400} > \frac{4.40}{4.50}$
		Ghana	$\frac{810}{380} > \frac{4.90}{4.50}$

(*Contd.*)

APPENDIX 8.7 (Contd.)

(1)	(2)	
	Burkina Faso	$\frac{810}{350} > \frac{5.20}{4.50}$
	Mali	$\frac{810}{330} > \frac{6.30}{4.50}$
	Tanzania	$\frac{810}{320} > \frac{6.80}{4.50}$
	Central African	$\frac{810}{310} > \frac{-2.00}{4.50}$
	Togo	$\frac{810}{310} > \frac{2.60}{4.50}$
	Somalia	$\frac{810}{300} > \frac{2.10}{4.50}$
	Madagascar	$\frac{810}{290} > \frac{2.90}{4.50}$
	Gambia, The	$\frac{810}{280} > \frac{3.80}{4.50}$
	Mozambique	$\frac{810}{270} > \frac{8.80}{4.50}$
	Chad	$\frac{810}{250} > \frac{14.10}{4.50}$
	Nepal	$\frac{810}{250} > \frac{2.50}{4.50}$
	Udanda	$\frac{810}{250} > \frac{5.80}{4.50}$
	Niger	$\frac{810}{210} > \frac{4.10}{4.50}$
	Rwanda	$\frac{810}{210} > \frac{5.20}{4.50}$
	Sierra Leone	$\frac{810}{210} > \frac{7.20}{4.50}$
	Guinea Bissau	$\frac{810}{160} > \frac{-1.20}{4.50}$
	Malawi	$\frac{810}{160} > \frac{2.90}{4.50}$
	Ethiopia	$\frac{810}{110} > \frac{3.60}{4.50}$
	Burundi	$\frac{810}{90} > \frac{2.70}{4.50}$
No. of Countries = 1	No. of Countries = 36	

Appendix 8.8
Development Gap Between Lower Middle Income Countries With Brazil as Target GNI per capita (Y_1 = 3000 US$) Growth Rate = 2.00

Gap Bridging (Decreasing) Name of Countries		*Gap Not Bridging (Increasing) Name of Countries*	
(1)		*(2)*	
Romania	$\frac{3000}{2960} < \frac{5.90}{2.00}$	El Salvador	$\frac{3000}{2320} > \frac{1.90}{2.00}$
Bulgaria	$\frac{3000}{2750} < \frac{4.80}{2.00}$	Guatemala	$\frac{3000}{2190} > \frac{2.30}{2.00}$
Tunisia	$\frac{3000}{2650} < \frac{4.30}{2.00}$	Dominican	$\frac{3000}{2100} > \frac{2.40}{2.00}$
Thailand	$\frac{3000}{2490} < \frac{5.40}{2.00}$	Colombia	$\frac{3000}{2020} > \frac{2.90}{2.00}$
Peru	$\frac{3000}{2360} < \frac{3.70}{2.00}$	Egypt Arab Rep.	$\frac{3000}{1250} > \frac{3.40}{2.00}$
Iran Islamic	$\frac{3000}{2320} < \frac{6.00}{2.00}$	Syrian Arab Rep.	$\frac{3000}{1230} > \frac{3.50}{2.00}$
Algeria	$\frac{3000}{2270} < \frac{4.80}{2.00}$	Phillippine	$\frac{3000}{1170} > \frac{3.90}{2.00}$
Ecuador	$\frac{3000}{2210} < \frac{4.20}{2.00}$	Indonesia	$\frac{3000}{1140} > \frac{4.60}{2.00}$
Jordan	$\frac{3000}{2190} < \frac{5.50}{2.00}$	Paraguay	$\frac{3000}{1140} > \frac{1.40}{2.00}$
Morocco	$\frac{3000}{1570} < \frac{4.70}{2.00}$	Honduras	$\frac{3000}{1040} > \frac{3.30}{2.00}$
China	$\frac{3000}{1500} < \frac{9.40}{2.00}$	Sri Lanka	$\frac{3000}{1010} > \frac{3.70}{2.00}$
Angola	$\frac{3000}{930} < \frac{8.10}{2.00}$	Bolivia	$\frac{3000}{960} > \frac{2.60}{2.00}$
		Nicaragua	$\frac{3000}{830} > \frac{2.50}{2.00}$
No. of Countries = 12		No. of Countries = 13	

APPENDIX 8.9
Development Gap Between Upper Middle Income Countries With Oman as Target GNI per capita (Y_1 = 9070 US$) Growth Rate = 3.00

Gap Bridging (Decreasing) Name of Countries		*Gap Not Bridging (Increasing) Name of Countries*	
(1)		*(2)*	
Trinidad & Tobago	$\frac{9070}{8730} < \frac{7.20}{3.00}$	Mexico	$\frac{9070}{6790} > \frac{1.50}{3.00}$
Hungary	$\frac{9070}{8370} < \frac{4.00}{3.00}$	Poland	$\frac{9070}{6100} > \frac{2.80}{3.00}$
		Chile	$\frac{9070}{5220} > \frac{3.70}{3.00}$
		Mauritius	$\frac{9070}{4640} > \frac{4.40}{3.00}$
		Malaysia	$\frac{9070}{4520} > \frac{4.40}{3.00}$
		Costa Rica	$\frac{9070}{4470} > \frac{3.90}{3.00}$
		Botswana	$\frac{9070}{4360} > \frac{5.50}{3.00}$
		Panama	$\frac{9070}{4210} > \frac{3.30}{3.00}$
		Gabon	$\frac{9070}{4080} > \frac{1.60}{3.00}$
		Venezuela RB	$\frac{9070}{4030} > \frac{-1.20}{3.00}$
		Uruguay	$\frac{9070}{3900} > \frac{-1.20}{3.00}$
		Turkey	$\frac{9070}{3750} > \frac{4.20}{3.00}$
		South Africa	$\frac{9070}{3630} > \frac{3.20}{3.00}$
		Argentina	$\frac{9070}{3580} > \frac{-0.10}{3.00}$
		Jamaica	$\frac{9070}{3300} > \frac{1.50}{3.00}$
No. of Countries = 2		No. of Countries = 15	

Appendix 8.10
Growth Rate and 22 Selected Economic Development Variables: Graphical Presentation

Fig. 1
GDP Growth Rate 1980-2004 and GNI per capita (Current US $) 1980

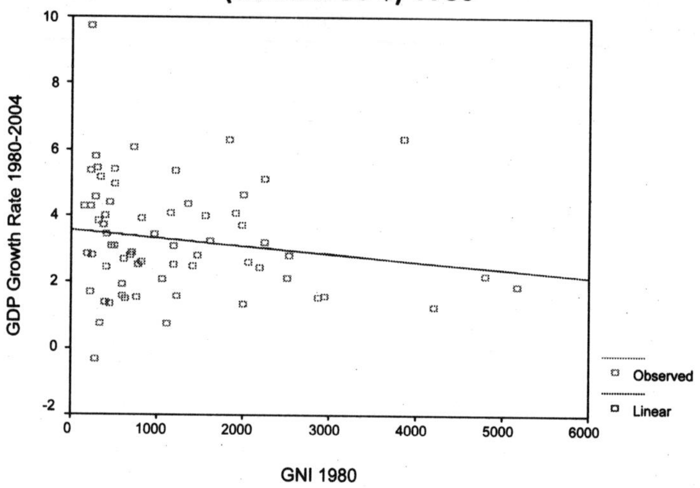

Fig. 2
GDP Growth Rate 1980-2004 and GNI per capita PPP (Current International $) 1980

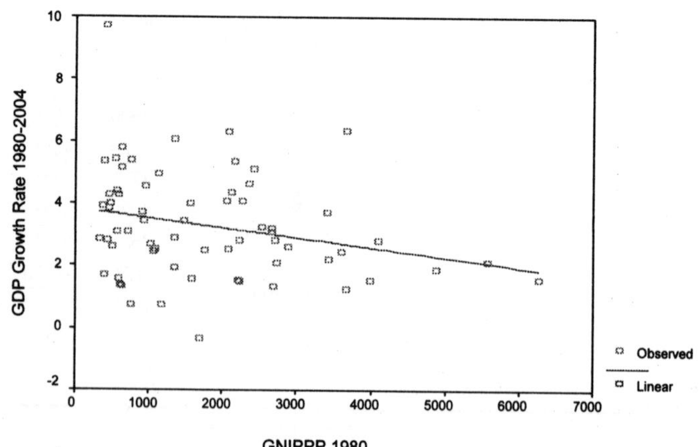

FIG. 3

GDP Growth Rate 1980-2004 and Industry Value Added (% of GDP) 1980

FIG. 4

GDP Growth Rate 1980-2004 and Services Value Added (% of GDP) 1980

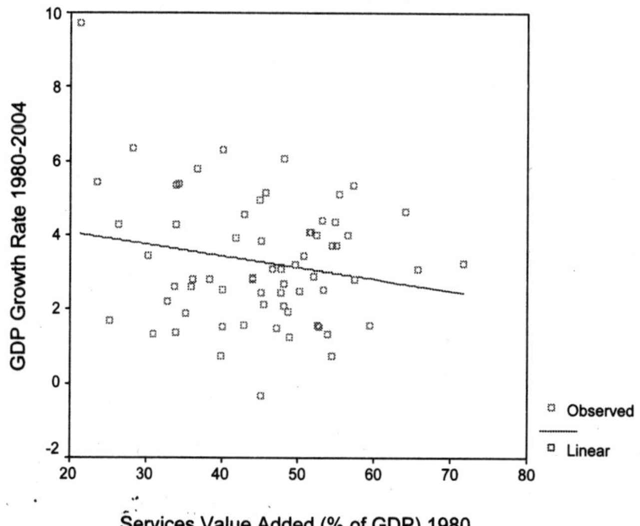

Fig. 5
GDP Growth Rate 1980-2004 and Daily Calorie Supply (Per Capita) 1980

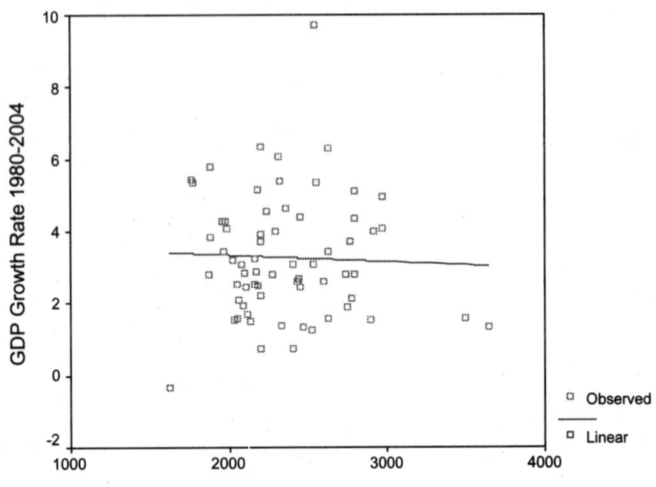

Fig. 6
GDP Growth Rate 1980-2004 and Energy Use Per Capita (kg. of oil equivalent) 1980

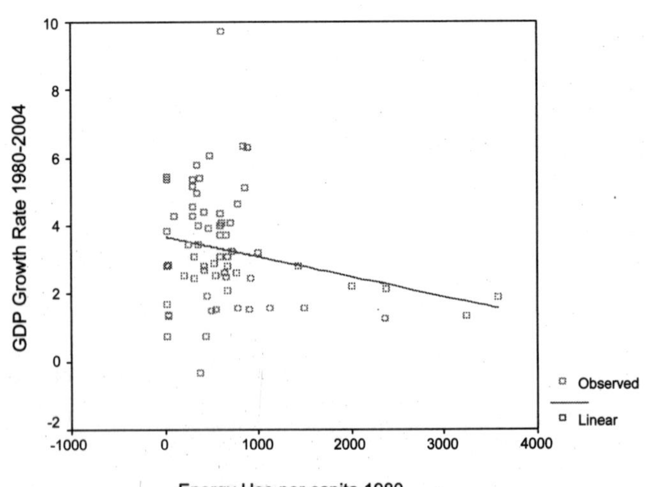

Fig. 7
GDP Growth Rate 1980-2004 and Fuel, Ore and Metal Exports (% of Merchandise Exports) 1980

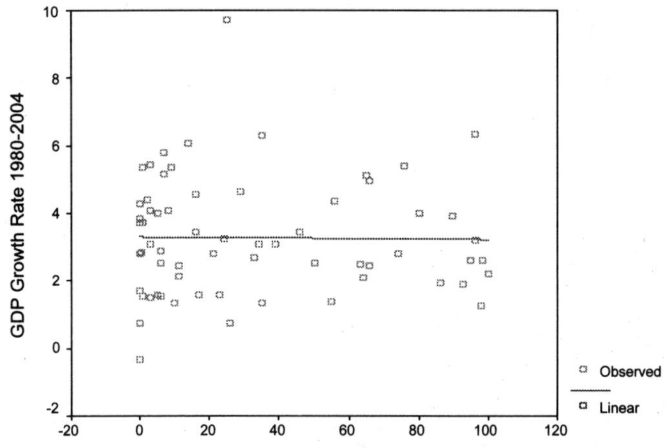

Fig. 8
GDP Growth Rate 1980-2004 and Life Expectancy at Birth 1980

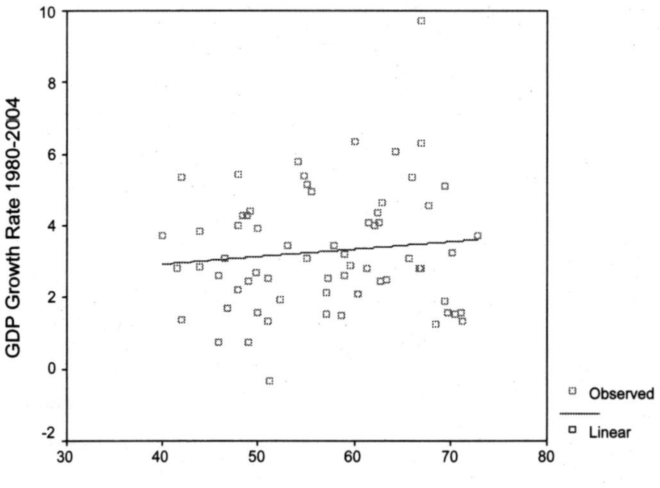

Fig. 9
GDP Growth Rate 1980-2004 and Employment in Services 1980

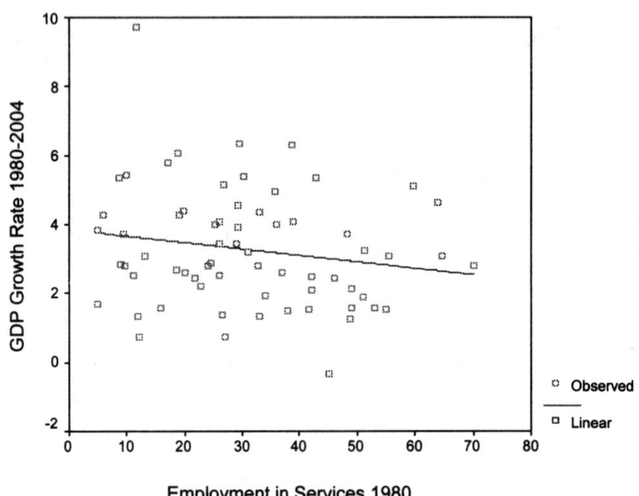

Fig. 10
GDP Growth Rate 1980-2004 and Population of Working Age (% of Total) 1980

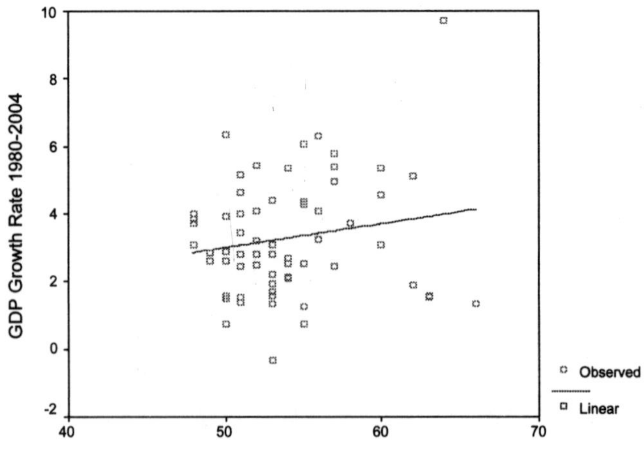

Fig. 11
GDP Growth Rate 1980-2004 and Physicians (per 1000 people) 1980

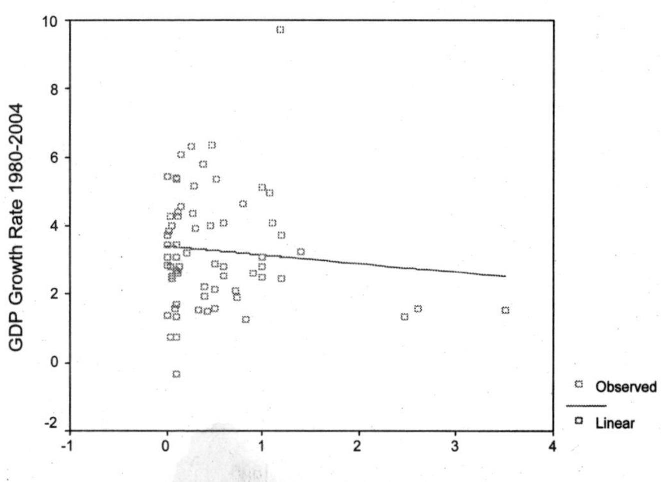

Fig. 12
GDP Growth Rate 1980-2004 and Urban Population (% of Total) 1980

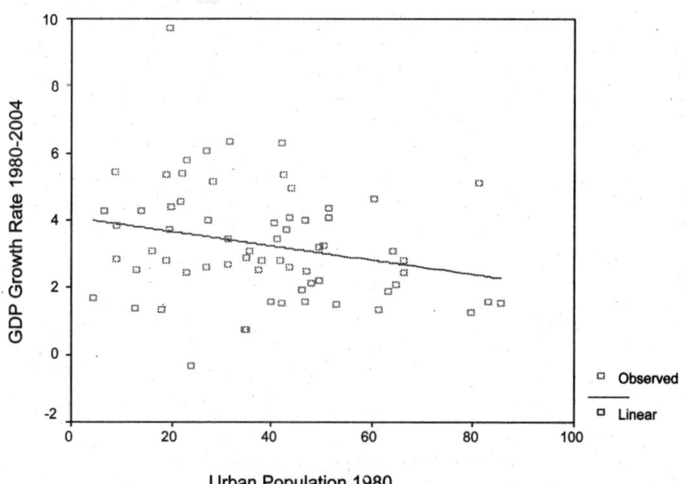

Fig. 13
GDP Growth Rate 1980-2004 and International Migration Stock 1980

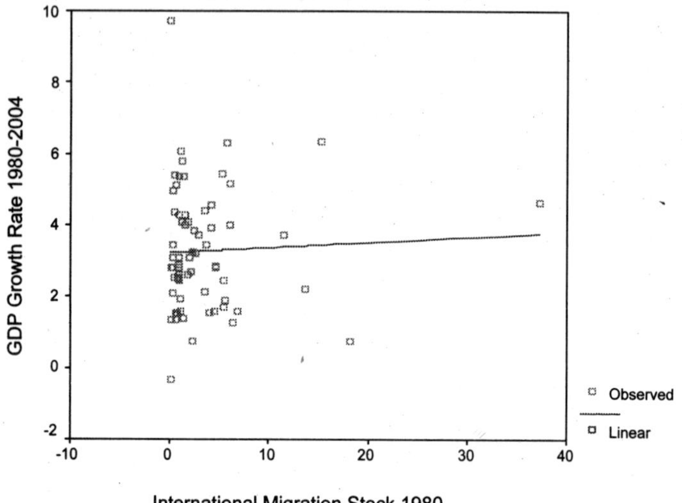

Fig. 14
GDP Growth Rate 1980-2004 and Gross Domestic Savings (% of GDP) 1980

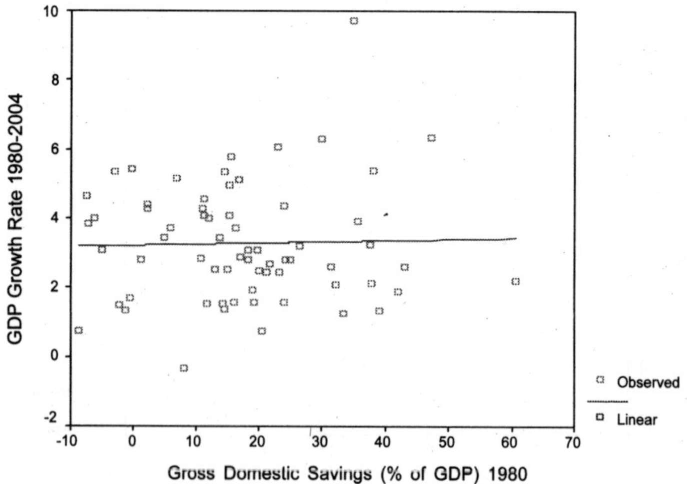

FIG. 15
GDP Growth Rate 1980-2004 and Manufacture Exports (% of Merchandise Exports) 1980

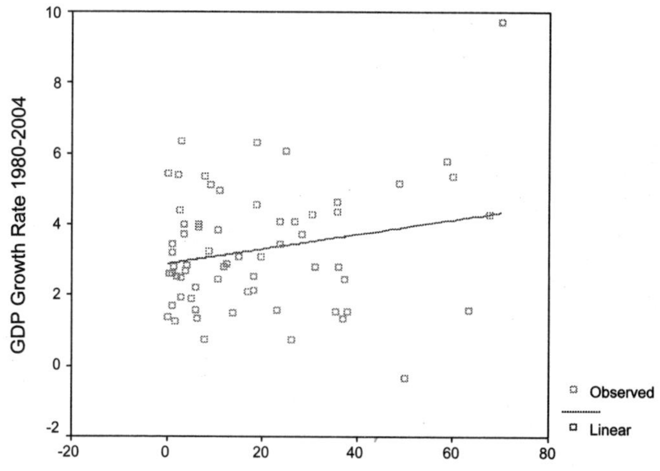

FIG. 16
GDP Growth Rate 1980-2004 and Exports of Goods & Services 1980

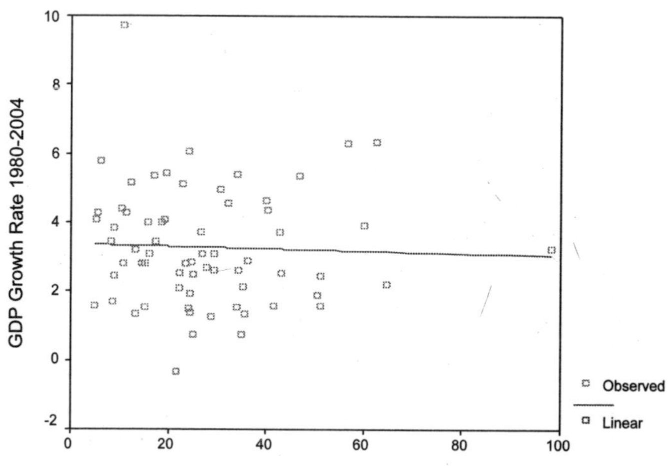

FIG. 17
GDP Growth Rate 1980-2004 and Imports of Goods & Services 1980

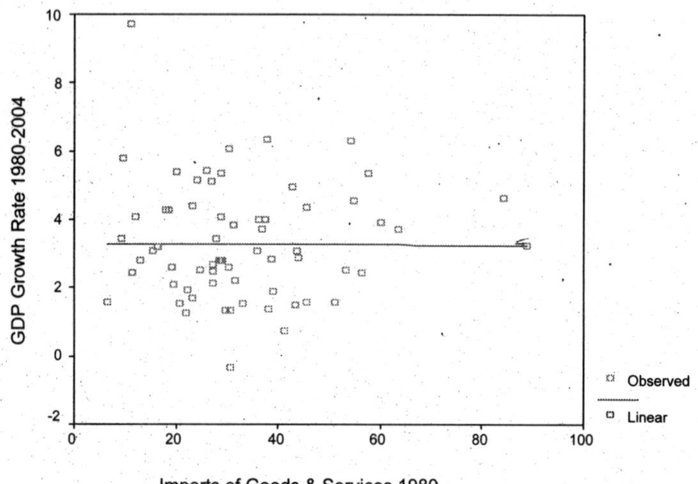

FIG. 18
GDP Growth Rate 1980-2004 and Degree of Openness 1980

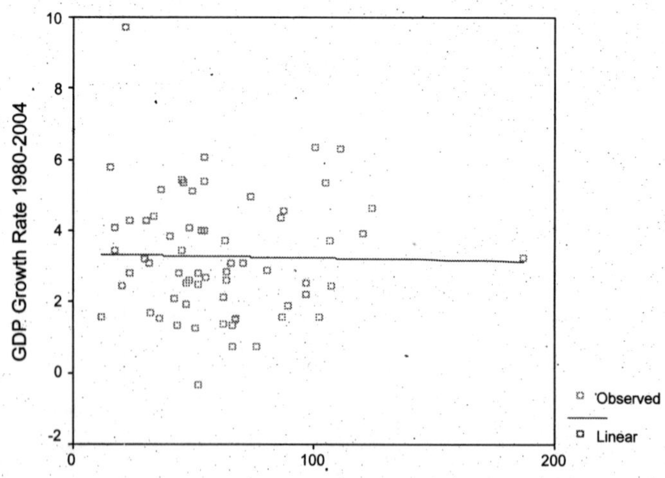

FIG. 19

GDP Growth Rate 1980-2004 and Gross Private Capital Flows (% of GDP) 1980

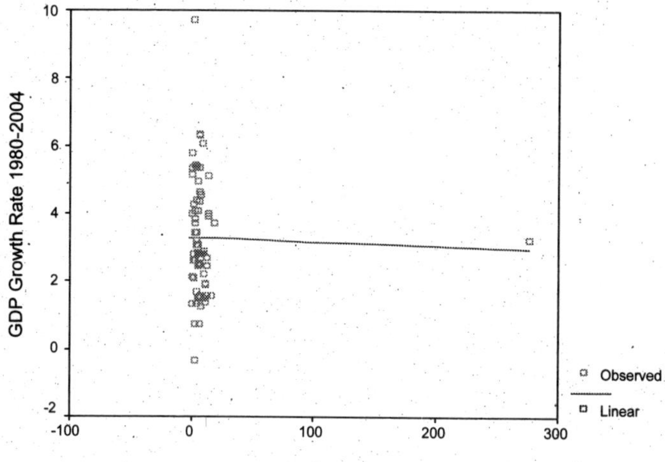

FIG. 20

GDP Growth Rate 1980-2004 and Gross Capital Formation (% of GDP) 1980

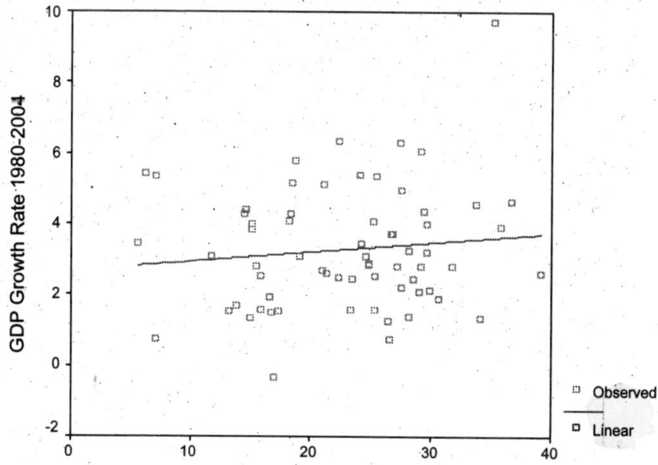

FIG. 21
GDP Growth Rate 1980-2004 and Merchandise Trade (% of GDP) 1980

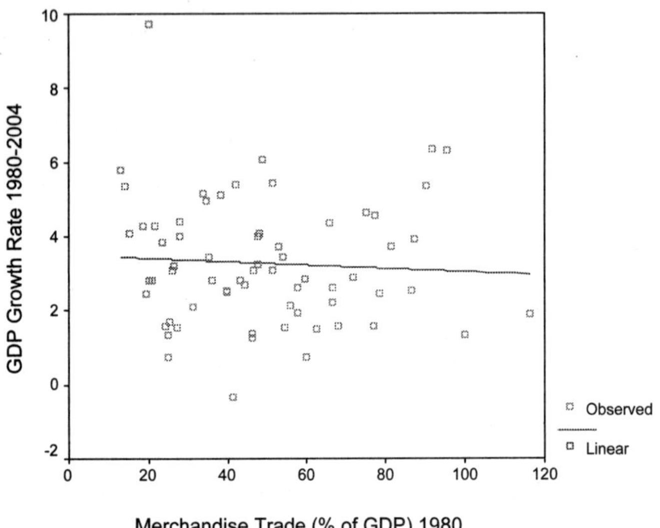

FIG. 22
GDP Growth Rate 1980-2004 and Trade in Services (% of GDP) 1980

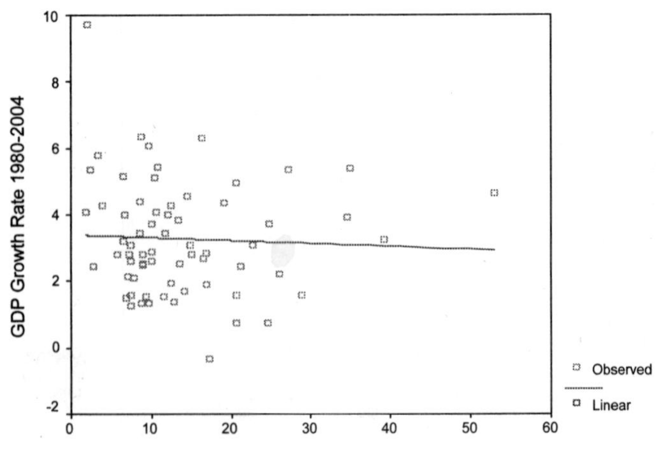

APPENDIX 8.11
Growth (Average Annual %)

Sl. No.	*Country Name*	*1980-2004*	*1980-90*	*1990-2000*	*2000-2004*	*1980-2000*	*1990-2004*
(1)	*(2)*	*(3)*	*(4)*	*(5)*	*(6)*	*(7)*	*(8)*
1.	Algeria	2.59	2.70	1.90	4.80	2.27	2.57
2.	Argentina	1.59	-0.70	4.30	-0.10	1.65	3.52
3.	Bangladesh	4.29	3.70	4.80	5.20	4.27	4.94
4.	Benin	4.00	2.50	4.80	4.50	3.78	4.68
5.	Bolivia	1.94	-0.20	4.00	2.60	1.97	3.45
6.	Brazil	2.45	2.70	2.90	2.00	2.18	2.55
7.	Bulgaria	1.35	3.40	-1.80	4.80	0.49	0.23
8.	Burkina Faso	3.86	3.60	4.00	5.20	3.74	4.39
9.	Burundi	1.69	4.40	-2.60	2.70	1.46	-0.30
10.	Cameroon	2.67	3.40	1.70	4.50	2.52	2.34
11.	Central African Republic	0.76	1.40	2.00	-2.00	1.45	0.84
12.	Chad	5.35	6.10	1.90	14.10	3.94	6.01
13.	Chile	5.10	4.20	6.60	3.70	5.20	5.71
14.	China	9.73	10.30	10.60	9.40	9.90	10.14
15.	Colombia	3.09	3.70	2.80	2.90	3.07	2.65
16.	Congo, Rep.	3.92	3.30	1.20	3.10	3.38	2.06
17.	Costa Rica	3.71	3.00	5.30	3.90	3.87	4.79
18.	Cote d'Ivoire	0.76	0.70	3.30	-0.70	1.57	1.60
19.	Dominican Republic	4.08	3.10	6.10	2.40	4.31	4.98
20.	Ecuador	2.48	2.10	1.90	4.20	1.97	2.62
21.	Egypt, Arab Rep.	4.97	5.40	4.70	3.10	5.01	4.23
22.	El Salvador	1.55	0.20	4.80	1.90	2.17	3.82
23.	Gabon	2.20	0.90	2.80	1.60	2.29	2.21
24.	Gambia, The	3.74	3.60	3.00	3.80	3.48	3.62
25.	Ghana	3.44	3.00	4.30	4.90	3.29	4.48
26.	Guatemala	2.54	0.80	4.20	2.30	2.51	3.61
27.	Haiti	-0.33	-0.20	-1.50	-0.40	-0.75	-0.84
28.	Honduras	2.87	2.70	3.20	3.30	2.89	3.33
29.	India	5.78	5.70	6.00	6.20	5.66	5.70
30.	Indonesia	5.41	6.10	4.20	4.60	5.42	4.46
31.	Iran, Islamic Rep.	3.20	1.70	3.50	6.00	3.48	4.52
32.	Jamaica	1.56	2.00	0.90	1.50	1.94	1.24

(Contd.)

APPENDIX 8.11 (*Contd.*)

(1)	(2)	(3)	(4)	(5)	(6)	(7)	(8)
33.	Jordan	4.63	2.50	5.00	5.50	3.70	5.36
34.	Kenya	3.09	4.20	2.20	2.70	2.98	2.19
35.	Madagascar	1.32	1.10	2.00	0.90	1.19	1.87
36.	Malawi	2.83	2.50	3.70	2.90	2.98	3.42
37.	Malaysia	6.29	5.30	7.00	4.40	6.63	6.40
38.	Mali	2.82	0.80	4.10	6.30	2.45	4.77
39.	Mauritius	5.35	6.00	5.20	4.40	5.53	5.03
40.	Mexico	2.79	1.10	3.10	1.50	2.71	2.98
41.	Morocco	3.46	4.20	2.30	4.70	3.19	3.10
42.	Nepal	4.29	4.60	4.90	2.50	4.90	4.43
43.	Nicaragua	1.50	-1.90	3.70	2.50	1.09	3.24
44.	Niger	1.36	-0.10	2.40	4.10	1.00	2.50
45.	Nigeria	2.62	1.60	2.50	5.40	2.00	3.43
46.	Oman	6.33	8.40	4.50	3.00	6.93	4.29
47.	Pakistan	5.16	6.30	3.80	4.10	5.12	4.00
48.	Panama	3.25	0.50	4.70	3.30	3.33	4.59
49.	Papua New Guinea	2.53	1.90	4.30	0.60	3.18	3.76
50.	Paraguay	2.80	2.50	2.20	1.40	2.41	1.91
51.	Peru	2.10	-0.10	4.60	3.70	1.78	3.88
52.	Philippines	2.79	1.00	3.40	3.90	2.44	3.32
53.	Senegal	3.08	3.10	3.20	4.40	3.10	3.44
54.	South Africa	2.13	1.00	2.10	3.20	1.69	2.23
55.	Sri Lanka	4.55	4.00	5.30	3.70	4.71	4.71
56.	Sudan	4.39	2.30	5.40	6.00	4.21	5.81
57.	Syrian Arab Republic	3.99	1.50	5.00	3.50	3.68	4.55
58.	Thailand	6.05	7.60	4.20	5.40	6.26	4.79
59.	Togo	2.45	1.70	3.50	2.60	1.85	2.52
60.	Trinidad and Tobago	1.89	-3.30	3.20	7.20	0.53	4.17
61.	Tunisia	4.36	3.30	4.70	4.30	4.18	4.68
62.	Turkey	4.09	5.30	3.80	4.20	4.47	3.72
63.	Uganda	5.43	2.90	7.10	5.80	5.33	6.50
64.	Uruguay	1.53	0.50	3.40	-1.20	1.62	2.20
65.	Venezuela, RB	1.25	1.10	1.60	-1.20	1.55	1.89
66.	Zambia	1.58	1.00	0.50	4.40	0.93	1.84

Source : World Development Indicators; Various Issues.

Bibliography

Adelman, I., and C.T. Morris (1967), *Economic Growth and Social Equity in Developing Countries*, Stanford University Press, California.

Agarwala, Amar Narain (ed.) (1969), *Accelerating Investment in Developing Economies*, Oxford University Press, Bombay.

Agenor, P.R. (2002), *Does Globalization Hurt the Poor?*, World Bank, Washington DC.

Agenor, Pierre-Richard and Joshua Aizenman (1996), "Trade Liberalization and Unemployment", *Journal of International Trade and Development*, Vol. 5, (September), pp. 265-86.

Ahluwalia, M.S. (1974), "Income Inequality: Some Dimensions of the Problem", in H.B. Chenery, *et. al.* (eds.), *Redistribution with Growth*, Oxford University Press, London.

Ahmed, S. (1990), "Foreign Capital Inflow and Economic Growth: A Two-Gap Model for the Bangladesh Economy", *The Bangladesh Development Studies*, Vol. XVIII, No. 1, March, pp. 55-71.

Aiyar, S.P. (1961), *Federalism and Social Change: A Study in Quasi Federalism*, Asia Publishing House, Bombay.

Alfaro, Laura, Areendam Chanda, Sebnem Kalemli-Ozcan and Selin Sayek (2004), "FDI and Economic Growth: The Role of Local Financial Markets", *Journal of International Economics*, Vol. 64, 89-112, NH Elsevier, USA.

Baffes, John and Anwar Shah (1993), *Productivity of Public Spending, Sectoral Allocation Choices and Economic Growth*, Working Paper Series, No. 1178, September, World Bank, Washington D.C.

Bagchi, A.K. (1987), *Public Intervention and Industrial Restructuring in China, India and Republic of Korea,* ILO/ ARATEP, New Delhi.

Barro, R.J. (1991), "Economic Growth in Cross-Section of Countries", *The Quarterly Journal of Economics,* Vol. 106 (May), No. 2, 407-43

Baster, N. (1972), "Development Indicators: An Introduction", *Journal of Development Studies,* 8 (January).

Bauer, P.T. (1973), *Dissent on Development: Studies and Debates in Development Economics,* Vikas, Delhi.

Bawa, R.S. (2002), "Challenges and Opportunities of Globalization; Implications for India", Presidential Address to 84th Annual Conference of Indian Economic Association, *The Indian Economic Journal,* Vol. 49(3).

Bawa, R.S. and P.S. Raikhy (Eds.) (1993), *Structural Changes in Indian Economy,* Punjab School of Economics, Guru Nanak Dev University, Amritsar.

Beckerman, W. and R. Bacon (1966), "International Comparisons of Income Levels: A Suggested New Measure", *Economic Journal,* Vol. 76, 1966.

Bhagwati, Jagdish (2004), *In Defense of Globalization,* Oxford University Press, New Delhi.

Bhardwaj, V.P. and Naseem H.A. Jamile (1992), "Some Aspects of the Dynamics of Economic Development—A Cross-Sectional Inter-Country Analysis", *Margin,* July-September, 1992, Vol. 24, issue 4.

Bhargava, Alok (2008), *Globalization, Literacy Levels, and Economic Development,* Research Paper No. 2008/04, UNU-WIDER, United Nations University—World Institute for Development Economics Research, Helsinki, Finland.

Bhargava, Madhuri (1951), *Inter-Governmental Financial Relations in India Since Independence,* Chaitanya Publishing House, Allahabad.

Caircrass, A.K. (1962), *Factors in Economic Development,* George Allen and Unwin, London.

Chenery, H.B. (1960), "Patterns of Industrial Growth", *The American Economic Review,* September 1960.

Chenery, H.B. and Moises Syrquin (1975), *Patterns of Development 1950-70.* Published for the World Bank by Oxford University Press, New York.

Chow, Gregory C. (2006), "Globalization and China's Economic Development", *Pacific Economic Review*, Vol. 11:3 (2006).

Clark, Colin (1940), *The Conditions of Economic Progress*, Macmillan, London.

Coale, Ansley J. and Edgar M. Hoover (1958), *Population Growth and Economic Development in Low-Income Countries: A case study of India's Prospects*, Princeton University Press, Princeton.

Cooper, Charles (1972), "Science, Technology and Production in Underdeveloped Countries–An Introduction", *The Journal of Development Studies*, Oct. 1972

Das, Ram Upendra (2005), *Trade, Technology and Growth: On Analysis and Policies for Developing Countries*, Bookwell, New Delhi.

Dhillon, S.S. and P.S. Raikhy (1993), "Economic Development and Structural Changes—Comparative Experience", in Bawa R.S. and P.S. Raikhy (eds.) *Structural Changes in India's Economy*, Guru Nanak Dev University, Amritsar.

Dhillon, Sharanjit Singh (1995), *World Development Experience*, B.R. Publishers, New Delhi.

Eatwell, John and Lance Taylor (2000), *Global Finance at Risk: The case for International Regulation*, The New Press, New York.

Fisher, A.G.B. (1935), "Economic Implications of National Progress", *International Labour Review, 1935.*

Frankel, J. (2000), *Globalization and the Economy*, NBER Working Paper, 7858, NBER, Cambridge, London.

Friedman, John, as quoted in, *Growth Centers in Regional Economic Development*, N.M. Hansen (Ed.) (1972), The Free Press, New York.

Ghani, Ejaz (1992), *How Financial Markets Affects Long-Run Growth–A Cross-Country Study*, Policy Research Working Paper Series, No. 843, January, World Bank, Cambridge, M.A

Goncalves, Aeinaldo and Jurgen Richtering (1987), "Inter-Country Comparison of Export Performance and Output Growth", *The Developing Economies*, XXV-1, March, Institute of Developing Economies, Tokyo, Japan.

Gorsuch, R.L. (1974), *Factor Analysis*, W.B. Saunders Company, Philadelphia.

Griffin, Keith B. and John L. Enos (1970), *Planning Development*, Addison-Wesley Publishing Company, London.

Gujarati, Damodar N. (2004), *Basic Econometrics*, McGraw-Hill Book Co., Singapore.

Haberler, G. (1959), *International Trade and Economic Development*, National Bank of Egypt, Cairo.

Hagood, M.J. (1943), "Statistical Methods for the Purpose of Delineation of Regions Applied to Data on Agriculture and Population", *Social Force*, Vol. 21.

Hansen, N.M. (Ed.) (1972), *Growth Centers in Regional Economic Development*, The Free Press, New York.

Harbison, F. and C.A. Myers (Eds.) (1965), *Manpower and Education: Country Studies in Development*, McGraw Hill, New York.

Harman, H.H. (1967), *Modern Factor Analysis*, Chicago : Chicago University Press.

Herberger, A.C. (Ed.) (1984), *World Economic Growth: Case Studies of Developed and Developing Nations*, San Francisco: Institute of Contemporary Studies.

Hicks, N.L. and P. Streeten (1979), "Indicators of Development: The Search for a Basic Needs Yardstick", *World Development*, 7 (June).

Hirschman, A.O. (1958), *The Strategy of Economic Development*, Yale University Press, New Haven.

Hogendorn, J.S. (1987), *Economic Development*, Harper and Row, New York.

Hovert, Branko (1974) "The Relation Between Rate of Growth and Level of Development", *Journal of Development Studies*, April/July, 1974.

Isard, Peter. (2005), *Globalization and the International Financial System: What's Wrong and What can be Done*, Cambridge University Press, UK.

Jain, S. and A. Tiemann (1973), "The Size Distribution of Income: A Compilation of Data", IBRD Development Research Centre, *Discussion Papers*, No. 4.

Johnson, H.G. (1967), *Economic Policies Towards Less Developed Countries*, George Allen, London.

Jorgenson, D.W. (1961), "The Development of a Dual Economy", *The Economic Journal*, June 1961.

Jorgenson, D.W. (1967), "Surplus Agricultural Labour and the Development of a Dual Economy", *Oxford Economic Papers* (New Series), Vol. 19, No. 3, November 1967, pp. 288-312.

Kakwani, Nanak (1991), *Growth Rates and Aggregate Welfare—An International Comparison*, Policy Research Working Paper Series, No. 647, April, World Bank, Washington D.C.

Kawai, Hiroki (1994), "International Comparative Analysis of Economic Growth: Trade Liberalization and Productivity", *The Developing Economies*, XXVII-4, Institute of Developing Economies, Tokyo, Japan.

Kay, G. (1975), *Development and Underdevelopment: A Marxist Analysis*, Macmillan, London.

Keyner, J.M. (1936), *The General Theory of Employment, Interest and Money*, London: Macmillan.

Khalaf, Nadim G. (1979), "Country Size and Economic Growth and Development", *Journal of Development Studies*, Oct. 1979.

Kindleberger, Charles P. (1965), *Economic Development*, McGraw Hill, New York and London.

Kindleberger, Charles P., and Bruce Herrick (1977), *Economic Development*, 3rd Edition, McGraw Hill, Tokyo.

King, Robert G. and Ross Levin (1994), *Capital Fundamentalism, Economic Development and Economic Growth*, Policy Research Working Paper, No. 1285, April, World Bank, Washington D.C.

Kravis, I.B., A. Heston and R. Summers (1978), *International Comparison and Real Product and Purchasing Power*, John Hopkins Press, Baltimore.

Krishnamurty, K. (1966), "Economic Development and Population Growth in Low Income Countries: An Empirical Study of India", *Economic Development and Cultural Change*, Vol. 15, 1966, pp. 70-75.

Kuznets, Simon (1955), "Economic Growth and Income Inequality", *The American Economic Review*, Vol. 45, No. 1 (March), 1-28.

Kuznets, Simon (1966), *Modern Economic Growth: Rate, Structure and Spread*, Oxford and IBH Publishing Co., New Delhi.

Larson, D.A., and Walton, T. Wilford (1980), "The Physical Quality of Life Index: A New Measure of Welfare?", *Indian Economic Journal*, 27 (3), 1980.

Lindeman, R.H., P.F. Merenda and R.Z. Gold (1980), *Introduction to Bivariate and Multivariate Analysis,* Scott Foresman and Company, USA.

Majumdar, P. (1982), *Development and Welfare Indicators—A Critical Appraisal,* Allied Publishers, New Delhi.

Malthus, Thomas Robert (1969), *On Population; Three Essays,* Oxford IBH, Calcutta.

Matsuyama, Kiminori (1992), "Agricultural Productivity, Comparative Advantage and Economic Growth", *Journal of Economic Theory,* Vol. 58, (December), pp. 317-34.

McNamara, Robert S. (1984), *The Population Problem: Time Bomb or Myth,* Washington D.C.

Meier, Gerald M. (1970), *Leading Issues in Economic Development: Studies in International Poverty,* Second Edition, Oxford University Press, London.

Meier, Gerald M. and Robert, E. Baldwin (1957), *Development: Theory, History, Policy,* Asia Publishing House, Bombay.

Mohanasundaram, V. (2000), "Globalization and Private Capital Inflows to Developing Countries", *Economic Affairs,* Vol. 45, Quarter, 4, December.

Morris, M.D. (1979), *Measuring the Condition of World's Poor: The Physical Quality of Life Index,* Overseas Development Council, Washington D.C.

Morris, M.D. and Michelle, B.M. (1982), *Measuring The Condition of India's Poor: The Physical Quality of Life Index,* Promilla, New Delhi.

Myrdal, G. (1956), *Development and Underdevelopment,* National Bank of Egypt Fiftieth Anniversary Commemoration Lecturers, Cairo.

Myrdal, G. (1957), *Economic Theory and Underdeveloped Region,* Duckworth, London.

Nagar, A.L. and S.R. Basu (2002) "Weighting Socio-Economic Indicators of Human Development: A Latent Variable Approach", in Ullah, A. *et. al.* (Eds.), *Handbook of Applied Econometrics and Statistical Inference,* Marcel Dekker, New York.

Nayyar, Deepak (2006), *Development through Globalization?,* Research Paper No. 2006/29, WIDER (World Institute For Development Economics Research), United Nations University.

Nayyar, Deepak (2006), "Towards Global Governance", in Nayyar, Deepak (Ed.) (2006), *Governing Globalization: Issues and Institutions*, Oxford University Press, New Delhi.

Neena and P.S. Raikhy (1993), "Structural changes in Industrial Production and Imports in India", in Bawa, R.S. and P.S Raikhy (Eds.) (1993), *Structural Changes in Indian Economy*, Guru Nanak Dev University, Amritsar.

Nurkse, R. (1961), "Patterns of Trade and Development", in G. Harbarler and R.M. Stern (Eds.) *Equilibrium and Growth in World Economy*, Harward University Press, Cambridge.

Otsubo, Shigeru (1996), *Globalization: A New Role for Developing Countries in an Integrated World*, Policy Research Working Paper, 1628, July, The World Bank, Colombia.

Panchamukhi, V.R, R.G. Nambiar and Rajesh Mehta (1986), "Structural Changes and Economic Growth in Developing Countries", 8th *World Economic Congress*, New Delhi (December).

Panchmukhi, V.R. (1998), "Globalization, Competition and Economic Stability", *RIS Occasional Paper No. 51*, RIS, New Delhi.

Patel, I.G. (1986), *Essays in Economic Policy and Economic Growth*, Macmillan, London.

Perkins, John (2004), *Confessions of an Economic Hit Man*, Berrett-Koehler, San Francisco, California.

Petras, James and Henry Veltmeyer (2001), *Globalization Unmasked*, Madhyam Books, New Delhi.

Pietro, Di William R. and Bansi L. Sawhnay (2002), "Foreign Investment, Externalities and Growth in Less Developed Countries", *Asian-African Journal of Economics and Econometrics*, Vol. 2, No. 1.

Pigou, A.C. (1932), *The Economics of Welfare*, London: Macmillan.

Prasad, Eswar S., Kenneth Rogoff , Shang-Jin Wei and M. Ayhan Kose (2003), *Effects of Financial Globalization on Developing Countries: Some Empirical Evidence*, International Monetary Fund, Washington D.C.

Rana, Pradumna B. and J. Malcolm Dowling (1988), "The Impact of Foreign Capital on Growth: Evidences from Asian Developing Countries", *The Developing Economies*, XXVI-1, Institute of Developing Economies, Tokyo, Japan.

Ranis, G. and J.C.H. Fei (1961), "A Theory of Economic Development", *American Economic Review*, Vol. 51, No. 3.

Rao, C.R. (1962), *Advanced Statistical Methods in Biometric Research*, John Wiley, New York.

Rassekh, Farhad (2007), "Is International Trade More Beneficial to Lower Income Economies? An Empirical Inquiry", *Review of Development Economics*, Vol. 11(1).

Reynolds, Lloyd G. (1969), "Economic Development with Surplus Labour: Some Complications", *Oxford Economic Papers* (New Series), March, pp. 90-97

Robbins, Lionel (1968), *Economic Planning and International Order*, Macmillan, London.

Roe, Terry, Agapi Somwaru and Xinshen Diao (2006), "Globalization: Welfare Distribution and Costs among Developed and Developing Countries", *Review of Agricultural Economics*, Vol. 28, No. 3.

Rogoff, Kenneth S. and Eswar Parsad and Shang-Jin Wei (2004), "Financial Globalisation, Growth and Volatility in Developing Countries", National Bureau of Economic Research, *NBER Working Paper No. 10942*, December, Cambridge, M.A

Sachs, Jeffery (2005), *The End of Poverty*, The Penguin Press, New York.

Santos-Paulino, U. Amelia (2002), "The Effects of Trade Liberalization on Imports in Selected Developing Countries", *World Development*, Vol. 30, No. 6, Elsevier Science, Great Britain.

Schmukler, Sergio L. (2004), "Financial Globalization: Gain and Pain for Developing Countries", *Economic Review*, Second Quarter, Federal Reserve Bank of Atlanta.

Schumpeter, J.A. (1934), *Theory of Economic Development: An Inquiry into Profits, Capital, Credit, Interest and the Business Cycle*, Galaxy Books, New York.

Seers, Dudley (1969), "The Measuring of Development", *Eleventh World Conference of the Society for International Development*, New Delhi.

Sen, Amartya (1973), *On Economic Inequality*, Oxford University Press, Delhi.

Sethi, A.S. and P.S. Raikhy (2001), "Changing Sources of Economic Growth in India: Implications for Second

Generation Reforms", in Ruddar Datt (Ed.), *Second Generation Economic Reforms in India,* Deep and Deep Publications Pvt. Ltd., New Delhi.

Shah, Anwar and Zia Qureshi (1994), *Inter-Governmental Fiscal Relations in Indonesia,* World Bank, Washington.

Shahi, M.A. (1989), "Sector Shares and Economic Development: A Re-Examination of the Cross-Section Evidence", *Asian Economic Review,* Vol. 31, Issue 3.

Sikdar, Soumyen (2002), *Contemporary Issues in Globalization: An Introduction to Theory and Practice in India,* Oxford University Press, New Delhi.

Simon, Julian (1981), *The Ultimate Resource,* Princeton University Press, Princeton.

Solimano, Andres (1999), *Globalization and National Development at the End of the 20th Century: Tensions and Challenges,* Policy Research Working Paper, 2137, June, The World Bank, Colombia.

Steger, Manfred B., (2006), *Globalization: A Very Short Introduction,* Oxford University Press, New Delhi.

Stewart, I.G. (Ed.) (1969), *Economic Development and Structural Change,* Edinburgh University Press, Edinburgh.

Stiglitz, Joseph (2006), *Making Globalization Work,* Penguin Books, London.

Stiglitz, Joseph E. (2002), *Globalization and its Discontents,* Penguin Books, New Delhi.

Streeten, Paul P. as quoted in Todaro, M.P. and Stephen C. Smith (2003), *Economic Development,* (Eighth Edition) Pearson Education, Delhi.

Syrquin, M. (1988). "Patterns of Structural Change", in Chenery, H. and T.N. Shrinivasan (Eds.), *Handbook of Development Economics,* Elsevier, Armsterdam.

Taylor, L. (1986), "Theories of Sectoral Balance", *8th World Economic Congress,* New Delhi (December).

Thirlwall, A.P. (1972), "A Cross-Section Study of Population Growth and the Growth of Output and Per Capita Income in a Production Function Framework", *The Manchester School of Economics and Social Studies,* Vol. 40(4).

Thorbecke, E. and M. Nissanke (2006), "Introduction: The Impact of Globalization on the World's Poor", *World Development,* 34(8): 1333-37.

Todaro, M.P. and Stephen C. Smith (2003), *Economic Development* (Eighth Edition), Pearson Education, Delhi.

UNDP (1990), *Human Development Report*, Oxford University Press, New York.

UNDP (1992), *Human Development Report*, Oxford University Press, New York.

UNIDO (1979), *World Industry Since 1960: Progress and Prospects*, New York: United Nations.

United Nations Educational, Scientific and Cultural Organization (UNESCO), *Statistical Yearbook*, Various Issues, Paris.

United Nations (1965), *Planning the External Sector: Techniques, Problems and Policies*, New York.

UNRISD (1995), *States of Disarray: The Social Effects of Globalization*, UNRISD, Geneva.

Wheare, K.C. (1956), *Federal Government*, Oxford University, London.

Wood, A. (1986), *Growth and Structural Change in Large Low-Income Countries*, World Bank Staff Working Papers, No. 763, Washington, D.C.

World Bank (1992), *Development and Environment*, Published for the World Bank, Oxford University Press, New York.

World Bank (1992), *Governance and Development*, Washington, D.C.

World Bank (2007), *Global Economic Prospects: Managing the Next Wave of Globalization*, Washington, D.C.

World Bank, *Annual Report*, Various Issues, Washington, D.C.

World Bank, *Social Indicators of Development*, Various issues, Johns Hopkins University Press, Baltimore.

World Bank, *World Bank Atlas*, Various Issues, Washington, D.C.

World Bank, *World Development Indicators*, Various Issues.

World Bank, *World Development Report*, Various Issues, Oxford Press, New York.

World Bank, *World Tables*, Various Issues, Baltimore: Johns Hopkins University Press.

World Commission on the Social Dimension of Globalization (2004), *A Fair Globalization: Creating Opportunities for All*, Academic Foundation, New Delhi.

Yotopoulous, P.A. (1976), *Economics of Development: Empirical Investigations*, Harper and Row, New York.

Yusuf, Shahid (2001), *Globalization and the Challenges for Developing Countries,* World Bank Policy Research Working Paper, 2618, Washington, D.C.

Zind, Richard G. (1990), "Comparative Development Gains: An Empirical Assessment", *The Development Studies,* Vol. XVIII, June, No. 2, pp. 1-21.

Index

Addman and Morris, 38
Adult Literacy Rate, 131
Alfaro, 55
Average Annual Growth Rate of GDP :
  Level of Growth, 85
Average Annual Growth Rate of Services :
  Level of Growth, 83

Baldwin, 1
Baner, 39
Barro, 46
Bawa, 17
Bhagwati, 27
Birth Rate and Level of Growth, 124
Bridging of Gap, 69
Bridging the Development Gap :
  Hogendorn's Concept, 215

Cairncross, 18
Chenery, 36
Chi-Square Test, 64
Chow Test, 73
Coefficient of Variation, 72
Concept of Globalization, 14
Correlation Analysis, 65
Correlation Analysis of the Selected Variables, 203
Correlation Matrics, 144

Death Rate and Level of Growth, 125
Democraphic Changes and Economic Growth, 123
Developing Countries :
  GNI Per Capita, 210
Development Indicators :
  Coefficients of Variation, 217
Dhillon, 49
Different Groups of Countries :
  GNI Per Capita, 209
Different Measures of Economic Development :
  Rank Correlations, 202

Economic Development :
  Factors, 143
Economic Growth and Structural Changes, 75
Energy Use Per Capita, 92
Export Volume, 101

Factor Analysis, 66, 154
Fastest and Slowest Growing Countries, 231
FDI (Foreign Direct Investment), 23
Fisher, 4
Friedman, 3

Globalization and Economic Development, 12, 208
Globalization-Related Variables, 175
Goncalves and Richtering, 43

Hansen, 3
Herrick, 41
Hogendorn, 44

ICT (Information and Communications Technology), 31
IMF (International Monetary Fund), 53
Import Volume, 102
Infant Mortality Rate, 127
International Migration Stock, 138
Isard, 26

Jamile and Bhardwaj, 47
Jorgenson, 38

Kakwani, 46
Khalab, 41
Kindleberger, 41
Krishnamurthy, 37
Kuznets, 37

Level of Growth and
- Daily Calorie Supply, 112
- Adult Literacy Rate, 131
- Average Annual Growth Rate, 101-02
- Average Annual Rate of Industry, 81
- Exports-GDP Ratio, 97
- Employment in Agriculture, 113
- Employment in Services, 116
- Employment in Industry, 114
- Energy Use Per Capita, 92
- FDI Net Outflows, 109
- FDI Net Inflows, 207
- GNI Per Capita, 86
- Gross Private Capital Flows, 107
- Gross Domestic Savings, 89
- Imports-GDP Ratio, 99
- International Migration Stock, 138
- Infant Mortality Rate, 127
- Life Expectancy at Birth, 128
- Merchandise Trade, 104
- Number of Physicians, 129
- Primary School Enrolment, 132
- Percentage of Population of Working Age, 135
- Private Consumption Expenditure, 87
- Secondary School Enrolment, 134
- Share of :
  - Agriculture in GDP, 76
  - Industry in GDP, 79
  - Fuel, 93
  - Manufacture, 96
  - Food, 94
- Trade in Services, 105, 185
- Total Debt Services, 110
- Urban Population, 137

Measuring Economic Development, 166
Meir, 1
Merchandise Exports, 93
Mohanasundaram, 51

Otsubo, 50

Percentage of Population of Working Age, 135
PQLI (Physical Quality of Life Index), 70, 166
Primary School Enrolment, 132

Rank Correlation Analysis, 66, 201, 228
Regression Analysis, 69
Regression Parameters :
  Stability, 235

Secondary School Enrolment, 134
Services in GDP :
  Level of Growth, 82
Sikdar, 15
Solimano, 50
Step-wise Regression Analysis, 221
Stiglitz, 31

Tabular Analysis, 64
Thirlwall, 39

Urban Population, 137

World Commission on Social Dimension of Globalization, 25, 57
WTO (World Trade Organization), 53

Xioping, Deng, 58

Yusuf, 51

Zind, 46